A Sea Dog's Tale

SANTOS

Don Kreuter photo

Brave spirit of a dog, burning more brightly than any tiger yet.

Chasing the hoofed intruders of the world through high and low, thick and thin.

Leaving no stone unmoistened, no passing boat unbarked.

May your little light shine on, wherever you are

—and may your spirit roam free on the endless beaches of the hereafter.

—Raf Muilenburg

A Sea Dog's Tale

The True Story of a Small Dog on a Big Ocean

Peter Muilenburg

Distributed by University Press of New England
Hanover and London

Printed in the United States of America

Copyright © 2012 by Peter Muilenburg

Library of Congress Control Number: 2012931696
ISBN 978-1-937644-07-9 (pbk)
ISBN 978-1-937644-08-6 (eBook)

Front cover design by Harrah Lord, Yellow House Studio; Cover photo of Santos by Don Kreuter Photography; Cover photo of *Breath* by Don Brown; Author photo by T. A. Carter; Back cover panel and interior design by Janet Robbins, North Wind Design & Production, www.nwdpbooks.com

Cadent Publishing
9 Gleason Street
Thomaston, ME 04861
www.cadentpublishing.com

Distributed by University Press of New England
1 Court Street
Lebanon, New Hampshire 03766

CONTENTS

PROLOGUE

A biography of a dog?

Why not? Since long before Zoroaster declared them sacred, people have loved dogs; and ever since Plutarch's *Lives of the Noble Greeks and Romans*, literature has valued accounts of exceptional lives, for their own sake as well as for the light they cast on their times.

So . . . this book details such a life, that of Santos, a noble dog. Hey, don't laugh; after all, the choice spirits of an age come to animals as well as to people. As much as Pericles or Brutus, the story of Santos illuminates its little corner of life and history, and it provides a new twist on a timeless subject—seafaring.

And after all, people are a lot like dogs. Of all the animals, dogs are probably the closest to us in spirit (if we charitably draw a veil over war, soccer hooliganism, child abuse, and classroom massacres), and they present us with a model of life that is recognizably close to our own.

To use an automotive analogy, if people were Ferraris, dogs would be Model T's. Ferraris are more advanced, more complicated, more likely to break down, and *much* more likely to end up in a fiery high-speed wreck. Anyone trying to deduce the basic operating principles of an automobile engine would learn more looking under the hood of a bare-bones Model T than peering at the mass of wiring and computerized components under the stylish cowl of a Ferrari.

All of which is to say, watching dogs is a way of watching ourselves.

Santos, a schipperke, came to us as a tiny puppy and sailed with us all his life, 75,000 deep-sea miles. He sailed four times across the Atlantic, crisscrossed the Caribbean, ranged far up African rivers, gunkholed the Eastern seaboard of America, and explored the Med.

7

He survived kidnap, hurricane, raging surf, and being lost overboard. We gave him up for dead twice. His adventures were written up in *SAIL* magazine and were the subject of two *Reader's Digest* articles. Time and again people who met him on charter aboard his boat *Breath* went home and acquired schipperkes of their own. He was a celebrity on his home island of St. John. Charisma streamed off him. He may have been an 11-pound dog, but he strode through life like a lion.

While writing this book I periodically wondered if my unbridled memory was galloping afield from reality. Yet every time such doubts assailed me, as if on cue, someone who'd sailed with us years ago would show up in Coral Bay or hail us at the bar at Skinny Legs or on the old Moravian dock, and always the first question would be, "Do you still have that amazing dog?"

In fact it happened again just the other night, as I finalized the last draft of this story. A friend who'd sailed with us up the Gambia River years ago had just returned to Africa to see how the friends we'd made there were doing. "You know," he told us, "the first thing everybody wanted to know was, 'How's Santos?'"

Santos joined us during *Breath*'s maiden voyage and was there, an integral member of the crew, throughout our family voyaging, when *Breath* made her most memorable trips and when our two sons formed their tight bonds with each other, with their dog, and with the sea. He was a third brother and an inspiration to our family—an authentic, questing adventurer, without fear or compromise, true to himself and to us. Climbing a mountain in the Cape Verdes, running before a North Atlantic gale, discovering ancient ruins on the coast of Turkey—always the dog's keen spirit augmented the event.

When our sons left the nest, our era of family voyaging passed, and, not long after, Santos left us, too. He checked out quick and clean and left a lasting memory behind—of an incandescent spirit like a bright, steadfast little flame.

He showed us how to live, and he showed us how to die.

One thing we know for sure—we'll never have a dog that cool again.

ONE

INDIAN RIVER GIFT

White water exploded from *Breath*'s bow as she forged through the river chop, her hull as sturdy as a 20-ton boulder, her two stout masts silhouetted against the sky.

"Heavy squalls coming, boys! Better pack up the cards," I shouted down the companionway. "Get your foul-weather gear on and stand by. . . ." Two boys, 6 and 13, still blond-haired from the salt sea and tropic sun, wriggled quickly into rain wear and took their places on deck. Right behind them came their mother, pulling the companionway hatch shut behind her with a bang.

Thunderheads towered over the flat Florida terrain. Sickly daytime lightning flickered like a snake's tongue. A powerful, rapidly moving cold front was on a collision course with our boat and there was no avoiding it—we were hemmed in on a river, and intense black line squalls stretched both ways to the horizon. Already powering at hull speed up the broad stretches of the Indian River, we were trying to reach the shelter of the Eau Gallie anchorage before the weather did.

Like outriders sent to lash the river's back, gusts raced ahead of the storm and rattled *Breath*'s halyards fiercely against her solid spars—a warning of what was to come.

As the anchorage drew nearer, so did the approaching storm clouds, diminishing the daylight until it was eerie as an eclipse. Close ranks of whitecaps were goose-stepping down the river, but close to shore, protected by a narrow, rocky island, was a V of smooth water. We eased in past the stony outcrop into its lee and headed for the only other cruising boat in that little cove, an immaculate Chesapeake pinky with a sweeping sheer and dainty pointed ends.

As we approached it, a jet-black head with a bristly mane and pointed ears suddenly popped above the cockpit coaming, regarded us warily, then barked a sharp warning. We heard the scrape of a hatch being thrown open, and a man stuck his head out. His eyes narrowed as he beheld our bowsprit coming straight at him like the ram on a trireme.

"Look mom! A dog!" Six-year-old Diego wanted a pet more than anything else in the world. His cat had jumped ship in Nassau.

"It's a neat little dog," agreed Dorothy.

The sky overhead darkened even more as a sudden blast of cold air announced the arrival of the first squall. It rushed toward us, putting the treetops in a frenzy and raising a traveling shriek from the fleet of small craft moored outside the cove's confines as halyards flogged against aluminum masts, sounding like a wind chime in torment. I swung the boat around to face the squall and shouted, "Drop it now!" Raff, poised at the bronze windlass, struck off the brake and stood back. The big CQR anchor plummeted toward the bottom, pulling out its heavy chain so fast it rattled and jumped like a runaway freight train barreling through the boat.

The blast of wind caught our bow and veered it off sharply. It stretched out the chain, blowing us down on the little pinky and her man and dog, who huddled in the shelter of the cabin wall, watching us fixedly. Then, to everybody's relief, our bow fetched up with a sudden jerk and the boat spun around to face the wind as the big CQR bit deep into the mud bottom and its half-inch chain stretched link by link out of the water, dripping as it rose.

There she rode as the norther set on in earnest, one squall following another while we watched the fury from the warmth of the cabin. The big diesel radiated back the heat accumulated from the day's run while Dorothy boiled up cocoa to go with the hot loaves of banana bread just drawn from the oven.

* * *

The little dog next door had made a distinct impression on the boys.

"Did you see how the dog called his master when he saw us getting close? That's a smart dog," said Diego.

"Right," said Raffy. "And did you notice that as soon as the dog barked the man came up on deck, even in the rain? That means he must trust the dog's judgment."

Not much escaped The Raff's keen mind. A skinny 13-year-old, a voracious reader with memory like a black hole, he was way ahead of grade level but took no pride in that. What he really wanted was muscles, to be unequivocally "buck."

"Pretty useful on a boat, don't you think Dad?" Diego continued with a wistful look at me. I nodded but said nothing. I knew what he was thinking, what the whole family but me was thinking—*wouldn't it be nice to have a pet on board?*

The discussion had come up regularly ever since Theresa, the best cat we ever had, inexplicably jumped off the stern in the wee hours one morning. We were anchored off Paradise Island in the Bahamas when Dorothy and I both heard a low, strangled meeow, then a splash, but didn't get out of our comfortable bunk in the after cabin, not believing our ears. But in the morning she was gone, and no searching aboard or on shore turned her up. The obvious possibility was that she hadn't made it. The current ran strong in the cut between the islands. Now there was a void in our lives.

Especially Diego's. Since the cat had disappeared, he'd clung more to Dorothy and been quicker to tears. We often thought that Diego should be a vet. He loved animals and they loved him.

Well, I loved animals too, but the time wasn't right for another one, especially an untrained puppy. Our boat was still under construction inside. We had enough cleaning up to do without a puppy piddling in the sawdust or tracking wet paint all over the floor. When I got started on this line of talk, the rest of the family would reluctantly agree and subside, but they remained unconvinced.

* * *

An hour later the norther had blown through; the wind moderated, the sun broke into a rapidly clearing sky, and the temperature dropped. On the pinky, *two* black heads with pointed ears were alertly cocked our way. Perfectly silhouetted by the late afternoon light, they stared intently at *Breath*'s crew, who stared back with equal interest.

Soon the man reemerged from the companionway hatch of the pinky. He gave a friendly wave, and we all waved back, glad he didn't feel we were anchored too close to him—some boaters petulantly demand excessive "swinging room" even in obviously tight anchorages.

He was a lean and leathery man in his thirties with a taut look but a ready smile, as we soon found out when he got into his dinghy and rowed over for a chat. In the bow rode the bigger of the two dogs. It lay on the bow cover with its forepaws over the edge, a dignified look on its sensitive, fox-like face. A striking ruff, distinctive as a lion's mane, spread out behind his head, the sable hairs silvered enough to show.

"Nice boat you got here," he said, looking up and holding on to the rub rail. "Some kind'a solid! Massive!" he said, his eyes taking in the mainmast and rigging.

"You got a nice boat yourself. Very fine and dainty."

"Yeah, she's a sweety. Small, though. Just right for two . . . but right now there's nine of us living aboard."

"Nine!?" we exclaimed in disbelief.

"Well, seven of us are dogs. This here's the dad, Winnie the Pup." He gave the old dog a scratch behind its ears.

"Cool. . . . What kind of dogs are they?" asked Raff, as we all stared down at the dinghy and its crew. Vince—that was his name—chuckled fondly and said nothing for a moment as if trying to decide how best to impart something momentous.

"Why, these dogs are pure-bred schipperkes, the Belgian canal barge dogs, genuine boat dogs, bred for centuries just to live and work on boats. And let me tell you something." His eyes squinted conspiratorially. "They are the smartest damn dogs you ever seen. And the two you've seen are just the tip of the iceberg," he said. "Down below are their five puppies—cutest little bear cubs you ever saw! And," he continued, avoiding my eyes and shamelessly focusing on Dorothy and the boys, "they're for sale—got all their shots and papers."

"Hold on a second," I interjected hastily, wanting to nip this in the bud. "We're not in the market for a pedigreed dog. We have to watch our bucks, and besides, we always get mongrels from the pound."

"Good for you! I did the same 'til I moved in with Jean. She breeds skipps, and I guess I just fell in love with the little black devils. Now it's the only dog I'd have. . . . Then again, I'm a seafaring man, and these dogs are just so good aboard a boat!"

Then he set the hook. "But hey, I understand about money being tight . . . story of my life . . . but that shouldn't stop you from just coming over to play with them. It's good for the pups to socialize with people."

He hit a responsive chord there. It didn't take long for Dorothy and the boys to take up his offer, and so, what the hell, I went along too.

The puppies were down in the tiny cabin, fast asleep atop each other and so uniformly black they were hard to distinguish from the shadows. Vince threw open the main hatch and sunlight streamed below. The tiny black felt ears started to twitch, their eyes opened, their heads wobbled to attention—then they were clambering all over each other, little limbs propelling comically round bellies. Each one was bright-eyed, fat, and jet black from nose to closely cropped tail—everything except their bright pink tongue tips. With their blunt muzzles and their ears cocked over, they looked exactly like little black bear cubs.

"Aren't they cute . . . ?" said my wife adoringly.

"Yes, they're marvelous tiny beasts, but we've never paid $500 for a dog and we're not about to start now."

"Oh I know . . ." she said, not really hearing. She picked one up and held it wriggling while she kissed its muzzle. "Actually, he said only $350 for boat people—and they have all their shots."

"Dorothy, if you want a dog let's go rescue one from the pound. Anyway, now is a terrible time to take on a leaky puppy. Remember, the boat is still under construction inside."

"Oh really . . . still?," she said tartly.

I winced.

* * *

I had built the boat under a palm tree next to the beach of a remote cove at the end of the road in St. John, the smallest of the U.S. Virgin Islands. After the project had taken three years and all of our money, rock fever struck my wife. We had to set sail, finished or not. She needed a change. So we packed the essentials aboard, stored the rest of our belongings in the old West Indian rum shop that had been our home, and set sail for the U.S. Eastern seaboard, where we had been alternating between working for money and working on the boat.

Hence there was still no door on the bathroom, just a curtain. Lumber and plywood were stacked beneath the main saloon table. Dorothy had to climb over boxes of caulking and paint to get into our bed. I had often been told by single sailors that they couldn't understand why she stayed.

Sometimes I wondered myself. Dorothy was definitely unusual by middle American standards. On the one hand she had been born with a silver spoon in her mouth, a doctor's daughter with seven ancestors on the *Mayflower*, the family's only girl in whom her dad and four brothers delighted. A girl of her background could have every expectation of a comfortable home and a steady income.

On the other hand, born of missionary parents and grandparents who had served in China, she'd grown up hearing stories of hardships surmounted, dangers run, and suffering endured. Her mother remembered living for days on a train stopped in the dead of winter by battling warlords. Dorothy's aunt had been literally beheaded by Chinese bandits in the 1930s. Her doctor father had spent all of World War II in a Japanese prison camp in Manila, defying his captors and emerging a hero. Dorothy, the result of his return home, was of that same stock, indifferent to material indulgences. Hardships alone wouldn't make her leave.

However, there *had* been questions about building a boat in the first place. How was an ex-1960s radical—a history major and, some said, a mechanical idiot—going to build a 42-foot, 20-ton gaff-rigged ketch? Would the result be a joke or a disaster?

Dorothy believed in me but questioned the wisdom of putting all our money and so much time into a boat, not only because she had tendencies toward seasickness but because she had just started a preschool program. If I needed a big project, I might consider getting behind her school.

On the other hand she loved the water, loved to travel, and knew from experience that going by boat had big advantages—you could sail to the earth's ends and yet, at the end of the day, make a cup of tea just the way you like it and fall asleep in your own bed.

It also mattered to her that both sons loved the idea. They could swim and dive like otters. Raff had already acquired some Spanish from voyages in our first, smaller boat to Venezuela and Puerto Rico. And she also knew that life on the sea taught children the value of work and bred responsibility, self-reliance, and a familiarity with foreign cultures. She had cautiously acquiesced.

"With the proviso," she had added, "that . . . sometime . . . we'll have a house . . . just a little one . . . where I can feel bedrock beneath my feet and grow flowers on the mountain."

"You got it babe, I swear."

So, yes, she was well aware that the boat was under construction . . . still.

* * *

Just then, as if to back me up, the puppies started to leave little dollops of what looked like expensive gourmet mustard on the varnished cabin sole. Vince sprang into action with paper towels and cleaned up one mess, then another, lifted a third and fourth dog to the newspaper just in time, but missed with the fifth. For the moment, my point of view gained the upper hand.

The weather was clear but freezing, typical of a norther's passage, and we decided to stay a couple of days until it warmed up. Jean and Vince were Bahamas-bound and we were northbound, so we traded the usual cruising shoptalk—favorite anchorages, where to get water, grocery stores near a free slip.. And of course we talked about schipperkes. Jean passionately felt that each dog she raised should fulfill its function—to live and work aboard a boat.

"That's what they were bred for," she asserted crisply.

She told us that back in medieval times, schipperkes were bred down from Belgian shepherds to develop a small, alert dog, powerful for its size, to work on canal and river barges, where they were as useful as any crew member. They guarded against thieves, scared off rats, gave the alarm if a child fell overboard, swam ashore in the cold canal water to nip at the heels of the tow horse when it slacked off pulling, and even helped the captain navigate in fog.

"Why did you cut their tails?" I asked. "Just for style?"

Jean looked stung. "I didn't cut them! The vet did, when they were just three days old. There's hardly any feeling there then—it's not nearly as bad as being circumcised."

"You circumcised them too?"

"Of course not!"

"Just kidding, Jean."

"Anyway, it's for their own good," she added.

"How's that?"

"Well, the tail grows in a curl like a husky or chow, and it can chafe the dog's back when it wags—a happy dog can rub a hole in its skin, get infected, and die."

This seemed farfetched to me, as did the bit about helping the captain navigate. Would the law of evolution devise a tail that killed its owner? But I let that pass, never suspecting the real explanation, which is both practical and aesthetic. In the close confines of a boat, a happy dog's thrashing tail can knock over a coffee cup, a paint can, or worse.

One afternoon Dorothy took the dinghy over to Jean's boat to drink tea and play with the puppies. Vince was ashore walking the two grownup dogs. He burst back into the cabin with a calamitous look on his face.

"Your dinghy! It's sunk!"

Our old inflatable leaked air out of the pontoons and water in through the floor. By bailing, pumping, and patching, we were keeping it afloat until we could build or buy a better one. This time one of the pontoon valves had leaked out all its air; the dingy swamped, the oars and gas tank floated away, and the dingy anchor went to the bottom. The outboard engine was still held up by the surviving pontoon, but just below the surface.

Vince retrieved the oars and the gas tank, which thankfully hadn't leaked into the river. While I worked on the faulty valve and pumped it back up, he and Raff dredged the river with a grapnel for our anchor and line.

Since Vince worked in maintenance on an oceanographic vessel, he knew mechanical stuff and insisted on helping me resuscitate the outboard. We talked as we worked, and he told me that the boat was Jean's, as were the dogs and most of the funds. He wanted to get certified as an engineer, but drink and drifting had interfered. He and Jean's future together was uncertain; still, they were enjoying their cruise and meshed well. They both loved schipperkes, she kept him off the sauce, and he kept the boat together.

"And what about you?" he asked me. "You got it made. Great boat, lovely wife, good kids. . . . All you need now is a schipperke."

"I wish!" I replied. "It wasn't a terribly successful maiden voyage. Dorothy's not convinced she wants to live indefinitely on the boat. She gets seasick."

"She'll get used to it," he said, with the blithe assurance of one who'd never suffered mal de mer.

"Actually, Diego is a bigger problem—he nearly died of dehydration on the way up here. . . . Couldn't hold down a thing for days."

"Why didn't you put into a port?"

"We couldn't." And I told him the story of our maiden voyage

* * *

When we left the Virgin Islands to sail to the States, Raf had gone to summer camp and was not with us. Diego was 6, the age most susceptible to seasickness. He had been living ashore and doing occasional overnights in the protected waters of the Sir Francis Drake Passage without serious trouble, but when we went four days straight down the rough north coast of Puerto Rico and Hispaniola, he fell into a cask of misery and couldn't climb out. We tried to put in when we reached the Dominican Republic but were prevented by weather. When the wind moderated and Diego started to feel better, we opted to continue on another 150 miles to Great Inagua instead.

As soon as we were far enough to leeward to make beating back a prohibitive ordeal, the wind picked up again with a vengeance, raising a steep sea between Hispaniola and the Caicos Banks a hundred miles north. *Breath* roared down the waves with a rush of white water in her wake, making great speed but rolling violently as well. Diego promptly relapsed into nausea, and I could hear him gagging down below even over the wind. "I hate sailing," he moaned. I *hate* this boat!"

"I'm worried about him, Peter," Dorothy said. "Look at his face. I think he may be getting dehydrated. He can't even keep down water!" Her face accused me as she cuddled the moaning boy's head.

His skin did have an unhealthy pallor. Sweat bathed his brow, there were dark shadows under his eyes, and his lips showed a bluish tinge.

"He doesn't look good," I said, a weak reply. Diego retched again, painful dry heaves that brought up a little bile and left him wracked and panting. It was pitiful to see, and a bit scary. Were prolonged spasms dangerous? Could a person die of seasickness? A young, delicate child? Neither of us voiced our fears, but there was no masking the apprehension in his mother's eyes.

"You've got to do something!"

"Well, what. . . ? Go on deck, spread my arms wide, and command the sea to be still?"

"What about heaving-to? The way we read about in the Hiscock book, so they could rest in a gale?"

"I don't know, honey. . . . Might not be such a great motion."

"It's got to be better than this if that's what they did to get some sleep!"

"Well, let's try it." The truth was, I'd practiced the technique once or twice in the sheltered waters of the Virgins, but never at sea. Heaving-to is a way to stall a boat so that she won't need steering and won't go anywhere, and it's said to be especially effective on heavy, long-keeled boats like the ones Eric and Susan Hiscock sailed around the world—and like *Breath*. I went back on deck and dropped the jib, backed the stays'l by lashing it against the wind to a shroud, sheeted the mizzen close, let the mainsail out until it luffed, and tied the helm hard to leeward.

The boat stopped and just hung there, nicely balanced, her mizzen levering her bow up into the wind and the backed stays'l pushing it back down. The motion, however, was atrocious—she was bucking like a bronco with a burr under its saddle cloth. All the dishes clanked with every heave, and everything that wasn't nailed down rolled or shifted, creaked or clacked. Sleep was out of the question—the heaving was too much. Suddenly Dorothy convulsed and ran up topsides to kneel at the rail. Just then a fluke wave rolled up and broke against the hull, apparently with the sole purpose of soaking her. She knelt there for a while, wet, sick, sorry for herself, and then came back below to comfort her son, pausing only to inform me, icily, "If a ship comes by and is willing to rescue us, I'll give them my half of the boat!"

"Look, I've been studying the chart. Let's try making for the lee of the Caicos Bank. It's shallow enough to maybe stop the worst waves."

The Caicos Bank is a huge area of shallows that comes to within feet of the surface. Much of it consists of long, skinny sandbars and flats that dry at extreme low tides. Breaking reefs and uninhabited barrier islands border some of its perimeter, and the whole of it is the domain of seabirds and fish. Sailing behind it had to be an improvement over the open sea. Our new course, a beam reach for the lee of West Caicos, was so much steadier that Diego managed to hold down some soup and fall asleep with Theresa by his pillow.

He woke up to the seas subsiding as we got farther behind the bank, and in mid-afternoon we anchored behind the low cliffs of West Caicos with a profound sense of relief. The boat lay still and silent. There wasn't a soul in sight. The water was incredibly clear, and we could see coral thirty feet below the keel. A soft fluttering came to our ears, the sound of thousands of minnows jumping into thin air to escape a mackerel slashing past beneath. To help Diego recover his spirits, we baited a hook with chicken skin and tossed it over the side. The boy sat on the aft cabin roof with the hand reel, looking hopeful, a little color back in his wan cheeks.

"Fishing should be good here," I opined. "It drops off like a stone just behind us to a quarter of a mile deep. Anything could cruise on up out of the depths. Feeling any nibbles, son?"

"Yes. . . . Something's eating my bait right now!" He gave a tug on the line to jerk it away from a hungry little fish and immediately got a hit that almost tore the hand reel out of his grip.

"Wow! It's huge! I can't hold it!"

"Give it line, more line!" I shouted, scrambling over the cabintop to help him. He let out line as best he could but was just about to lose his grip when it suddenly relaxed.

"He got off?"

"I still feel a weight . . . but it's not fighting." He pulled it in hand over hand and up came the head of what must have been a 40-pound grouper. Everything below the gills was gone. A stunned look was in its eyes, fading.

That did a lot to improve the mood aboard the good ship *Breath*. There was enough meat in the grouper's head to make a fine meal, which Dorothy served up at sunset and which Diego devoured with a four-day hunger.

"This is more like it, eh guys? I wish we could stay here and never leave," said Diego feelingly.

"What's the next leg like?" asked Dorothy.

"Piece of cake from here to Florida. All downwind, mostly behind islands, flat water. No sweat, we've done the worst."

* * *

While Vince and I got the outboard engine back together, Dorothy and Jean cooked a great dinner. During the course of the evening both guests made much of *Breath's* seaworthy lines, her traditional rig with solid yellow pine masts, and especially her immense room below. In contrast with their tiny cabin, our interior seemed like a huge cave. Vince appreciated the sheer labor of building her, and Jean admired Dorothy for raising a family aboard without recourse to washer/drier, microwave, blender, and all the other American "necessities."

We had to push on in the morning, so this night was a farewell, fonder because the dinghy disaster had brought us closer together. Vince raised a glass and made a final toast.

"You've got a fine vessel—a young ship. May she always fare well on the ocean highway." He emptied his drink and sat back, glowing with contentment.

"And here's to the crew," chimed in Jean. "May their wishes be granted."

Next morning we waved goodbye and the boys started cranking

up the chain, when suddenly, although we'd said our goodbyes the night before, Jean and Vince got into their dinghy and came alongside. Jean had a glow in her face that wasn't from the cold.

"Vince and I have decided that your ship needs a schipperke. We want you to take your pick of the litter. It's our gift to *Breath*."

There was a hushed silence on board. I cast about in my mind for a way to refuse tactfully, but looking into my boys' happy eyes, I could see that anything I said would be like slapping them in the face. I was also aware of an electric charge of lightning-like proportions behind my back, where Dorothy stood. I got the strongest possible vibes that the whole family was holding their breath and begging me to accept. Faltering, I turned to Dorothy.

"What do you think, do we want a dog . . . ?" I was going to continue with how it really wouldn't be fair to the dog right now, the usual line, but they didn't give me the chance. A williwaw of delight almost blew me off the deck. "YES!!!!" The boys were hopping with delight, excitement cresting in their faces. Dorothy's eyes burned with a brilliance that caught my breath.

I turned and said, "Thank you! A great addition to the crew! Boys, you go over and pick your favorite. Take your time. Your mother and I will do some chores down below."

So Raff and Diego went over to select a pup. My parting words of advice were to pick the liveliest one of the litter, wisdom I had received from my father years before. Appropriate as that advice may be for normal breeds, it should be reversed for schipperkes, but the boys followed it to the letter. The little ball of jet-black fluff they brought home sat jauntily in my palm, looked me dead in the eye— and growled.

Our life with Santos had begun. Hindsight is 20/20, but in retrospect, it was entirely fitting that Santos came to us on the heels of a storm.

TWO

CLOSE CALL ON THE INDIAN RIVER

Our brand-new puppy very nearly died its first night aboard.

He came to us not yet six weeks old, the first of his litter to leave his mother. Jean gave Dorothy a little baby bottle along with elaborate instructions, but Dorothy knew just what to do. She was in her element, tending a young creature that couldn't live without her care.

The little rogue looked like a cross between a panda and an ewok, something created by a Disney or Starwars studio for the express purpose of being cute. He had a squarish, foreshortened muzzle with very fine, silky hairs on his face, the most expressive, soulful black eyes, and quick pointed ears that lay back, perked up, or tilted forward according to mood.

His first acts were characteristic—explore and get into trouble. We put him down on the floor, and immediately he began exploring every cranny of his new home with martial vigor. He flung himself in a wobbly headlong rush at the stack of teak lumber stored beneath the table, clambered with great difficulty over the boards as if assaulting a city wall under a rain of arrows and boiling oil—and got stuck between the stacks.

Nothing deterred, he pushed headfirst into one of Raffy's boots, intrigued by the smell of old leather and sweaty feet. Following his nose, he worked tightly up into the toe and then couldn't get out. Only the quivering of the leather uppers alerted us to his whereabouts.

Diego rescued him and brought him into the cockpit to see the wide world. Tracing its perimeter doggedly, he found, while we weren't looking, the cockpit drain that opened onto the deck. Scooting through the dark tunnel of 3-inch PVC pipe, he almost fell overboard through a scupper hole in the bulwarks before we could react.

Like a 2-year-old child, he had boundless energy, little control, and absolutely no fear. Diego, concerned, went around on deck blocking the scupper holes with 2 x 4 scraps and duct tape.

The puppy needed a name. We sat in the cockpit and brainstormed as we motored up the protected Intracoastal Waterway—the ICW, or what boaters call "the Ditch"—mugs of cocoa steaming in the brisk air. The day was beautiful with a crisp blue sky. An invigorating wind whitened the tops of the wavelets and rippled and furrowed the tall golden marsh grass. Small gray dolphins worked the low tide, their smooth, wet skins gleaming against the rich brown mud as they wriggled halfway out of the water up the slippery banks looking for food.

Theseus, Napoleon, Houdini, or Zorba would have been good had we but known. We tried Odysseus, but a dog, like a boat, needs a name one can call out from a dock loud and clear without hissing. We tried Jet . . . Sable . . . Bear . . . Apocalypse . . . even Sun King, the name I'd wanted to give Raf. Then when the conversation had drifted to other subjects, Raf suddenly said, "Hey, how about Santos?" That was the name of a 16th-century mestizo boy who roamed the Caribbean with a profane old parrot named Jack—characters in an ongoing story I had told the boys to entertain them on long passages. "Because he's such an explorer and he's going to sail all over the West Indies and have lots of adventures—just like Santos."

Santos he was.

The boys put him on the floor midway between them and started calling his name, beating the floor to get his attention, luring him with bits of cookie to see who he would go to first. He wobbled back and forth, confused but clearly delighted to be the focus of the excitement. He growled excitedly, a ridiculously comical sound! Barely old enough to leave his mother, tripping over his own belly—he couldn't even bark yet—but here this preposterous little hoodlum was, growling! It was a stitch to see how seriously he was already training himself to be a warrior. Though he barely weighed a full pound, nothing pleased him more than combat. Given the corner of a washcloth, he immediately clamped his needle-sharp teeth into it and hung on for dear life, growling ferociously. He might be a fluffball, but he would be a formidable one.

* * *

All day, meanwhile, the big Ford diesel exuded power and warmth, driving the boat against the rhythmic slap, slap, slap of chop blown down the broad reaches of the Indian River. As the afternoon wore on we found a deserted side canal, which allowed us to anchor well out of the river's mainstream. The sun set over the Florida flatlands, sinking into a wavy field of grass below a crisp blue sky. It looked like another cold night; the stars shone like ice crystals.

We had not expected freezing temperatures in Florida, and the boat still lacked a heater, so when it came time for bed we had to figure how to keep the dog warm. All we had was the Aladdin, a pressurized kerosene lamp. Too hot to use in the tropics, it was on nightly duty now, the family clustered around it. Now Dorothy put it next to Santos's bed, a cardboard box lined with a blanket. Seeing how active he was, we had selected a high-sided box whose lowest edge he could barely reach with the tips of his forepaws, even when standing on his hind legs as straight as his puppy belly would let him.

Securely mounted close to his snug bed, the Aladdin radiated a small circle of light and warmth that took the edge off the chill. With the blankets and his thick baby down, he would handily survive the night. He fell asleep with a dribble of milk bright about his whiskers, his little tongue tip at rest outside his closed mouth, looking for all the world like a tiny teddy bear. We watched him for a moment, fondly and already a little proud, and then retired.

Night settled in. The sky and the river leached out the last warmth stored in the hull by the engine and the afternoon sun. We humans closed all hatches and ports and wrapped up like mummies in our blankets.

Dorothy got up to check on him in the night as the cabin temperature dropped. He took a little milk and then fell back asleep. She returned to our aft cabin bunk with a fond smile and cuddled up to me for warmth.

"How's the dog?" I asked.

"Fine," she murmured, already drifting back to sleep. The boat was still and cold; the wind had dropped away to a crisp calm.

Early the next morning, well before light, Dorothy woke again. The portholes were rimed with ice.

"I'd better go check on the pup," she said.

"Save yourself the trouble. When he wakes up we'll hear about it."

"Well . . . I guess so," she said uneasily. Ten minutes later she slipped silently out of the covers to go check on her charge, stopping to put a baby bottle of milk to warm in a pan of water on the stove.

I had drifted back to sleep when I heard her cry of distress.

"The dog! The puppy's gone! He got out of the box!"

The whole family jumped from their bunks and converged to stare in disbelief at his empty box. How had he gotten out? Pulled himself up by the claws? It was a feat worthy of a gymnast—and he so fat and roly-poly!

We got a first glimpse of the little dog's monomaniacal will.

The search began in the pre-dawn dark, assisted by flashlights in the dark corners. At first I wasn't overly concerned, expecting to find him curled up somewhere near the lamp—but we didn't. We spread out, calling his name, looking first in all the obvious places. No response.

"Let's get organized," I said. "We'll go from bow to stern. Raffy, Diego, you start in Diego's cabin and work back. Dorothy and I will work from the stern, and we'll meet in the middle. Be methodical, take your time, and leave no stone unturned."

The two boys started right in the point of the bow, where Diego had his little bunk on the port side and a simple desk with a bench to starboard. Beneath were cubicles stuffed with shoes, clothes, toys, and books. Raffy searched their cabins thoroughly, looking under piles of laundry and in the folds of the awning. I looked under the main saloon table between the stacks of tools and lumber. Dorothy checked the galley, under the stove, under the sink amidst cleansers and big pots. I looked in the engine crawl space and behind the battery boxes. Together, with mounting alarm, we examined every shoe and boot on the floor in the aft cabin bedroom.

He had disappeared.

"What on earth happened to our little dog? I wonder how long he's been out of his box? He could have . . . he might have. . . ." Dorothy's anxiety turned horror struck. None of us dared voice aloud the "f" word. Lying for hours in the cold interior, a 30-degree cave, might have *frozen* him!

Now we renewed our search in high gear, disrupting everything from its resting place. He had to be somewhere, for Pete's sake! Suddenly we were tearing things apart, dumping out the laundry on the floor, overturning crates of tools and supplies, checking increasingly improbable spots. But the rascal might have wormed himself anywhere if he could hoist that fat belly out of such a high-sided box. A regular Houdini! Where the hell could he be?!

Suddenly Raffy stopped, revelation illuminating his face.

"Could he have gotten into the bilge?"

"The bilge!" we gasped. It was possible—and though bone dry, it was the coldest place in the boat—the low spot where the coldest air pooled.

One of many unfinished interior details was a narrow gap in the floorboards where the mast went through to its step on the keel. The plywood floors were unashamedly makeshift, meant to be replaced soon with hardwood planking. In the meantime we had tacked a scrap of carpet over the gap, but it tended to get accidentally knocked open again. So far, the worst that had been lost there were socks and playing cards. But yes, the hole did happen to be in its open phase and yes, a puppy that was tiny, impetuous, and very determined could have wriggled down that opening.

We picked up the floorboard nearest the mast and looked under the floor with a flashlight. We saw lengths of old chain and hose, spare turnbuckles, and metal scraps stored there, along with cobwebs and sawdust, but no trace of a dog. We removed the next one and shone the beam at the rough gray pigs of lead placed there as trim ballast. Still no dog.

There was only one more floorboard to check. With bated breath we watched Raffy stick his head and flashlight below the floor—and give a muffled shout. "There he is!"

We had finally found him in the remotest reaches of the bilge, as far as he could get from where he had entered, but it looked like we were too late. The little form lay very still on the 8-ton lump of lead and concrete that was our keel, as if he were lying on a block of ice in a morgue.

What had possessed him to explore this subterranean wasteland, the coldest, blackest place in the boat? A pathetic image came vividly to mind of him wandering in the pitch dark, bumping into sharp-edged bricks of lead, feeling his way blindly through a maze of rusty chain and gaping hoses like an Alice who had popped down a rabbit hole and found herself lost in a freezing Dante-esque hell. We imagined him trying to find some way back to the light and warmth, getting ever farther from the source, losing strength and consciousness, and finally collapsing on the killing slab.

Raffy delivered the body to Dorothy, and I braced myself to see its legs sticking out rigid with rigor mortis. But when she took him with infinite tenderness, he drooped around her palm, cold, limp, but not yet stiff!

Dorothy cradled him close to her breast, breathing on him, surrounding him in the warmth of her body, radiating concern from her eyes. The rest of us gathered around in an agony of hope.

"Get the lamp," she said, and Raffy rushed to fetch it and hold its warmth close. It illuminated a timeless crèche, mother and stricken infant. She rubbed the puppy's limbs gently to stimulate circulation.

"Get me the bottle," she said. Diego dashed to the stove and fetched the bottle, still dripping from its heating pan. She held the warm bottle to his belly for a minute, then tried to work the nipple into his mouth, but his little jaws were clamped shut. She dribbled warm milk on his tongue tip, which, even in extremis, protruded just slightly from his lips.

Then the tongue gave a twitch. His mouth opened spasmodically. He shuddered, his eyes blinked, and all at once he came to life, frantic to get the nipple in his mouth. Twice he had it but didn't know it, dislodging it as he struggled to find it. Finally he cornered it and loud, steady slurps reached our ears. Dorothy held him between arm and breast, singing a lullaby, while he lay there like a lord, glutting down milk, looking like he'd lost himself on purpose to get the attention.

Why hadn't he made a sound? Most dogs would have whimpered or barked, but this tiny fellow would keep his silence to the grave. As we were soon to find, this was no accident. Six months later he was vocal to a fault, with a hair-trigger bark in defense of the boat, yet he never made sound or complaint when *he* was in trouble. It was part of his code never to show fear, never to ask for help. Small and vulnerable he might be—he couldn't help that—but he didn't accept it and never let it stop him.

In his mind he was a bull mastiff.

THE BARGE DOG'S BOAT

The next day we passed through the locks that connected the river to the inlet at Port Canaveral, where we made arrangements with the Cape Marina boatyard to haul out.

A crowd gathered when the crane started up. *Breath* was in the slings and slowly rising out of the water, to the powerful roar of the travel lift's diesel. As the boat lifted, Diego and Raffy heard a red-bearded, seam-faced old salt tell the crowd at large, "Now that's what I call a serious boat! Look at that long deep keel, those buoyant ends—and check that prop. Some unit, eh?" People grunted approvingly, and the boys came running to tell us what they'd heard.

Breath was a 42-foot Venus design. The class name owed something to its designer's obsession with the opposite sex and to the ancient Mediterranean myth that the goddess of beauty had come from the sea. She was an unusual boat, uncompromisingly designed to cross oceans and built strong enough to survive (God willing) a hurricane. She looked salty with her jaunty bowsprit, her shiny varnished teak wheel, her double-ended stern with outboard rudder, and especially her two solid masts, hewed from whole trees like the masts of the sailing ships of old. Bright with varnish, these two stout spars immediately set *Breath* apart in any harbor

On deck, the boat felt underfoot as if it had been carved from a granite boulder. The U.S. Coast Guard had tested hull cutouts from the first Venus and declared the fiberglass skin as strong as the 4-inch-thick oak "Old Ironsides" was planked with. An anvil could be dropped on her deck, children could jump up and down on the hatches—it didn't matter. A friend from Georgia, impressed by the way the boat barely moved when he climbed aboard amidships, quipped, "This ain' no boat. . . . Thi' shere's a yoaung shyip!"

I'd only sailed once on a 42-foot Venus before I decided to build my own. John Frith, who owned *Moon*, one of the original Venuses built in Bermuda, was a friend. Knowing I was considering building one, he invited me to sail with him in the 1979 St. Barts regatta.

The day of the race was muggy and calm—"Not our preferred weather," observed John—but a decent breeze came up just in time for the start, and we were among the first over the line. Then the wind died away and the lightweight racing boats flying their drifters and genikers passed us one by one until we were dead last in a long file of boats heading for the mark, a pinnacle of rock at the tip of a little island.

We had opened cold beers and accepted that it was not to be our day when we noticed dark clouds building above St. Barts. We watched them getting blacker, clinging to the top of the island until they attained critical mass, then spilling violently down the slopes. The clouds' charcoal underbellies writhed and morphed as if in madness or agony, and the sea beneath turned electric with breaking crests.

"Hang on," said John. "If this reaches us . . .!"

The squall line reached the lead boat and knocked it flat. Sails flogged maniacally until the jib split with an audible crack and the main was clawed down.

Like a bowling ball knocking down ten pins, the gust front went down the line of boats. Some managed to drop their sails altogether, some luffed up and hung there, and others were knocked on their beam ends and pinned over by the blast.

Then it was our turn. A downdraft of chill air from aloft warned us, and then it came, a 40-knot drop-hammer, rasping white water off the sea surface. John let the main well out, but even under headsails and mizzen alone we almost suffered a knockdown. *Moon* heeled *way* over—seawater flooding the scuppers and climbing the side deck almost to her portholes—before she started to move. Then we sheeted in the main and she strode away, rail down, powerful, pulling a swelling stern wave—in short, simply hauling ass! In five minutes we passed the entire fleet, weathered the rock, and took up a new course for the next leg.

Then the squall passed, it got calm again, and in due time we were once again last in the fleet. We ended up motoring back to Gustavia, but I had seen all I needed to know. She might not be much in light airs, but I planned on a big engine anyway. How she performed in a gale of wind was far more important in a boat that would be crossing oceans with my wife and boys aboard. We didn't know about our madcap dog yet, but as it turned out, *Breath*'s seakeeping qualities probably saved his life more than once.

I called up Dorothy, who was teaching back in St. John, told her about the day, and she agreed. That night I sent a letter with a check for the plans to the designer, Paul Johnson, who was already a legend in sailing circles on both sides of the Atlantic. He wouldn't get it for several weeks because he was halfway to England on the original big Venus.

* * *

We had met Paul years before when we sailed *Venceremos*, our 28-foot sloop, from St. John across the Anegada Passage to St. Barts for the first time. The island was charming, just beginning to be developed, and when jobs were offered to us we decided to stay for a month or two. We anchored in the inner harbor—there was plenty of room in those days—near the public dock where West Indian schooners and island sloops took on cargoes of spirits to smuggle back into the Windward Islands. The hills surrounding the harbor were dotted with quaint old shingled houses.

Late one night—a bad one with furious squalls and occasional thunderbolts—I heard the flog of sails, then the rattle of chain. In the morning when I went on deck, a 28-foot gaff-rigged ketch rode to her anchor close at hand with her tan bark mizzen still up, sheeted tight to keep her bow into the wind. She was different from the other boats in the harbor. Besides being gaff-rigged, her masts were solid trees and she had a full yet jaunty stern, an out-thrust bowsprit, and high-crowned decks. She looked as rugged and buoyant as a stout barrel.

A man emerged on deck, about 35 with a full curly beard and deep, weather-beaten crow's feet about his lively eyes. He had a booming laugh and a shock of unruly hair. When he saw me, he shouted over that he had just sailed across the Atlantic from England via the Canaries, couldn't be bothered to wait for dawn, and so had threaded his way into Gustavia's teacup harbor, past outlying rocks and shoals, without benefit of chart or engine. His name was Paul Johnson.

We got to know him pretty well. Paul was a most talented, flamboyant character. Artist, sailor, boat designer, and builder—what a boatbuilder he was. He had the vitality of a Rasputin. Night after night he drank rum into the wee hours, his booming laughter audible across the harbor, and still rose early to work in the morning. He was a fount of wit, especially original and genial obscenities thrown out to make men laugh and enliven a job.

Paul had forgotten more about boats than most sailors ever learn. He had been born on a boat, a Colin Archer design well-known for its seaworthiness, whose lines were the departure point for Paul's own designs. Before he turned 21 he had rebuilt an 18-foot Shetlands fishing boat and sailed it around Europe and across the Atlantic to the West Indies. There he picked up odd jobs (and I do mean odd, as in improvised underwater demolition and delivering old boats that no one else would touch) and cruised the Lesser Antilles, the Bahamas, and the U.S. Eastern seaboard. A lot of people called him a genius, a lot of women called him sexy, a good many found him egocentric—there was truth to all of it.

Though tireless on a boatbuilding project, Paul loathed conventional work and did as little of it as possible. His solution to the problem of money was draconian—he rarely spent any. He lived on $200 a month, built what he needed himself, generally out of scraps other people had thrown away, and did without the things he couldn't improvise. He did without ice, electricity, new clothes, and fresh vegetables. He once set off across the Atlantic with less than $90 and with only onions in the vegetable locker. Two things saved him. He was so charismatic, authentic, and broke that people vied with each other to give him stuff they didn't really need; and his conversation was so interesting that he rarely had to buy drinks.

He excelled at doing things well, quickly, and cheaply. His most stunningly cost-effective stroke was building his first original design, a 28-foot Venus, from the timbers of a 70-year-old church that was to be torn down. Paul offered to dispose of the lumber and the deal was struck. The minister saw a pile of used-up wood from the preceding century, while Paul saw old-growth pitch pine cut from trees that had grown for centuries in virgin forests before being felled. There are no more 300-year-old pitch pine trees, and a more impervious wood for a boat is hard to find at any price. Suffused with pitch, the wood is proof against rot, marine worms, termites, and waterlogging. As far as Paul was concerned, 70 years in a church had properly seasoned his lumber. He borrowed a truck, rented a sawmill for a night, and by dawn had cut up all the frames, strips, and timbers he needed.

He worked dawn to dusk building the hull in a girlfriend's backyard, salvaged bronze hardware from wrecks, and sewed his own sails at night—all of which inspired admiring onlookers to donate spare hose, a coil of line, a length of chain, and old tools that had been collecting dust in an attic. He claimed he had spent just under a grand in cash by the time the boat was launched. Paul did exaggerate, and mightily, but still. . . .

Although the same length on deck as *Venceremos*, Little Venus had twice the room below, sailed as well off the wind, and looked a lot saltier. I told myself that if Paul ever designed a larger version, that would be the perfect boat for our family. Years later, when he sailed his new Venus 42 down to the Antigua Race Week, we met him there and were amazed at the strength, the seaworthiness, the amount of space below, and the boat's capacity for water and stores. This was the perfect cruising vessel.

The only trouble was, I'd have to build it myself. Venuses didn't come made to order off the shelf, and if they had, I couldn't have afforded one.

* * *

Building a boat where we lived, at the remote East End of St John, had its difficulties. Supplies were a problem, since the road was so steep and treacherous. I ended up using a small barge to deliver shipments right to the beach. It was a tiny landing craft built with plywood, painted military gray, and named *JAWS* after its most prominent feature—the sharks' teeth painted on its hinged bow ramp. The barge was run by an old sailor with a quiet manner and a face seamed and battered like a boat fender that had been jammed between a barge and a rough concrete dock in a gale. Every time we loaded her up in St. Thomas with lumber, barrels of resin, and pallets of fiberglass cloth, I wondered if we would get to Round Bay before we sank, but the old girl and her weatherworn owner never let me down. Her demise came when a front-end loader lowering something heavy from a high dock into *JAWS*' hold overreached and fell in on top of the cargo.

When it came time to lay up the fiberglass hull, expert help lived close at hand. Within the previous year, six smaller vessels of Block Island cowhorn design had been built by friends in nearby Coral Bay. We all helped each other do the hull fiberglassing. My boat was the last to be ready for building, by which time we had become expert fiberglassers. All the guys were good friends and conscientious. There had been jokes that by the time I was ready they'd be gone sailing, but now, determined that I should not lose from having been last, they delivered their best efforts, and the result was one of the finest fiberglass hulls possible, a true labor of love.

Breath's wheel, main boom, bowsprit, anchors, and much else were salvaged from the classic English yacht *Armorel*, which had piled up on Johnson's Reef, not far from East End, the day before a hurricane struck. Its crew of one called in vain on the VHF for help to pull her off, as the damage of the grounding had been slight, but the constant stream of boats passing by were panicked at the approach of Hurricane David, a category 4 or 5 storm that was due in 24 hours, and they made a beeline for Hurricane Hole, anxious to find a good anchorage in the protected mangrove creeks before the protected spots filled up. David ended up going south of the islands, sparing us a direct hit but sending enormous seas, 25 feet from crest to trough, directly into Coral Bay. They flung the *Armorel* high upon the reef and broke her back.

But it's an ill wind that blows no good. I helped salvage the boat, and the captain rewarded me handsomely with gear I could use, notably the wheel. Crafted from 19th-century Burmese teak with bronze ring plates, it was a beautiful piece of work with carved spokes, all varnished and gleaming in the sunlight as it spun.

The big day finally came.

The hull had been launched five months previously and towed to the creek in Coral Bay, where I added lead and cement ballast, stepped and rigged the masts, spliced the strops for the halyard blocks, bolted the stanchions to the bulwarks, strung the lifelines, and did half a million other jobs. At last she was ready to sail, the moon was full, and the tide was high enough for us to get past the bar.

"Let's go for it."

Word spread, and people came to watch as several outboard dinghies pulled her out of her berth, the diesel engine having yet to be fitted. For the first time we raised the bright white unblemished sails, caught the breeze, and started to slip through the water. At that moment a fellow emerged onto the foredeck of a cruising boat that was passing through. He was dressed in kilt and tartan cape with a set of bagpipes under his arm, and he began to play. The unexpected sound of that blood-stirring music that has propelled men against the odds for so many centuries triggered in me a fierce joy and gratitude that came close to tears as we sailed through the boats and out the harbor, the piper playing on and on until the wind slowly muffled his sound. It was an incomparable way to start *Breath*'s career under sail.

Her performance far exceeded my expectations. She turned out to be much faster than I had hoped and handy enough to sail anywhere. Immensely strong, stable, and roomy, she carried 400 gallons of fresh water, had a powerful engine, and best of all, looked beautiful under sail. Dorothy and the boys were at the house in East End when they heard conch horns blowing and looked out over Round Bay to see *Breath* under sail for the first time. I drove in to get them in the skiff, and we all drank her in. With topsail and flying jib and her high-peaked gaff boom, she looked like a miniature tall ship cutting through the water on her way to Cathay. I could scarcely believe I'd built her.

Best of all, she was simple throughout, made of materials we could repair ourselves at sea—wood, sail cloth, fiberglass, leather, rope. We had no electronics save a tape deck and a VHF. The sextant helped us find our way, and instead of an electronic depth finder, we used a lead and line—infallibly accurate, and nothing to break. When we finally lost it years later halfway up the Gambia River, where it snagged the bottom, we just went ashore and made a fire on the riverbank. While Santos sniffed up a storm and secured the perimeter against baboons, we melted lead and cast it into a Guinness bottle that we buried up to its neck in wet sand—all in keeping with Paul Johnson's fervent adherence to the KISS principle: Keep It Simple, Stupid.

FOUR

PORT CANAVERAL

A defining moment of Santos's life came after we'd been hauled out at the boatyard for a week. Morning and evening we took him, on a leash of red yarn, to a quiet part of the yard where boats were stored on land. There, away from the commotion of vessels being readied for sea, he could be released to run around in a couple acres of scrub grass and sand and begin to learn about business—his business—namely, that the best place for a boat dog to do his business was ashore, and the sooner he learned, the better.

This part of the boatyard gave him powerful cues as to what was expected of him. Towering above him were boats in storage, giant monoliths to Santos, the keels of which rested on baulks of timber that kept them from sinking into the sand. These bare wood timbers retained odors of previous dogs in the grain and had an olfactory history that, for all I knew, went back decades. The little dog would sniff at the blocks, quivering with excitement, until he found a corner where he could make his statement.

All went well at first until he put together the connection—that shortly after he transacted his business, the walk would end. So the pup began to take his sweet time about it, first practicing his jungle warfare exercises. He would creep up behind a dandelion and then charge through, scattering the ephemeral flower in a satisfying explosion of petals.

Doing this one day he startled a big lizard, green like weathered copper, with yellow markings, which had been dozing in the sun. Panicked, it scuttled away, shaking the grass as it went. Santos immediately gave chase, struggling frantically through the tufts, getting spiked by chest-high blades of grass and stepping heedlessly on sharp sand burrs, oblivious to pain and anything else save the pursuit. This was the first creature ever to run from him, and the ego boost was monumental. Now he had a mission; he became the terror of the grassy tufts. Henceforth all lizards take note!

His walks took ever longer to accomplish their crucial item of business, and what had been a peaceful place for a reptile to warm its blood was now twice a day subject to alarums and uproars. We caught up on our reading while Santos roamed farther in quest every day. And day by day he grew bigger; within a couple of weeks he had grown into his puppy belly, so that it no longer ballasted him down. In his daily walks and stalks, it became apparent that this once roly-poly mite would grow into an exceptionally agile, fast little animal. At the time none of us realized how chasing validated him, and we certainly could never have guessed the astonishing extreme to which he'd take it.

* * *

One weekend we took a break from the boat and drove in a friend's car to Orlando, a trip during which we had the first of many encounters with lodgings that disallowed pets. When hotels feel free to issue prohibitions, what's a traveling family to do but feel free to flout them? We tried to find a motel as darkness fell, but each one we passed was either full or wouldn't take pets. Desperate, we finally decided to smuggle Santos in; Dorothy slipped him into the big pocket of her parka and kept her hand on him as we walked past the front desk, which was staffed by a gaunt, pinch-faced dowager with lines of irritation etched permanently around her mouth.

We needed this room. She knew this, and also knew she would have no trouble filling it with some other party. This pitiful trifle of power corrupted her in a trifling, pitiful way. She honed in on us, squinting her beady eyes suspiciously at Diego. "Does this one still wet his bed?" Diego went scarlet and started a hot retort, but I choked him. One peep from Santos and we were through. We held our breaths as she guided us to the room, then fumbled with the key for ages before finally opening the door. Still she wouldn't leave, but had to warn us, glowering at the boys, not to get the floor wet.

Just as she was turning to leave, Santos gave a restless peep. The woman whirled, eyes glinting, but Dorothy, thinking quickly, said, "Excuse me! I have to use the bathroom right away!" and vanished within it, shutting the door with a decisive bang. Trumped, the woman left.

The place was dingy enough that a little puppy piddle on the rug would never have been noticed, but we took turns watching him and lifting him to newspaper at the first sign of hesitation. Whenever he whimpered, one of us jumped to silence him. We smuggled him back and forth again for supper, stuffed him with scraps at McDonalds, and placed him on an old shirt in the bathroom. He woke only once in the night; his whimper dragged us out of deep sleep, and his first tiny, sharp bark catapulted us out of bed to his side.

On that trip, amid crowds of strangers, we began to appreciate the little dog's charisma. When Dorothy walked up to Disney World leading her jet-black teddy bear on a length of bright red yarn, she caused a small sensation. Everybody she passed smiled, stared at the dog, reached down to pet him, and asked her a question we were to hear a thousand times in the future. "What breed is that?" A tall, burly, weather-beaten man wearing richly tooled boots and a Stetson hat stands out in my memory—he immediately brought to mind John Wayne. He gestured at Santos with a twinkle in his eye. "Scuse me, ma'm . . . but that critter o' yourn thar. . . . Is it a dawg, or a b'ar?"

Santos's lack of a tail, his squarish body, his spiky mane, and his odd sideways gait confused people. No one who looked him in the face could doubt he was a dog, but over the years people asked us if he was a fox or bear cub—or a Vietnamese pig, porcupine, dwarf wolverine, or even a Tasmanian devil. In Africa he never failed to draw a crowd of fascinated onlookers, who invariably wanted to know if he was a baby "buki," or hyena.

But it wasn't just his looks that caught the eye. There was also the intensity with which he did everything. When we picked up our dog at Disney's free pet-care facility, we found the entire staff of clean-cut teenagers gathered around Santos, watching his antics and laughing while he "went on bad," as West Indians put it.

It was only a matter of time before Raffy found a use for this natural resource.

When we went to watch a space shuttle launch we found ourselves a couple of cars down from a station wagon with Michigan plates and two pretty girls. Raff, who was stealing surreptitious glances their way, fidgeting while he tried to concentrate on a book, suddenly looked up with a Eureka! expression on his face, whipped the dog's leash out of the glove compartment, and said, "C'mon Santos, let's go for a walk." He strolled away from the girls' car, closely inspected some apparently notable lichens growing on a chain link fence, and then oh so nonchalantly turned and sauntered toward his objective.

Santos obligingly hurled himself over and over again at the leash, like the lead dog on a fairies' sled team, pulling until he gasped, drawing all eyes upon him.

The two girls waltzed out of their car, proclaiming their adoration. They asked Raffy if they could pick the puppy up. They hugged Santos close, stroked him, fluttered their eyelashes, vocalized, and generally carried on as if for an event in a beauty contest—("using this furry animal as a prop, each contestant shall exhibit the range of her feminine charms, to the max, in five minutes").

Such extravagance was permissible when directed toward a puppy but by no means wasted on Raffy either. He lingered fondly, talking and bantering with the girls, exchanging addresses, while his younger brother, glued to the windshield, admiringly denounced such an egregiously brazen ploy and catalogued it carefully for future retrieval.

Many were the outings Santos enjoyed because a pretty girl walked by. In Seville, Santiago de Cuba, Caracas, Key West, Charleston, and Charlotte Amalie, Santos reeled 'em in every time.

* * *

Despite the regular walks, housebreaking was not an overnight success. It was a process, a give-and-take that evolved over time into a mutually acceptable accord. As Dorothy noted, he trained us as much as we trained him. One thing quickly became crystal clear—given the choice between a big dog or a little dog aboard ship, little is better.

Like every other puppy owner, we began with a newspaper on the floor. But no, his offerings were too painfully obvious in the middle of the floor on clean newsprint. He opted instead for a guerrilla campaign, clandestine drops, making his mark in the dark, and eventually came to favor the narrow, shadowy walkway between the engine and my desk. Here the floorboards, anointed by previous visits, announced "this is the spot."

However this was also *my* spot—my study and navigation table, where I determined the fate of the ship! It impeached the captain's dignity to have to get down on his knees to clean the cracks in the floorboards with an old toothbrush . Naturally, it was here that the most memorable accident of his house-training career occurred.

We were beat. I'd been up until 2 A.M. the night before doing last-minute jobs, but at last the boat was in the slings, the travel lift was roaring, and she was easing back into the water.

Then Dorothy shouted, "Peter, water is *gushing* into the hull!"

Instantly I remembered. Sometime after midnight I'd removed the engine's old saltwater intake hose without turning the seacock off!

An inch-and-a-half-diameter hole in the water with 20 tons of boat pressing down on it shoots a jet of water straight as a fire hose into the air. From the deck, the gusher sounded like Niagara Falls diverted into my boat. Adrenaline pumping, my gaze riveted to the seacock, I dropped through the companionway, slipped in something, and landed with an oath of surprise, flat on my back.

One part of me found the seacock handle and shut off the water while the rest of me lay there stunned. Holding my afflicted leg in the air as if it was leprous, I could hear the crack of pistol shrimp through the hull and Dorothy bustling down the companionway.

"Are you all right? What about the leak?"

"The dog . . .," I croaked. I pointed to my foot. "He got me good."

"Oh my poor dear! How awful!" She nervously looked for the dog out of the corner of her eye, ready to interpose her body between me and him. I had recently made intemperate remarks about what I'd do to the little devil if he used my office as a privy again.

"Right at your desk . . . the *worst* place," she commiserated. "Stay right there while I get you some paper towels." She kept up a lulling patter, meanwhile darting up the companionway to give the kids hushed orders to take the dog on a very long walk and not to return until dark.

I came to myself, sat up, and turned on the seacock again. It blasted out, cold and clean, and I bathed my foot in the stream, washing carefully between my toes until they were impeccable.

"Oh, you must be furious. . . ." She looked at me warily, waiting for the outburst that, unfortunately, she had cause to expect. But this time I was calm.

"Not really, it's too . . . farcical. The little brat really nailed me that time. I should wring his neck."

My wife laid me down solicitously, soothing my brow with a cool cloth, then got up to put a bottle of wine on ice and started cooking stir-fried chicken. When the boys returned, Raffy came circumspectly aboard to scout the situation. Satisfied, he gave Diego the all-clear sign, and the dog returned. I insisted that he stay on deck, and everybody was quick to agree, but come morning I noticed that someone had brought him down during the night. He was sprawled out cheerfully on the saloon floor, back legs splayed to either side like he owned the place.

* * *

Rivers are deceptive. One thinks of the ocean deeps as being most dangerous for a boat, while a river seems inherently safe because land and help are always near. Land is a two-edged sword, though. A boat on a river is always potentially close to hitting the shore, and rivers, during anomalous conditions, can attain currents of devastating velocity. The closest *Breath* ever came to sinking was on a river, and a river almost killed Santos on two different occasions.

The first time was right there in Port Canaveral, where we spent a few days in a slip on the river several miles from the sea, readying the boat for the resumption of our voyage. Here the tide ran swiftly past our hull—six hours out the inlet and then six hours in, regular as clockwork. A hundred yards away, in the middle of the river, the ebb stream attained four knots and boiled and rippled as it ran out the inlet.

Plenty of work needed to be done getting the boat back into cruising mode from haulout mode. All the tools and supplies had to be restowed, the sails bent on, the anchors readied.

Oblivious to the commotion around him, Santos played "Canine the Barbarian," a puppy war game of his own devising, which featured all three pounds of him hurtling down the deck to disembowel or otherwise mutilate and impress the hell out of an imaginary enemy. He'd start his sprint at the mainmast, heading aft, his teeth bared and flashing white, a bloodcurdling snarl issuing from his throat. Velocity and ferocity were the desired results—control was a distant second. Typically, by the time he reached the front wall of the cabin, his momentum bounced him head over heels into the bulwarks. After picking himself up and shaking his fur, he'd trot back to the mainmast to do it again, faster, badder, perfecting his charge, honing his snarl. It was comical but also endearing how the little dog was obsessed by his need for respect. He had to have it; he conceded nothing to size; he *would* be feared.

When lunchtime came we went down for a quick bite and then moved into the aft cabin to rearrange stowage under the bunk. There we gradually became aware of a strange sound—not the pistol shrimp that live in the Intracoastal Waterway and make a loud cracking sound audible through any hull, but a very slight scratching or scraping. And it seemed to be coming not from the riverbed but from our waterline. Suspecting a can or twig caught in a trailing rope and marring my freshly painted boottop, I jumped up on deck, looked over the side—and there was Santos! He was treading water, dog paddling almost vertically, scratching his forepaw claws against the boottop.

"Dorothy! He's in the water!"

A short shriek of alarm scarcely preceded her arrival on deck, followed closely by both boys. Raffy and Dorothy grabbed my legs as I bent way over the hull and scooped Santos out of the water. He must have lost control while charging down the deck and went out a scupper hole. How long had he been scratching there? Would he be all right? What about hypothermia?

Then we remembered the tide. It was slack just then, and slack tide didn't last any more than 15 minutes there. That was the longest he could have been swimming in the cold February water, and it didn't seem to have harmed him any. He'd been damned lucky the current was slack—a few minutes later and he'd have been riding a fast track out the inlet and into the Gulf Stream.

Of course attention was lavished on him. Dorothy hugged him and put her radiant brown eyes close to his face, kissing him and telling him what a wonderful dog he was to survive, what a smart dog to pick slack tide to tumble into the drink, what a little athlete to swim like an otter his first time ever in the water. We all hovered around.

Big mistake. We gave him all the wrong signals. He learned that hairbreadth escapes and dangerous games made him a hero and brought adulation and an unusually good supper. To the young furry immortal, that was the best game of all.

He resolved to make a career as a Cossack.

FIVE

LEARNING THE ROPES

By the time Santos was nine months old, we were ready to return to St. John, our adopted home in the U.S. Virgins. We'd gotten a good dose of continental U.S. culture gunkholing from south Florida to North Carolina and back, a land of incredible freeways and grocery stores, national parks and industrial parks, housing projects and space projects. Life for better or worse on the point of the world's forward thrust had satiated our "rock fever" for awhile. We were tired of always being strangers; we missed our friends and the beauty of the islands. It was time to go home to the "rock," put the kids back in school, make some more money.

The only problem was that St. John lies about 1,200 miles to the east of Florida, dead against the easterly trade winds. Sailing against the wind is known as "beating to windward," and the choice of verb is deliberate. Smashing against seven-foot seas can be exhilarating for a couple of hours in a bathing suit, but doing it day after day is an ordeal. A well-found boat can take it, but the crew is often another matter. We worried about Diego and wondered about Santos. How would they fare on the high seas? There was, of course, only one way to find out. After carefully stowing everything below and tightly lashing everything on deck, we motored out between the long stone breakwaters at the mouth of the narrow inlet, onto the wide ocean.

A fitful southwest wind was blowing off the low, endlessly stretching beach as we rounded up at noon and started raising sail—first the mizzen to hold her bow into the wind, and then the big main, Raffy pulling the peak halyard while I hauled on the throat halyard, together raising the heavy gaff.

Santos was underfoot, growling and tugging at the halyards, until Raff, throwing himself back to sweat up the peak, accidentally stepped on his paw. There was a sharp yip from the dog and he backed off to nurse his first seagoing lesson—stay out of the way of work.

He wandered about the deck inspecting changes. Inanimate objects that had always just lain there had suddenly come alive—like the jibsheet block, which now stood eagerly erect and creaked with strain. The steering wheel turned to and fro, back and forth, pacing like a caged bear. The staysail boom, which had always been tethered quietly to the lifeline, was lifted high off the deck by its taut white sail and flogged back and forth like a truncheon whenever it lost its wind.

Dorothy kept the dog leashed to a cleat in the cockpit for his own safety, but he hated being restrained, and I finally unclipped him for a minute. He snuggled underneath my foul-weather jacket and gave a sigh of satisfaction, but when I went to check the lashings on the life raft he scampered halfway down the deck.

"Santos, come!" I said urgently. He adopted his mischievous "come catch me" posture, his head and shoulders low, his rump high and ready to spring. Meanwhile a big sea was rearing up behind him.

"Santos, dammit, come here right now!" I lunged for him, but catching that dog was a hopeless proposition for just one person. I left the helm too long, the boat started rounding up, and he was still thinking himself clever when green water crashed aboard, sweeping him head over paws across the deck and slamming him up against the lee bulwarks. The streaming water tried to sluice him through the scupper hole while the hungry sea boiled past, but he knew enough to splay his limbs. When the water was gone and the boat rose to meet the next wave, he obeyed "come!" with alacrity. It was the first of many attempts by the ocean to swallow him.

This was a true "shake-down" cruise, another nautical expression that means just what it says. After months in a calm port, many items are insufficiently stowed for a sea voyage. They come crashing down in the first rough weather, when the boat lurches up a steep sea, gyrates off its back, rolls in the trough, and slams into the next.

Dorothy and I held our breaths over Diego, hoping his stomach had improved. Months of flat calm had convinced him that seasickness was a thing of the past, especially with his older brother there to coach him through. In the morning before we left, Raff and Diego held an intensive session, their heads together as Raff exhorted and Diego absorbed. "You have to psyche it out, Diego. Get tough! It's a war—build up your mental defenses. You can do it!"

Diego emerged from his pep talk confident.

"It's mind over matter, Dad," he said almost jauntily. "I just have to psyche it out."

He was fine as we left the inlet, remained so in the smoother waters of the continental shelf, but started to lose it quickly as we entered the choppy seas of the Gulf Stream, that great ocean river.

"Are you feeling alright?" I asked him upon noticing he'd been quiet for awhile—always a warning sign of seasickness.

"OK . . .," he answered, lackluster. "Not great." His face looked wan and fragile. He sat in the cockpit clinging to the boom gallows while his brother sat by his side and kept up a line of encouraging patter, tried to distract him with jokes, and urged him to keep his eyes on the horizon, the only fixed line left in a tossing world. Then even that faint comfort was blotted out by swells that heaved up over the line.

Tears came to his eyes as nausea overwhelmed him and he hurriedly sought the rail on his knees.

"I'm having a very, very bad day!"

The seas had been increasing. *Breath* sidestepped most of them adroitly, but one boxcar of a sea rose up from nowhere and body slammed the hull, sending a shudder through the ship and raising an explosion of spray. It was as if the rough hand of God had reached suddenly from a cloud and wrenched the masts over. The impact caught Santos scampering when he should have been clinging. His footing disappeared, his paws scrabbled in thin air, and he landed in the cockpit just under the wheel, whose spinning spokes gave him a bastinado of cudgel blows. The dog gave a short shriek of surprise.

"Santos! He's hurt!" Diego forgot about being sick and cradled the dog, who was gasping for breath. A little later Diego retired to his bunk and Santos was put down below for his own safety. When we saw them next, both youngsters were curled up together, fast asleep.

In the morning we had crossed the Gulf Stream and the seas were much improved. Gradually we rounded the northeast side of the Little Bahama Bank, a vast shallows rimmed by long, stringy islands and peppered with reefs, rocks, and sandspits like scattershot discharged from a giant broadside. When Diego awoke he felt well enough for a bite of breakfast. The sky was a bright, promising blue, and we were smoking along on a broad reach for Nassau.

One question had been answered. Santos was *not* prone to seasickness. This took a weight off our minds, because dogs do get seasick and there's no training them to vomit over the lee rail. Where they are is where you get it—the galley floor, your berth, the middle of the cockpit.

* * *

Nassau had once been a nice town with character and breeding. Island sloops laden with conch had sailed up to their moorings in the blazing blue channel that separated the bustling waterfront from the long, narrow island that gives Nassau its harbor. Palm trees grew in well-tended gardens behind the walls of substantial waterfront buildings, and stately hotels built of pink sandstone gave the town class.

Now the place seemed tacky, the waterfront overbuilt, docks and bars and television antennas extending everywhere in haphazard clutter. Gone were the old wooden sloops. Now the boats that caught the eye were fast, flashy smuggling craft—Scarabs and Cigarettes, chromed and gelcoated daggers thrust by huge horsepower—and their opposites, overloaded, battered Haitian traders with planks showing at their tired seams, their box-sided cabins fitted with one or two tiny windows that revealed nothing of the interior, their cabintops piled high with bicycles, poultry, a pig, and other unassorted goods.

Everywhere ashore, Haitian vendors sold an overflow of cheap carvings dominated by grotesque masks. Their unemployed countrymen sat around on empty crates and on the curbs in the dust of the street, conversing in Creole. They were ubiquitous, the native Bahamians scarce. And when a native did accost me, it was at night on a dimly lit shabby street.

"Yo . . . bro! . . . Hey! . . . Hey mon! Wan' buy some crack?"

"No way Jose!"

"How 'bout some ganja den?"

"No thank you."

"A girl? Something special . . ."

"What's so special? She your sister?"

"Huh?"

"Or a Chinee girl?"

"Uh . . . no mon." He seemed taken aback. "You know . . .," his tone plaintive now, "just a big, nice, black Haitian girl. . . . Sweet." He lapsed back into the doorway of a late-night chicken fry shop.

Oh well, the Bahamas is not the only country whose biggest city is its least attractive place. The best parts of the Bahamas were yet to come—the out islands and the out-out islands, a chain of stepping stones suffused in light that shines down from the sky and refracts up from the sea. They lie to the southeast of Nassau, stretching all the way to Hispaniola, and provide stops for the Caribbean-bound voyager in waters of matchless clarity. We left the capitol in midafternoon and headed for those clearer waters, setting a course for the Exumas, a day's sail away.

SIX

EXUMA EPIPHANY

In my last year of college I read a book that changed my life. It wasn't the Bible or *Das Kapital* or even the *Kama Sutra*. It was the *Skin Diver's Travel Guide to the Caribbean* that I read during deep winter New Hampshire nights when snow hung heavy on the pines outside the windows. I read about the seas and reefs of South Caicos and Anegada and Aruba, dreaming of clear warm water glowing with light. The image of plunging off a pure slope of sand into that shimmering aquamarine plucked longingly at some ecstatic string within me. That book drew us down to the islands, and of all the places it described, the choicest were the islands and cays of the Exuma archipelago.

Santos stood in his favorite landfall position—poised precariously on the bowsprit—as we approached the Exumas close-hauled to a fresh breeze. The seas became progressively flatter as we neared the lee of the islands. We had left Nassau the previous afternoon, sailed all night, and in the morning had carefully picked our way across the Yellow Banks, where occasional coral colonies grow in massive heads to the surface. There had been nothing to see or smell for hours, and he was bored when finally the wind started carrying snippets of information to him, intimations of shrubs and grass and birds and the pungent whiff of a salt pond. Land.

The cays and islands of the Exumas run north to south for a hundred miles, making an eastern boundary to the vast area of shallows known as the Grand Bahama Bank. The bank, extending from the Exuma archipelago toward Florida in the west and Cuba to the south, covers thousands of square miles under a mantle of water as clear as distilled air.

Exuma geology is schizophrenic. On their western, leeward sides, the islands descend into the sea so gradually that even a mile from shore you can stand in water only three feet deep. Broad expanses of beach are skimmed by only an inch or two of water. Looking down from a jetliner's window, one is hard put to tell where the sea stops and terra firma begins.

Yet the windward shoreline is just the opposite. The beaches are narrow, mere ribbons of sand, and much of the coastline consists of low cliff. The bottom drops away steeply to the east, then plummets to the ocean floor almost a mile deep. On this side of the islands, the visual boundary between water and land couldn't be more distinct. Seen from a jet, the endless expanse of cobalt blue to the east comes to an abrupt westward halt at a narrow strip of vivid—blazing—aquamarine. Shoreward of that is a ribbon of surf and beach, then the dry Bahamas tan of scrubby, sandy soil and salt ponds.

The long, skinny islands, separated only by narrow cuts, form an almost continuous barrier against the sea. At high tide the sea piles up on the banks, pushed in through the cuts by the easterly trades and retained there by the dike of islands. The ebb then races back out through the cuts, sluices of tumbling water carrying streams of whitecaps well out to sea.

Six hours later, on the way back in, the flood tide funnels through the same rocky cuts and scours deep ditches of electric blue in the soft sandy seafloor of the banks. But as the tidal stream escapes the confines of the cuts, it spreads out, slows down, and carves ever more fanciful patterns in the sand—galactic spirals, French curves, and fish-scale scallop as of clouds in the sky. Gradually over time, the contrasting sworls of vivid blue and muted sea-grass green fade, diminish, and die away.

* * *

As we approached the Exumas, the bottom came into constant view through water so clear we could see every coral head and sea fan and constantly feared going aground, though the lead showed a steady fathom—six feet—of water beneath our keel. Raffy climbed the ratlines to search ahead for a blue channel of deeper water. From 30 feet up the contrast of colors appeared more distinct, and he eventually conned us through a maze of shoals and reefs and into a broad pool of turquoise protected from every direction by islands and reefs.

The tide was high when we dropped the hook between a sandbank that was just awash and a small, rocky cliff. The next morning when we came on deck the tide had dropped and the sandbank had emerged as a half-acre of freshly washed and rippled sand. That beach was pristine; it called to us in a primal tongue, "Come make your mark !" The boys, Santos, and I couldn't resist.

Our dinghy nudged the beach with a soft grating sound, and for a moment we were spellbound in the presence of a cosmic prototype. Blue-edged water, translucent as a gem, intersected a soft loaf of pure white sand. This was the most perfect beach we'd ever seen, without the least impurity of coral fragments or half-buried shells or grass. Its surface was gently curved, and every inch was intricately, flawlessly rippled. That bar of sand was as elemental and refined as a bar of the purest gold.

Santos reached the end of the sandbar and doubled back at the boys with his tongue lolling, his ears back, and his eyes full of play. They charged, trying to catch him, but he dodged them with ease. Whooping at his marvelous agility, they gave chase, trying to trap him at the water's edge, but he ducked and dodged, then accelerated like a bullet past their outstretched hands. The little dog was uncannily swift and evasive; he could turn on a dime and hit full stride in the opposite direction as though he'd been bounced off a taut trampoline. Even on this circumscribed half-acre they couldn't catch him. I joined the chase and Santos redoubled his efforts, a wild ecstasy in his eye. The sand was so soft we could fall on it with impunity, and soon the three of us were making extravagant flying tackles and landing harmlessly, laughing with the almost psychedelic freedom of it, the exhilarating release from the normal consequences of gravity. Shouting with exuberance, we finally cornered him at the water's edge and hurled ourselves into the crystal, exploding it into foam, like lords at play in the firmament.

What a great game it was. Finally exhausted, we surveyed our work. Nothing remained of the pristine cloudlike ripples we had met—the surface of the beach was completely cratered, plowed, and churned. We swam back to the boat towing the dingy, diving down to get the fine sand out of our hair and dunking the dog to get it out of his eyes and nose, delighting in the warm-cool water, swimming through a shimmery emerald brilliance that sorry potentates only knew to hoard and wear, congealed and useless, on their fingers.

As we climbed back on board, the aroma of French toast drifted through the galley portholes and Dorothy's melodious voice gave us good morning and bade us to get ready for breakfast. The meaning of her words was no sweeter than the sound of her voice on that enchanted morning. Dorothy epitomized Shakespeare's Cordelia;

"her voice was ever soft and low, a good thing in woman."

Breakfast followed under the cockpit awning, with canned Dutch butter and homemade syrup spiced by fresh key lime. The tide rose all that morning and covered the sandbank as the boys did their chores. In the afternoon it fell, and by the time they had completed the day's home schooling and the parents had put in a good day's work on the boat, the beach had reemerged, as perfect as it was at the dawn of time when God delighted in his creation. And the five of us—mother, father, two young sons, and roguish dog—threw ourselves into the water, swam ashore, and played the game again, leaving the field happily and thoroughly trashed, only to wake up next morning to find it waiting in pristine splendor once again, washed and combed and arrayed by the sea.

This interlude was one of the high points of our lives, as I look back on it now. We stayed anchored next to that miraculous sandbar that, like the basket of loaves and fishes, was constantly renewed, until the cycle of the tides gradually changed to a single low at midday, and we moved on to another anchorage.

The experience shaped Santos to his dying day. Always, more than anything else in life, he loved to sprint down a beach in early morning.

SEVEN

AWOL AT WARDERICK WELLS

A week later *Breath* lay to two stout anchors at Warderick Wells in the central Exumas. As the tide funneled through the narrow, curving channel between the island and a broad shoal that was almost awash, the boat stood taut to her anchor chain like a bird dog pointing to a pheasant, leaving a distinct wake behind her. When the tide reversed, she fetched up on her other anchor and pointed the opposite direction. Only at slack tide did she face into the wind.

The channel was lovely, glowing with blue light, carved by eons of tide between a long white sand beach and glimmering flats tinged with green and yellow. Here we were content to spend a few days, Santos getting his fill of beach, the boys catching up on their lessons under Dorothy's tutelage while I put the finishing touches on a plywood dinghy I was building on deck to replace our afflicted inflatable.

Deflatable would be a better description. The rubber dinghy had a terminal skin disease—its fabric had gone flaky, and it wheezed from a dozen open sores that had been patched time and again. Water leaked in through the floor, air leaked out the pontoons; the time had come to take it ashore and shoot it. The new dinghy would be light, fast, and leak-free. The boys were looking forward to trying it out after lunch with the outboard motor.

"Lai lai lai!" Dorothy called from down below—a summons to eat that had originated from her mother's childhood in China. I put down my plane and headed below, leaving Santos on deck. The awning was up, and he was snoozing a brief puppy power nap in the shade with the cool sea breeze blowing over the deck—the finest of climates. I let the sleeping dog lie.

"Beans and rice again? When are we going to have meat?" groaned Diego.

"When you kill a cow," Raff offered, digging in. He had a healthy omnivorous appetite, whereas Diego was picky and hated all but "brown" vegetables—i.e., meat.

A paroxysm of barking assailed our ears. The dog was awake and at it again as a dinghy from one of the other boats passed by. We shouted at him to stop, but the noise continued unabated. Nobody wanted to get up and go on deck to hush him, so we waited him out. The other boats in the harbor were far enough away not to be disturbed. Finally the barking tailed off and stopped with an odd, plaintive, aggrieved yelp. It meant nothing to us at the time, but we were to learn.

We lingered over lunch, discussing Raffy's history lesson, the Mongol invasion of India. Raff wanted to know what enabled the Mongols to suddenly burst out of the steppes and sweep all resistance before them, and I tried to explain the role of momentum in history and the power of a new weapon or mode of combat like the chariot, the iron blade, the phalanx, the long bow, the gun, or the sailing ship.

Already Raff loved long, deep discussions of history and politics and would keep me up an extra hour at night. He always got more intense as the hour got closer to bedtime—mine, at any rate. His mind was catching fire as he moved into his teens, concepts breaking over him like a wave of champagne, intoxicating him and tumbling him forward. A youth's awareness leaps forward at certain times during adolescence, and this was one of them.

He would thrive at a university, but where was the money to come from? How would we come up with $17,000 or $20,000 a year? The boys had known from an early age that they'd have to be bright and deserving enough to win scholarships if they wanted to go on to college.

Dorothy used to remark that Raff had an unusually long attention span for a two-year-old, but I'd put it down to a fond mother's bias until the day a few years later when he stopped me in my tracks. We were trolling in the skiff, slowly, through the narrow channel that runs behind Lovango Cay and Congo Cay off St. John Island. We were living on the other side of Lovango at the time, and Congo was one of our favorite spots, a long, narrow, steep-spined cay like a blade of the chiseled and fluted rock that showed silver-gray through the glossy profusion of its tire palms. At the end of the island, gnarled rock dropped into the sea and kept dropping to the bottom 90 feet down. This was our favorite diving and fishing spot, where anything might strike. In recent visits I'd speared a 40-pound amberjack, had mackerel snapped off my spear by lightning-fast barracuda, seen large schools of bonito flash by, and been persuaded to exit the water by an overly curious 8-foot bull shark.

On this occasion Dorothy had caught a fish and hauled it in without much struggle, and we all stared at it. Being avid free divers, we prided ourselves on knowing the fish, but none of us had seen this one before—none of us, that is, except skinny little tow-headed Raff. The six-year-old looked at it carefully and said, "I think this is the *Synodus intermedius* . . . or something. I don't know how to pronounce it."

"What . . . ?!"

"It's in the book."

"What book?"

"Our fish book."

"That's the Latin name?"

"I think it's also called a sand diver."

"You have *GOT* to be kidding!"

He had learned to read a year before, and for the last several months his favorite book had been *Caribbean Reef Fishes*, which gave a fish's Latin name as well as its English under the picture. He would pore over that book for hours at a time, fascinated. But come on. . . .

But when we got home, there it was in the book, exactly as he had said. Six years old and he knew the Latin names of half the fish in the book!

* * *

Back in the Exumas, the meal ended, the table was cleared, the scraps were collected, and the dog was called.

No dog.

Not again!

A familiar drill reenacted itself. The family swarmed pell-mell up the companionway and out the hatches and beat the deck, shook out the topsail, and looked under the dinghy and between the jerry jugs stored on the after side decks. The dog was gone—again—but how? We had blocked the accessible scupper holes with scraps of 2 x 4 lumber to prevent a repeat of the accidental skid into the drink that had happened in Port Canaveral.

Over the side the tide was running hard toward the open sea—could he have made it to the beach? Looking toward shore, we saw no sign of him. But there was another dog, loping down the beach, looking from a distance to be a yellow lab. Where had he come from? No matter, that must have been what caused Santos's furious barking, and that explained what had happened to our puppy. He must have willfully jumped overboard to go socialize with that dog. He had a powerful urge to be noticed by other dogs, especially big dogs. We'd seen that already.

"What are we going to do?" wailed Diego, dancing from foot to foot, his face a grimace of worry.

"We're going to go look for him, right Dad? We'll take the new dinghy—it'll be a lot faster," suggested Raff. It seemed a good idea, so we launched the dinghy for the first time ever and screwed the 8-horsepower outboard to its transom. Raff and I jumped in, and I started the engine, put it in gear, and gave it some throttle. The cockleshell shot off like a scared rabbit. It was fast all right, maybe too fast to be stable. It tore over the surface like a low projectile from a cannon, leaving a rooster tail.

We headed for the beach and cruised its length, calling Santos by name. The yellow lab came bounding up, but without our dog. That was compelling evidence that Santos hadn't made it ashore—he would have been playing with this one if he had. At the very least he'd have been on the beach; our boy wasn't one for exploring the xerophytic cactus and thornbush typical of the low, dry Bahamas.

"We'd better go check the drop-off," said Raff worriedly, and I nodded. The current would have taken him through the calm water of the channel and then abruptly spit him into the open sea, pushing him beyond the line of the islands. Out there, where the ebb tide flowed east to the sea, it ran against the oncoming waves and wind, and on windy days this conflict created a race of turbulent water that visibly whitened the sea with breakers. Not good for Santos.

Nor for us. When we got to the mouth and started encountering the steep swell, I brought the dinghy to a halt, but even with the engine in neutral the tide funneled us out into more confused water. Suddenly, all about us, the waves were agitated, jumping up, forming into peaks that broke and tumbled, making a sound like whitewater rapids. The agitated sea slapped alarmingly at the thin plywood sides of the dinghy and slopped a couple of gallons in. That got our attention; suddenly fearful of being swamped, we motored back into calmer water, sitting on the floor to keep the cockleshell more stable.

For a few minutes we patrolled the edge of the race, but we didn't dare venture out into that welter even to get around the corner and down the coast, and we couldn't see anything so tiny as a schipperke's head among the tossing waves offshore.

"Well, decrepit as it is, the deflatable is still more seaworthy than this hot rod. We'd better go pump it up and bail it out and come back here to search farther out," I said.

As we approached *Breath*, Raff and I were hoping that Santos had turned up in our absence, but Diego and Dorothy's anxious body language told us no. We all fell to work in a hurry, scooping water from the inflatable, pumping the bellows to tighten the pontoons, transferring the fuel tank, and unscrewing the clamps that held the outboard to the transom.

We were all so busy that we didn't register the approach of a skiff. Up came a proper inflatable—a new one—with Santos dancing on its bow! A vigorous-looking man in his late thirties with a black beard and wearing the top to a wetsuit guided the skiff alongside and said with a grin, "This is a dog, right? If it's not yours, I'm going to keep him. Feisty little guy!"

"Santos!" we exclaimed in relief. His whole body expressed such delight that there could be no doubt he was ours. The eyes in his eager fox face shot out affection, and his tail stump wiggled his rump as he balanced precariously on three legs, gesturing toward *Breath* with a forepaw.

"I was out spearfishing, and on my way back I caught sight of something swimming. I knew it was mammal, but couldn't figure just what . . . an otter? . . . a seal? But he was eager enough to be fished out, and he shook like a dog. Then I see you all scurrying about, getting the dinghy ready, and I put two and two together."

That made three close calls in as many months. This time he hadn't accidentally fallen though—he'd purposely jumped. As we were to learn from future incidents, that reproachful final yelp was his signal that he simply had to go. He must have climbed the rail or gone up to the bow where the anchors pass over the side. No mesh, no netting would stop this creature from jumping. He was agile as a cat, nimble on his feet, and, once he got used to the boat, at no time in his life did he fall in by mistake. I began to realize that we were dealing with a wild man, a force of nature, and we might as well let him live life his way and hope for the best, because there'd be no stopping him.

Then again, if I'd known how far he was going to take it and the hair-raising dangers he was destined to risk, maybe I would have locked him up—if not for his good then at least for our peace of mind.

EIGHT

DOWN THE OUT-ISLAND CHAIN

On our way southeast to George Town on Great Exuma Island, we stopped at Norman's Cay, where a novel sight presented itself inside the anchorage. In the shallows of the large lagoon sat an airplane, perhaps a DC-3, its line of round windows just clear of the water's surface. Next to the lagoon was a long airstrip and buildings, all padlocked, with prominent signs forbidding entry. Carlos Lederer, a notorious cocaine smuggler, had shipped untold tons of drugs into the U.S. from this sanctuary, and sanctuary it was by virtue of his having high—very high—Bahamian government officials in his pocket. Eventually he was caught by U.S. officials and locked up for a very long time.

The half-sunk plane illustrated one of the peculiar hazards of transporting cocaine—the temptation to sample the cargo a little, then just a little more, with its attendant increase in confidence disastrously juxtaposed with a sharp decline in judgment. Stories of crashed cocaine planes form the modern equivalent of the wrecks of Spanish galleons loaded with gold bullion. Curiously, in the heyday of the Spanish empire, gold and silver were extorted from the Indians in the same region of northern South America from which cocaine—powdered gold—comes today. And the most likely place to find the wreck of a smuggler's plane is in the same archipelago of low, remote islands between Hispaniola and Florida where the galleons piled up.

* * *

Buddy joined us in George Town, to the satisfaction of all on board.

Buddy and I had met when I was constructing the wooden male mold of the boat. Almost finished, it stood by the deserted East End road, reminiscent of the huge skeletal blue whale near the entrance of the New York Museum of Natural History. Buddy was driving heavy equipment for the crew paving the road from Coral Bay to East End.

Each day while the crew was working near our house, Dorothy made a big, ice-cold pitcher of limeade from our prolific lime tree and sent Diego out to the crew with it. Diego was about four and cute as a button, absolutely unabashed. He and Buddy clicked right away. When he showed up painstakingly conveying the heavy, full pitcher, Buddy's face would break into a big smile.

"Amee-go! Slap me five, dude!"

Diego was incredibly impressed by heavy equipment like bulldozers and fire trucks, and he thought the world of Buddy, who took him up into his seat and let him put his hands on the controls.

Buddy was impressed by the mold and offered to come over on weekends to help me. I thanked him for his generous offer and forgot about it—it was an offer that a lot of people made, and I took it and appreciated it as an inconsequential expression of support—but a month later he called to say he was bringing a friend over for the weekend to help me fiberglass the deck. And he did, then and numerous other times, especially when I needed a gang of friends to do a big job like put the deck back onto the boat. No crane on the island in those days could get over the steep East End hills. We became good friends. When *Breath* left for the States he sailed with us as far as San Juan, but then had to return to work.

I had called him up hoping he'd be able to get away for a couple of weeks.

"The Bahamas are beautiful, Buddy—clear water, great diving, some of the best sailing."

"Sounds good capi*tan!* But . . . you sure you got room? Don't want to be in the way," he said, sounding me out.

"Well, you know the boat, and there are two empty bunks in the main saloon. If you don't think it's too crowded, we certainly don't, and I could use the help, another man on board. Pulling the anchor, dealing with the diesel . . . you know."

"Dorothy OK with it?"

"Actually, it would give Dorothy an ease when she's seasick—somebody else to share the watches."

"For true? You shoulda call me earlier. I'll be there in two days."

When he got off the plane, I asked him how long he could stay.

"Ain' gettin' off 'til we reach . . . .!"

"St. Thomas? All the way?"

"That's right."

Buddy was one of the best shipmates you could have. Not only was he a good diesel mechanic and a strong deckhand, but more important he was one of the steadiest, most positive people I knew. He never wasted time complaining, even when he had ample cause. He reminded me of Horatio, Hamlet's friend, "a man that Fortune's buffets and rewards hast ta'en with equal thanks . . . [who is] not a pipe for Fortune's finger to sound what stop she please."

God knows he'd taken a buffet in Vietnam. He'd been inside an armored personnel carrier when an armor-piercing NVA artillery round set it afire. By the time he got out of it, he'd been horribly burned. Somehow he survived, but he spent eight months in agony, both mental and physical, recovering in a burn center in Texas. When Buddy left that hospital he had learned what mattered in life and what didn't.

Buddy was about 40, with some white in his beard and grizzled dreadlocks framing his widening bald spot. His "dreads" attracted attention everywhere we went; dreadlocks don't commonly go with gray hair and a bald spot, and the overall impression was of a genuine Rasta, one who had aged in his beliefs. Which was mostly true. He didn't believe that Haile Sellasie was god, but like a serious Rastafarian he drank no alcohol, ate no meat except "anything that comes out of the sea," was devoted to his family, and believed passionately in agriculture as a way of life that brought spiritual as well as material benefits to the individual and society. He couldn't go anywhere in St. Thomas without people calling to him, a sudden fond smile easing their faces for a moment. He was the kind of guy that everybody loved.

And he had a love of dogs that went back to the hospital in Texas, where the main treatment for his burned flesh had been to keep it moist with the raw inner surface of a dog's skin. Many dogs had died to save his life. He took to Santos right away, especially when he saw Santos outface and put to flight a skittish rottweiler at the airport.

"This dog have a lot of heart," he said admiringly. Buddy became Santos's trainer and taught him tricks, took him on walks, and spent a good deal of time talking to him, encouraging his ardor. He loved it when Santos, by sheer brains and bravado, intimidated some dog ten times his size. "That dog *game*, you hear?"

And he took Diego under his wing, too. "Amee-*go!*" he'd call out cheerfully when Diego was getting queasy, and would listen to Diego's bitter recriminations and slowly jolly him up. "Wha' you mean, you 'hate dis boat?'"

"I do—it makes me sick!"

"Not the boat. It's the sea makes you sick. This is the boat your daddy built! To carry his family safe across the sea. Wha' you mean, hate dis boat? You love this boat. It's the strongest, finest boat on the sea."

"I don't care—I still hate it."

"Well, do you hate it when we catch a big wahoo? Huh? You look happy then. That's the boat, ain't it? How 'bout when we go spear diving? You like that, eh? That's the boat too. What you hate is bad weather, but bad weather is what makes you a man, makes you strong—you should be glad for bad weather."

From the Exumas we continued on down the chain of beautiful islands, Santos always seeking cool, shady spots beneath the sails where he could watch the scenery glide by and sample the air.

Concepcion Island came first into view, a green fringe on the horizon over a long, pristine arc of beach. We dropped anchor there by mid-afternoon after idling slowly over the coral gardens that spread in profusion over the floor of the bay, looking for a sandy aisle between. The day was marvelous, calm and clear the way the weather gets before a norther arrives, with islands far away seeming to float on the horizon, their ends curling up and lifting slightly above the sea. The water of the bay was an incandescent blue that leaped off the bottom and hovered above the surface.

Ashore the sun was lowering but still hot enough to melt the resinous buds of wild herbs in the brush, which added their essence to the tang of salt air. Crickets whirring in the bush counterpointed the coo of mourning doves, plaintive, soft and clear, like notes from the pipe of a pensive Pan.

As we neared the shore, Santos crouched in the bow of the dinghy, taking in whole packets of information denied to us who lacked his keen black nose. He had gone into his half-mad mode, a subdued frenzy of quivering and whimpering. He leaped into the sea when the dinghy neared shore and stormed the beach, looking for a lucky shrub. Then he bolted off down the half-mile length of sand, swam a turn or two, then sprinted back again for the sheer joy of speed.

The boys ran off to look for whelks—an edible gastropod found clinging to rocks throughout the Caribbean—and Buddy fished from some rocks while Dorothy and I spent a glorious hour walking the beach as the sun lost its bite and imbued the world with a slanting glow that highlighted everything it touched. Not a footprint did we see—only the three-toed tracks of sandpipers and soldier birds in the smooth sand and the distinctive trails made by lizards dragging their tails across the soft dunes heaped up by the trade winds at the edge of a carpet of sea purslane.

"Well, this is what you built the boat for, isn't it?" she said with a smile.

"Yup. . . . Nobody out here but us and the sea turtles. It's not that I'm antisocial, but there's a thrill in getting to such a beautiful place and not seeing the slightest sign of man." Arm in arm we looked out to sea, her honey-brown hair lifting in the breeze.

"Is it worth it yet to you, too?" I ventured. "The boat . . . this life?"

"It is, Peter. . . . Just don't ask me that when it's rough. This part is great."

"But . . . ?" I probed.

"Oh . . . but don't forget about a piece of land, someday. We're not ready for it yet, but I like to think of a house waiting in my future. This is beautiful, but I'm here because you're here, and I want to be with you. I could be just as happy in a little bungalow somewhere up a mountainside."

The next day we set sail for Rum Cay, which coalesced as a scarcely discernible shadow out where the plane of the sea intersected the arc of the sky. From a couple of smudges on the horizon it grew into a series of low humps that gradually lengthened and connected, becoming a single dull green line of scrub. Then a beach began to glint below the scrub, and the ensemble became ever larger and more distinct until at last we were only a hundred yards from its westernmost point, where a dazzling extrusion of bright white sand, shot through with pink and gold and heaped high by the northerly swell, ran out from the island scrub into the ocean and dropped away steeply through surrounding layers of emerald and aquamarine, turquoise and sapphire, to indigo. It was a flawless example of the characteristic progression of color in the Bahamas, from palest green to deepest blue where pure water lies over a clear sand drop-off.

The famous psychic Edgar Cayce claimed that the Bahamas are the site of Atlantis, the vanished midsea continent whose civilization used energy derived from crystals. When one sails over this vast area of shallows filled with light, where blue radiance streams out of the water, tales of Atlantis seem almost credible. There is a feeling of underlying energy akin to that encountered in the high desert around Santa Fe and in the islands of the Aegean.

* * *

One calm day, crossing between Long Island and Crooked Island, Santos was standing with his forepaws over the caprail, gazing into the mesmerizing depths, when he noticed a small school of balahou take station along the prow. These slim little fish with indigo caudal fins and a long needle beak tipped with a splash of bright red or yellow were wriggling joyously through the incredibly clear water when three glittering green-and-gold projectiles streaked up from the abyss. The tightly bunched balahou exploded away as the dorado struck. In an instant there was nothing to be seen save one injured balahou, swimming spastically in a circle. One of the dorado reappeared far down and spiraled slowly upward for the straggler until, with a speed our eyes could scarcely credit, it struck again. Head on we saw its mouth flash open and shut, and then it was gone, like a space warp, leaving empty water and a swirl where the little cripple had perished.

Santos growled; his ruff hairs bristled. It was from this time that he started keeping a sharp lookout for life under the sea, often riding on the front of the skiff with his head craned far over the edge.

* * *

Together Crooked Island and Acklins Island provide a 70-mile stretch of low land and lagoon in the lee of which a sailor finds flat water and great wind. The daytime heating of the land accelerates the trades, and they come belting off the shore and out over the water. *Breath* heeled until her teak rubrail kissed the snowy foam of her wash, which tumbled like quicksilver, with never a drop on deck. We sat in the shade of the sails, feeling the clean wind invigorate our pores with the freshness it had picked up while skimming a thousand miles of tropical Atlantic.

Life is good in the lee.

Santos spent the day watching the shore go by, often standing on the coil of anchor line forward, his two front paws resting on the caprail, looking dapper and relaxed. His nose was constantly twitching, sniffing, snuffing—sampling the messenger breeze that blew over the island and out to us, carrying a cross-section of the olfactory life ashore, from pheromones of every bitch in heat to aromatic molecules of jettisoned chicken legs ripening in the sun.

Excessively furry and jet-black made a bad combination in the tropic sun, and Santos perennially searched for shade and breeze. The best spot was atop the bowsprit, between the two oversize teak anchor cleats. This perch was just wide enough for him to lie comfortably, held by the cleats so that no matter how the boat heeled, he stayed put effortlessly. The staysail above gave continuous shade, and here, at the very bow of the boat, he could survey everything ahead and listen to the rush of the stem cutting through the sea.

But when the end of the island slid by and *Breath's* bow began to bury itself in the growing swells of the unshielded ocean, it was time for Santos to seek refuge farther aft. The perfect choice then was the dinghy, upside down on the port side deck. Once underneath that he was safe as a turtle from sun and spray and running feet. No one would trample him in a sudden rush to take in the topsail as a black squall bore down.

Being hidden from view also gave him the luxury of deciding whether or not to answer a summons. Santos was not one to slavishly obey—he had to be convinced that there was either a need or something in it for him. Was the call he heard the idle salvo of a bored helmsperson baking in the sun, vapidly looking to be amused while all other crew were sensibly cooling out below, or did it signal a tasty skillet to be licked clean? Was it a call to a much-loathed bath or a generous invitation to share a cookie? He had no wish to be the subject of a nervous habit, to be petted the way some people finger worry beads or shred napkins or roll up beer labels. Heartfelt affection he always responded to in kind, but he was not a toy, not a Barbie Dog.

As we sailed southeast through the Bahamas toward the far-off lightning that flickered on clear nights above the 10,000-foot peak of Hispaniola, the weather grew steadily warmer and the dog older, enabling us to leave him with good conscience topsides for the night. By now he much preferred being on deck to being down below. Already he took his job, his life's work seriously. His mission was to guard the boat, and that required his presence on deck.

At the end of our long, idyllic run we arrived at Castle Island, off the southern tip of Acklins, and anchored by the light of an old moon in a broad patch of clean sand. We adults sat back with the sailor's traditional grog—rum and lukewarm water made delicious with the juice of a fresh lime and a spoonful of brown sugar. The boys played backgammon at the table below. Santos whimpered piteously at the rail, staring ashore, then came back to the cockpit and flopped down at our feet.

In the morning Santos got his wish. We went ashore to look around.

I caught up to him way down the beach, where he had his muzzle in a hole. I assumed he was looking for ghost crabs, but this time the dog had found something, and he was worrying it with his teeth and digging at it with his paws. When I pulled it out of the sand and rinsed it, a woman's blouse revealed itself, the fabric gaudy and cheap but the colors still bright. Odd . . . probably a yachtie skinny-dipping in the moonlight and misplacing her top on the beach.

But a few paces farther on the dog began pulling at something similar—a pair of purple trousers, also of cheap manufacture. On down the coast we went, and the clothing multiplied until we were finding things half buried all over the beach—shirts, panties, shoes, dresses, trousers, a belt, two suitcases—all of it garish and cheap. Slowly it dawned on me that this clothing must have washed ashore from a foundered Haitian boat. One could imagine one of those weary, marginal boats, crammed with desperate people who knew nothing about the sea. I pictured them heaping themselves aboard and setting off without enough water, without a compass, without sufficient anything but blind hope, and the boat springing a leak and going down, down, down.

Such horrific tales were told of the migrant smuggling voyages. We got to know the crew of a large U.S. Coast Guard cutter whose mission was to patrol Haitian waters and intercept illegal migrants. To a man they swore to two stories that I still find hard to believe—but then again, if I had been alive in 1940, I would have discounted stories about the Holocaust as preposterous, mere propaganda run amok. I pass on the following in the tradition of Herodotus, who reported what people told him and left it to his readers to believe or not.

One day on patrol they passed a Haitian sailboat filled with people—an apparent smuggler—but went on to stop another vessel first. By the time they got back to the first sailboat, all the people were gone, and the boat was empty save for three crew and forty suitcase filled with personal belongings. When asked about the luggage, the crew baldly asserted it was theirs. The Coast Guard was sure they had knocked their passengers unconscious and dumped them overboard, but they could find no bodies.

The other incident involved a boat that took on its desperate cargo in Cap Haitien, on the north coast of Haiti, and set sail for Miami. Once away from shore the crew murdered all the passengers, decapitating them so there might be no recognizable corpses floating back to shore. The boat went to the Bahamas, stayed for a week, then headed back to Cap Haitien. But the murderous crew hadn't reckoned on decomposition in the brain cavity creating gases that floated the heads back to the surface and eventually to the shore, where people recognized their loved ones. When the boat docked in Cap Haitien, the crew was met by an enraged mob that dragged them off their vessel and tore them limb from limb.

Are the stories true? When it comes to man's brutality, anything is possible, and it does sound like Haiti. What Herodotus realized was that the mere circulation and acceptance of a story—even if not literally true—might say a great deal about reality. Such stories aren't told about the Staten Island ferry.

The Haitian migration is only the latest chapter in the historical Caribbean diaspora. Previous eras saw worse—for instance, the slave trade circa 1500 in the Lucayan Indians, original inhabitants of the Bahamas, who were forcibly removed to Hispaniola. These people were, by contemporary accounts, physically and spiritually beautiful, so it goes without saying that they were mightily abused, scorched off the face of the earth in not much more than a decade. The trade had a huge mortality rate; it was said that a ship could navigate from the Bahamas to Hispaniola by following the trail of floating corpses. The trade lasted only until the Lucayans were extinct, then the second chapter opened and lasted a couple of centuries—African slavery.

The irony is that today's trade is voluntary. People are so desperate to leave Haiti that they embark in conditions that make the old slave ships look like cruise ships. At least the slave ships were seaworthy, were manned by professional sailors, and weren't so astonishingly overcrowded. The reports and the photographs of people crammed into open boats with scarce enough freeboard to cross a mill pond, much less reach Miami, are incredible. Sixty people found adrift in a 30-foot boat, out of water and fuel; 200-plus passengers in a 40-footer—how can people bring themselves to step aboard? What does it say that so many would rather die than continue to live in Haiti?

It's lucky that Great Inagua Island and, to its northeast, the Turks and Caicos are just across the 90-mile channel from Haiti. A common scam among the smugglers was to drop people off at Molasses Bay on Great Inagua, just out of sight of Matthew Town, and point to the beach saying, "Miami is just a two-mile walk down that path." Seasick and scared, the people wanted to believe it and walked off with their sacks on their heads. By the time they crested the low rise and could see the sandy streets and single-story buildings of Matthew Town amid the cactus, the boat was gone.

As a result the town of Grand Turk, capital of the Turks and

Caicos—575 miles southeast of Miami—was overflowing with Haitians when we were there, sitting on the sidewalks, under shade trees, looking for work or just looking. People living there said that now was the time to build a house, a fence, or anything. Skilled labor was dirt cheap, and unskilled laborers would work for a plate of rice and beans.

A southeast breeze sent us northeastward and we anchored off Grand Turk just before dark. In the morning there was another boat anchored nearby, this one no yacht but a Haitian cargo vessel with its sliding windows shut tightly and without the slightest sign of people on board. Nobody came on deck or even slid open a window. One sensed a mass of humanity packed secretly below, their hopes wavering in the air above the vessel, creating a tension by its very inattention, as if it had been abandoned or was a ghost ship of the Haitian migration with some deadly tale hanging about its cabinhouse.

That night the Haitian boat left without a sound. We woke up in the morning and it was gone, to God knows where.

NINE

SANTOS THE NAVIGATOR

Dog owners are notoriously partisan. I knew a yellow lab that would spend hours barking at a rock, yet its owner swore by its intellect. Few of us will admit we have a dumb dog—except owners of Irish setters.

Thus I scoffed when I heard the claims of landlubber schipperke fanciers that in medieval times these dogs helped barge captains navigate. My professional sailor's ego resented such a trivialization of the great art, and anyway, a navigating dog? I liked my dog a lot and thought he was pretty smart, but I had no need to imagine that he was capable of coastal piloting or dead reckoning.

But Santos surprised me one dark and nasty night in the far out-islands of the Bahamas, and now I'm a believer. I'm not suggesting that dogs will ever get proficient with a sextant or even learn to punch buttons on a GPS, but they have senses that surpass ours, and these senses can be invaluable when traditional navigation techniques fail.

Santos was mightily bummed when we so abruptly left the French Cays.

These two small islets soar to the sea surface but barely break it with a mere rim of beach and a rise of hardy scrub. Yet they offer a pleasant lee in settled weather, and there we lay, swinging from two hooks set wide apart along the narrow sandy shelf, enjoying calm days and the radiant water. The shallows showed pale green, the boat floated in three fathoms of blazing turquoise, and fifty yards behind our stern the drop-off plummeted to the ocean floor. There the sea reflected a Homeric shade of blue, almost purple, like the wine-dark sea of Odysseus.

A southeast wind had led us there from Castle Island and then died away, so we anchored and waited for the wind to return. As far as Santos was concerned, there was no rush—he could happily have spent weeks here. He was by now a connoisseur of beaches, and this one was a beauty. People rarely set foot there, only the rare passing yacht or fishing smack, so the sand bore no tracks save those of lizards and birds, and now and then a nesting turtle.

Our last day there unfolded much as the others had. In the morning Santos leaped out of the skiff the instant it grated on the shore, put his nose to the sand, and ran full tilt down the beach, omnipotently flushing sandpipers and red-legged soldier birds into the air. He played chase-me games with the boys, tearing up the beach with joyous abandon, then went swimming. In the afternoon he accompanied us on a diving trip to the nearby reefs, riding in the front of the skiff—always and without exception in the very front—his rear in the air and his head low between his paws over the bow, intently watching the bottom speed by in flashes of bright coral and darting fish.

We dove for our supper, gliding down through gin-clear water to ancient coral reefs where thickets of glowing golden elkhorn grew atop labyrinthine mounds of dead fragments. Taking a deep breath and diving down 40 feet brought on a rapture that spread the longer one lay on the cool corridor of rippled sand and peered into a shadowy cave at the base of a huge cracked brain coral, increasingly conscious of the weight of the sea above and the play of sunbeams bouncing at the distant surface.

Great groupers wandered up from their deep, dark caves beyond the drop-off to prowl the sunlit gardens of coral. A manta ray swam majestically past and looked me in the eye, knowingly. When Raffy discovered a huge lobster tucked into a crevice, a barracuda five feet long and thick as my thigh gnashed a mouth full of needles in agitation at being robbed of a subject. When we heaved the crustacean into the skiff, Santos attacked it barking and prancing, but the horned monster slithered toward him waving its thorny whips and creaking, and Santos retreated to the foredeck.

Back at the beach we built a driftwood fire and cooked a feast—lobster and fish, onions, rice, and plantains. Santos stuffed himself on lobster in garlic butter, then dug for ghost crabs, his paws furiously showering sand. He thrust his muzzle into the hole, whiffing and sneezing, finally withdrawing with sand everywhere—eyes, nostrils, ears—looking decidedly pleased with himself.

The rest of us lay in the lap of the surf, feeling a million particles of sand wash back and forth, softly scouring our skin, as we watched the light fade and throw broad shafts of pink and gold high into the ethereal blue sky. When sandflies started to bite we packed up and rowed back to the boat.

Since it was the height of hurricane season we religiously checked the evening weather broadcast on the Coast Guard's short-wave weather channel. All fall we had been listening to tropical weather advisories. We had been warned in time to take shelter when tropical storm Isidor hit St. Augustine, and again in the Exumas we'd heard of a suddenly formed tropical depression that made us scramble to find a hurricane hole—which, in the outer Bahamas, are few and far between for a vessel of 6½-foot draft. And now, just as digestive lassitude took hold, the radio announced that "a strong tropical wave" was headed our way and would arrive in two or three days at its present rate of advance.

A tropical wave by itself was no great threat. The danger lay in its potential to develop into something far more powerful. Most hurricanes start their lives as tropical waves, and two years before, in Eleuthera, just such a "strong wave" had become full-fledged tropical storm Barry overnight and almost wrecked us. We had awakened at dawn in 50-knot squalls to find ourselves dragging steadily toward breakers on a lee shore at Governor's Harbor. Our engine was down, and if not for the assistance of two Frenchmen who risked their lives in a small Boston Whaler to carry out our last anchor, we'd have been on the beach.

Once bit, twice shy. We had to find better shelter than the glorified sandbars that comprised the French Cays. Behind us, Acklins Island offered nothing suitable to our draft. Much farther back were the two small, shoal, rockbound harbors on Long Island, but these were not great alternatives, and giving up so much painfully won windward mileage made us cringe, so Mayaguana became our choice. Though 40 miles to the east—against the wind—Mayaguana offered Abraham Bay, which, if not a hurricane hole, was still our best option to weather a blow.

We had no time to lose. We had to start that night, the sooner the better. So much for the mellow sailing life, for moon gazing and a sound night's sleep. So much for the sailing fantasy. Now we were in for the dark side. Already the clouds seemed less fluffy in the moonlight, the wind less languid.

We prepared for sea, lashing down fuel jugs, stowing items securely above and below. Santos watched us guardedly, and when we lifted the dinghy on deck, he lapsed into a doleful resignation. From previous experience he knew that a long and potentially rough sail lay ahead. As he moped, head between paws, up came the anchors, up went the sails, and within the hour we were underway, rounding the spit of land that sheltered us and driving into the full swell of the open Atlantic.

By midnight the wind had reached force 6 on the Beaufort scale—22 to 27 knots—well over the misery threshold for a small boat beating to windward on the open sea. The clouds had multiplied and lowered, and dark squalls appeared on the horizon and bore down, each riding a pillar of rain. Waves mounted, broke, and toppled onto the deck as *Breath* buried her bow in the oncoming swells. The dismal sluicing of green water on deck sought out every leak in the mast boots and deck prisms and dripped, like smart bombs, precisely onto my bunk and the chart table. Down below the activated bilge gave off swamp gas, while up on deck a blast of exceedingly fresh air flung buffets of spray into unguarded eyes.

Around 3 A.M. the seas got rougher, and suddenly we hit a rogue wave. Like a mean bronco goosed by a cattle prod, the boat bucked skyward, then fell off the wave. The motion threw Buddy clean out of his bunk and over the leeboard, to hit the hardwood floor with a resounding thump. Simultaneously the top of the wave burst against the main hatch, lifting it enough to douse him with five gallons of seawater and eliciting an unprecedented oath of outrage. Buddy was the crew member normally most in control of himself.

Day dawned and waxed and conditions remained rough. The tropical weather update reported the wave steadily approaching but with no further development. The day dragged by slowly, everybody wishing they were somewhere else. Raffy, Buddy, and I tried to carry out the normal routine but were all on the verge of nausea—trying to cook, wash dishes, or find some piece of gear stored in the violently thrashing fo'c's'l brought it on, accompanied by pallor, cold sweats, and dull headache. Diego and Dorothy, as usual, suffered the worst and spent the day trying to sleep, huddled together on a mattress on the floor in the main saloon, where the motion was least. My long-suffering wife, who had regularly gotten carsick as a child, was now as an adult condemned to toss about on a small boat in rough seas. She complained sometimes but mostly suffered in silence. I went down to commiserate with her and asked her what she was thinking of.

"A house . . . cottage. . . . I'd be happy in a shack," she quavered, "anything as long as it's on shore. . . . I long for flowers . . . and solid ground."

Santos wasn't seasick, but he wasn't happy. The poor dog alternated between standing hopefully at the companionway hatch, swaying and bracing to the cant and pitch of the boat, and hunkering down in ever more sodden misery in the cockpit, taking what shelter he could, wincing as the bow crashed against another boxcar and the inevitable lash of spray found him. He was the picture of misery, eyes woebegone, fur bedraggled. We tried to cheer him up, but he'd barely lift his head, and then only to give us a deeply reproachful look. He desperately wanted to go below, but because it had been a day since he'd been ashore to relieve himself, he could not be trusted. The atmosphere in the cabin was rank enough already.

By now we had to be close to Mayaguana, but because it had been too cloudy to take sights our position was based solely on dead reckoning, the process of artfully guesstimating a vessel's position (which the Spanish call "por fantasia," a wonderfully apt description to the English ear). The chart warned that local currents were quite variable, much affected by wind. How much to allow for drift? I had carefully reasoned estimates, but they could be way off, which in these waters could be disastrous. Mayaguana was low, sparsely lit, and fringed by reefs—all in all, a likely place to wreck a boat.

We hoped to fetch its lee sometime after dark. By 10 P.M. I was getting perturbed. We should see something, feel something, a slackening of the sea. Could I have judged the currents so badly that we might run into the five-mile reef? Or, more likely given my caution, would we sail far short of it and go right by in the night, too distant to see any light or feel any lee?

As my calculations revolved yet again in my head, a remarkable change wrought itself in our dog. He began pricking up his ears, lifting his head, and twitching his exquisitely sensitive nose. For a moment he stood hopefully, then, with a despondent sigh, sank back down in dank misery.

But five minutes later he leaped to his feet and stood with his tender nose ardently thrust into the corrosive wind and spray. His whole body quivered as if electrified. A whimper of the utmost longing issued from his throat. Something windborne possessed him absolutely. What else could it be but the edge of land? We must have reached it, and the island's scents of dogs and salt ponds and pungent shrubs had mesmerized him.

He convinced me, at any rate. Land! We dropped the jib, strapped the other sails in tight, and motorsailed hard upwind in short tacks,

15 minutes on each board, following directly up Santos's olfactory bearing. Our little pilot continued to shake eagerly, heedless of the spray, as we neared the source of his revelation. Gradually we felt the seas subside, and after 90 minutes we picked up the Mayaguana light at Betsy Point.

From there on in it was a piece of cake. The approach was deep and clear, and we eased in carefully to the roadstead close under the low cliffs where the light stood. When we could see ripples in the sand below we dropped the hook and lay back gratefully. We opened the hatches and let the wind blow through the cabin, dispelling in a trice all the dankness of the trip. We took freshwater showers, changed our sheets, and opened a bottle of wine. Then we turned in, once again in a euphoric mood. From our bunks we could see, framed by the hatch, bright stars in the velvet night.

If not for Santos we would have passed the island unwittingly and would still be heaving around wet and lost on the high seas. His nose was better than a radio direction finder, the coarse and approximate means of wayfinding on the sea in pre-GPS days—just as accurate and much less likely to blow a fuse. It gave us a rudimentary but essential bearing.

This experience provided us an insight into the schipperke's historical place on boats, which reaches back as far as the Hanseatic League. What worked for us must have worked even more for the medieval skipper, who sailed without electronic aids. The dogs' acutely augmented senses—sight, sound, smell—would have been the next best thing before the 20th century.

Back then, for instance, good dogs must have been the precursor to radar. On foggy mornings on rivers and canals, a barge dog would be alert on the bow. As two barges approached each other, the dog on the downwind boat would smell the upwind dog and start barking. The other would take it up, each thus signaling the other's position through echo location until they were safely clear. Santos's ironclad compulsion to bark at every other dog on a boat suddenly made sense.

The little dog's equally vehement reaction to anyone jumping in the water—he would put up a frantic hue and cry when he saw someone about to dive in, even going so far as to grab their heels none too gently with his teeth—also had a purpose behind it that dated way back. The barges typically were a family business, and the barge was home, with curtains in the portholes and momma cooking in the galley. A smart dog to entertain the children on deck would be that much more useful if it could be absolutely, infallibly relied upon to go berserk if a child fell in. Since the canals and rivers of the Middle Ages were dirty and cold, few knew how to swim, and no one went in for pleasure. Somebody splashing in the water meant trouble, and no matter how many times Santos saw us jump in—in the thousands, counting charter guests—his reaction remained as urgent as ever. One had to marvel at the ability of medieval breeders to inculcate these traits so well, long before Mendel provided the theoretical underpinnings of genetics.

One thing was clear. A skipper who shared a close rapport with his dog had access to another realm of sensory and psychic awareness.

* * *

In the morning we entered the vast lagoon called Abraham Bay after spotting a narrow break in the five-mile barrier reef. There we found ample room in protected water and good holding sand to anchor. To the north and east stretched densely wooded low hills. To our south the sea tumbled onto miles of breaking coral. We finally anchored near the head of the long bay, about half a mile from shore. From there on in the water grew too shoal to proceed.

We drove the skiff a quarter-mile in, reaching the end of a very long and narrow dock that stretched out from shore across acres of flats to a sufficient depth for small boats. We pulled up to it with Santos straining at his leash, struggling to jump, whelping frantically with desire for land.

"Hold him, he's out of control," I said, stating the obvious, but as we nosed in, the outboard cut out and a gust of wind blew the bow off. Buddy lunged for the dock, grabbed it—and in that unguarded instant Santos leaped ashore and dashed down the dock as if shot from a cannon. Buddy commanded, I threatened, Dorothy coaxed, but he didn't look back.

Halfway down the dock, three boys were knelt in a circle, absorbed in a game of marbles. When they heard us they looked up and froze. A small maniacal beast with prominently bared teeth was charging them flat out, blood in its eyes, apparently unstoppable. Our shouts clinched it—this weird creature was some kind of trouble. They took to their heels and tore a dust trail down the dock, with Santos gaining all the while. The tall skinny boy in the rear kept whipping his head around, wide-eyed, to gauge Santos's approach, and just as the dog reached his ankles the kid catapulted sideways off the dock and into the water, looking for all the world like a ten pin knocked asunder by a hairy bowling ball. The other kids wasted no time looking back but redoubled their flight, pelted over a rise, and disappeared with the dog from hell at their heels.

Buddy was assassinated by laughter, doubled up, tears in his eyes. "Aaaaahhh! Aaaaahh!" he gasped. I was furious with the dog for very likely poisoning our reception in the village, but I had to admit it was funny. When he could talk again, Buddy could only say, "That dog *game*, you hear? *Game*, I tell you!" He liked to see a small dog project such confidence, such power.

We entered town with trepidation but found everything quiet. Customs was closed for lunch. Down the soft sandy street, several old wood-frame houses shaded by big fruit trees dominated a crossroads. From behind one of them came the loud twangs of country gospel from a missionary radio program.

Across the street we entered a grocery store that was dark and still inside. No fresh vegetables, no frozen goods did we see—just a few cans of evaporated milk, beans, and corned beef covered with dust. The proprietor was an old man, fat and feeble, who never rose. When we asked him how he was, he replied quaveringly that he was OK but suffered much from gas. Unsure how to respond, we left before he suffered an outbreak.

Santos dashed up from the yard of a nearby house where two boys had been playing with him, probably the two he had chased off the dock. They waved tentatively and ran inside. I half expected some parent to come out to upbraid us, but all was quiet—apparently there were no hard feelings. Our boys nabbed him and Buddy snapped his leash to his collar.

"There! No more roaming out of you, you little devil," said Buddy.

"He's our roving ambassador," said Raffy.

"Some ambassador!" I grumbled. "He'll get us arrested one of these days."

"Naah. . . . People admire he spirit. He don't hurt nobody. And for sure he make a strong impression."

"Yeah Dad," said Raff. "He's a good mascot. He represents our team . . . *Breath* . . . and us."

"He makes us look good," chimed in Diego, and even I had to concur.

TEN

IN THE SHADOW OF HISPANIOLA

The strong tropical wave went by without intensifying—a good thing, because Abraham Bay offered better protection in my memory than in fact. When the clouds and rain and lightning had passed we set out anew, this time for the Turks and Caicos islands. We stopped in Provo briefly—one didn't have to be there long to hear lurid stories of the international coke trade, which was using this island, one of the least inhabited of the Caicos group, as a refueling stop for small planes flying from Colombia to the U.S. Every night, sometimes two or three times a night, the electricity would be cut and traffic stopped on the main road until the last drone of a Cessna or twin Otter faded away to the northwest, bound for the U.S. East Coast with full tanks and an interior stuffed with bags of white powder. One of the planes had recently crashed in the island's desolate, scrubby interior, and bags of cocaine had scattered far and wide. People had gone out looking for the spilled cargo, some of them armed, a bad situation that got worse when they found it. Fifty-pound sacks of cocaine spread profligately about in a small, unsophisticated community can be remarkably disruptive to social order.

Not long after getting back to the Virgin Islands, we would read in the daily paper that a minister in the Turks and Caicos government had been arrested in Miami for smuggling. In any event, each lost cargo bore a heavy weight of bad karma that frequently undid those "lucky" enough to find it.

Clearing customs on Salt Island, south of Grand Turk, we met the small island's commissioner, formerly its schoolteacher for 30 years. She was a delightful lady, quick to laugh, articulate, curious about boating life—so Dorothy asked her out to *Breath* for tea. She met us on the beach, readily shed her shoes, hiked up her skirt, and waded out to the dinghy, getting in gracefully.

Her ease and nimbleness in the tippy dinghy typified the Bahamian out-islanders. Living in close harmony with the sea, men and women alike are at home on boats there. In a Clarencetown bar one night, a lady in her fifties walked in, shed a slicker, and settled down with a cup of tea. She was a midwife and had just sailed a 14-foot fishing sloop from a nearby island, in the dark, to get home.

Slavery had been minimal in these far-flung sand and coral-rock islands, which could be farmed only with difficulty, and fishing in small boats bred equality and self-reliance. The people living there are more prone to offer help than to ask for it. They respect the sea and anyone who makes his or her own way across it.

The commissioner stamped our passports at the main saloon table while Dorothy prepared tea. Taking to her instantly, Santos jumped up on the top of the water tank where she was sitting and nuzzled her forearm with his nose. She stroked him with real pleasure.

"What a pretty little dog, like a small fox, he face so silky like," she exclaimed, "and his eyes so sensitive and loving, like a child. What kind of dog is this? I've never seen the like!"

She took particular interest in the galley, getting down on her knees to examine the oven on its gimbals, and when she stood back up she gave a delighted laugh. Santos, back up on deck, had thrust his head and neck through the galley porthole to keep track of events below, and his thick black ruff filled the 6-inch opening and hid the rim.

"Look at him! He looks exactly like a . . . a. . . ." She searched for an analogy, reacting like most people upon seeing the head seemingly mounted on the cabin wall.

"Like a small game trophy," Dorothy finished.

"Yes! How adorable!" People loved seeing him that way—the resemblance to a mounted head was uncanny, particularly because the eyes and pink tongue were so bright and alive.

Dorothy brought the tea and biscuits from the galley and started telling our guest about the dog and his life aboard. The conversation flowed easily, each woman touching the other's arm for emphasis.

"I'm new at this job, you know," she confided. "But I like it. I like going out on the boats to inspect them. After all those years in the classroom I enjoy having the sea breeze on my face."

"Do you ever run across situations you can't handle . . . guns? Drugs?"

"Oh my, I can tell you a story or two. T'ree weeks gone by a Haitian sloop come into the roadstead and request clearance for his cargo to sell in Grand Turk. Mangoes he have, and getting very ripe. I went out to his boat—only 30 feet long—and look down the hatch and the hold filled to the top with mangoes, so I write up his entry and buy a few mangoes and I getting in the dinghy when up come Major Pickering, in a next boat. He's the chief of police and he ask me do I mind if he take a look since he more experienced this kind a t'ing. I say go ahead, mon, I will learn from you, and he come aboard, go down into the hold, and start flingin' de mon' mangoes dem. Pretty soon he see a foot sticking up an' he pull out a man. Keep finding more people.

"Could you believe that little sloop carry 28 people hiding under the mango, and one a' them dead! Lord! Lord! I could still see that poor young woman's body, her thin limbs all cold and stiff—and such a sweet face. Poor thing . . . she suffocate."

"So what happened?" Raffy asked. We'd all been listening spellbound.

"Well, Major Pickering arrest the captain for murder, and the people, them get send to hospital yonder," she said, nodding her head in the direction of Grand Turk. "You could see them on the street there now—along with all the rest a' them Haitians." She shook her head. "Too many Haitians! What we goin' a do with all a' them?"

* * *

From Salt Island we made the overnight passage to Hispaniola, raising its massive green mountains at dawn, an absorbing sight after weeks of flat, low islands covered with wizened scrub. We pulled in to the round bay of Puerto Plata, past the long fringing reef and the old colonial fort with its distinctive corner sentry boxes catching the light and shadows of late afternoon. Here we moored stern-to the battered concrete dock between sharp snags of rusty iron reinforcing bar, then confronted a small mob to negotiate who would take our lines and for what fee, who would get ice and fuel, and so on. Customs arrived with big guns and muddy boots and avaricious eyes, asking for our Walkman but settling for an old cassette. Then we repaired to the town plaza to sit at an outdoor cafe, drink the excellent local brew served in liter bottles, and watch the people go by. We left Santos in charge of the boat. Small though he was, he was also powerful, and his cropped tail gave him a compact, squared-off look. He was a formidable guard.

This was the kind of place where Santos came into his own. Any number of people ashore—stevedores, prostitutes, shoeshine boys, and unemployed hangers on—looked out at the boat with frankly

speculative appraisal. The port was infamous for petty thievery—
not armed in-your-face robbery but surreptitious lifting of whatever
could be made off with unnoticed. Santos knew it too, in his bones.
He'd been born and bred for this job, and he patrolled the deck
unceasingly, a constant low growl sputtering in his throat like a siren
in idle. When a small, battered dory came paddling by close, he went
ballistic. This was not lost on the dock denizens—a casual pass-and-
snatch was not in the picture with this pumped-up guard tirelessly
pacing the decks. He stayed topsides all night, and whenever he really
erupted one of us poked his head out a hatch and took a quick look
around just to show that we were not dead to the world.

The next morning we left Santos on guard and the rest of us took
a cable car up the mountain to spend some time away from the salt
sea and the dust and heat of the town. We returned mid-afternoon
to a restive and hoarse Santos. He was now a local celebrity, an obviously awesome guard dog in a culture that appreciated the genre;
several of the dock crowd pointed at him grinning and made gestures
to indicate that he had been *on the case!* To judge from his alert, com-
pulsive patrolling and the admiring laughter, he'd been put to the test
and had passed with flying colors.

We took him for a walk to the beach on the windward side of
town and ended up drinking pina coladas at a row of maybe thirty
little shacks under a border of palm trees where the boulevard lined
the beach. Each had a couple of tall stools at a small counter bar
under a thatched roof. Behind the bar stood the proprietor with a big
block of ice, a work-worn old blender, fresh pineapples, cans of Coco
Lopez, and bottles of Brugal rum on a high shelf. For the record, they
were the best pina coladas any of us had ever tasted, and remain so
to this day.

Buddy had Santos on a leash; he took the dog everywhere, having taken it upon himself to be Santos's trainer and personal coach
and to teach him obedience and tricks. The tricks came easy once
Santos identified performance with food, but obedience . . . that was
tougher. It's not obedience when you say "come" and hold up a slice
of sausage and the dog comes. Obedience is when you're ready to
leave and the dog isn't but he dashes to your side anyway when you
voice the command "come." Santos never got that. It might check his
stride—he might even come—but it was always a toss-up.

Buddy and the dog took a jog down the beach, and it was hard
to say which of the two drew the most stares. Dominicans weren't

used to seeing dreadlocks, since Rastafarianism is predominantly an English-speaking Caribbean phenomenon and is for the most part a style affected by young men. Buddy's old-grown dreads were an object of great remark, especially from the women, who constantly wanted to touch them.

When a small crowd had gathered, Buddy, to deflect attention, unleashed the dog to run, and Santos really put on a show that day, sprinting down the surf line at a speed that amazed the onlookers. They were blown away that such a little dog could be so fast. Some of the kids, at Buddy's suggestion, tried to catch him. He would let them get close, then spring away, accelerating like a rock from a slingshot, bringing shouts of laughter from the crowd, many of whom were already well disposed to merriment from having spent half the afternoon imbibing those delicious pina coladas.

As we left Puerto Plata, Buddy spoke up.

"T'was good havin' Santos aboard. We had a' get rip off for sure if we left the boat with no one on board. Dat place? *For sure*—you seen the way dey coopin' us. An' it go to show," he went on, cocking an eye at Diego, who was stroking the dog, "Don' matter how big or how small you is if you got heart. All a' dem t'iefs know . . . *know* . . . they gon' have to kill he before they get anything off dis boat.

"Size ain't nothin' without heart. Ah remember back in Nam, dem VC's were small, *small*. But fight? Me son?! Dey could fight . . . an' live on next to nothin'. Ain' had but a han'ful o' rice a day to eat . . . sandals on dey feet, no boots. Ain' never get a hot shower even when they home. But dey were bad." Diego was hanging on every word. It was good to hear because it was so obviously true.

"What about the guy who pulled you out of the burning tank?" Diego asked. "Was he a big guy or a small guy?"

"It was a white guy who burn he hands to the *bone* to pull me out. I owe him my life. What a good dude . . . John F. Kennedy, jus' like the president. Can't remember . . . guess he was medium build, about my size. Anyway, body size were irrelevant. It took a big heart to grip that white-hot handle and wrench it open. The APC—not a tank—had roll over, the driver dead, he hair burnin'. I thought I was dead but then I see that hatch open up and I see them hands reachin' to grab me. I'll never forget that fresh air—and then the pain! Oh God!"

We sat there in the sunset as the boat responded to a fresh gust, her wake suddenly burbling like birdsong, and tried to reconcile the ways of this world.

* * *

By our second night out of Puerto Plata the wind had slowly died off. We motored through calm seas as the wild stars came out, their reflections undulating freely on the languid swell, counterpoised by the domesticated lights ashore that ran in lines and never winked or danced. We were on our last leg, and lulled by being so far along and by the beauty of the night, I tuned in too late to catch the weather on the coast guard radio—the first time in weeks that I'd missed a day. For the last several days the same conditions had been reported—a persistent stationary low south of Puerto Rico. Anyway hurricane season was basically over; only a fluke would come up now in early November.

Buddy and I sat for several hours, extending our watches, reluctant to leave the beautiful night. We talked while he brushed Santos's coat and played with him. We discussed what we'd do when we got back to the Virgin Islands, and I found myself worrying out loud over money and what I should do with my life. He listened gravely, nodding his head, letting me talk.

Finally he said, after a long silence, "The trouble with you, Pete . . . you got it made but you don't know it."

I guess I looked a bit diffident, so he continued, hesitantly at first but with growing conviction.

"You got the most important things in life. Look at Dorothy, beautiful, hard-working, great cook. . . . Cyan't ask for no better woman—and she still with you! Mos' woman woulda lef' you long time now. Livin' on a boat, an' she seasick so? You lucky, mon. Got to respec' that woman." Buddy's head was close to mine, his voice low, raspy, warm.

"Den the boys—good dudes! You could see they goin' places . . . ain' gon' be no burden. You should be proud!

"And you build dis boat—a fabulous accomplishment. You could go anywhere on dis boat—baddest boat on the seven seas! That's your life . . . sail to Europe . . . Africa."

"Yeah. . . . Yeah, you're right . . . once I get some money."

"Money! Wha' you need so much a' money for? Security? Don' care how much money you make, you never safe in this world. You could die tonight . . . or worse, one a dose . . . how you call . . . riggin' blocks drop on one a' yo' chirren head and what good money gon' do you then? Important thing is to live the life Jah give you doin' the bes' you can at what's mos' important to you." A long pregnant pause ensued.

"You need money you could always charter, or. . . ." He left it unspoken.

"Or what?"

"Write dose books you always talkin' 'bout."

Ooooh . . . a body blow. He'd said it, named the source of my angst. I wanted to be a writer but I lacked the confidence to pursue it, to spend so much time working at something so insubstantial as words words words on a piece of paper. Yet whatever else I did, I pursued half-heartedly, because that wasn't what I was going to be when I started my real life.

"See this here dahg? Jus' a dahg, but he know somethin' about life. He don' go with he head, he go with he heart—and when he go for something, ain' nuttin' gon' stop him. He don' be worryin' about what if, what if—he too busy doin' he utmost. Which right now be sleepin'."

"It's simple. Be like Santos," I said. Buddy laughed his great laugh, a warm, deep-throated chuckle.

"You know what I mean," he said.

* * *

After midnight the wind came up a bit and we sailed or motor-sailed as conditions warranted, and the morning found us close to the coast, still working our way east. As far as we could see, a tan beach of coarse sand ran to the southeast, backed by continuous coconut plantations. Low knobbly peaks with patchwork fields and occasional forest rose in the distance above the glistening palms.

By late afternoon we finally breasted the eastern tip of Hispaniola—fabled Hispaniola, scene of untold suffering, where the Spaniards first settled in the new world, where they met the Arawaks and made an end of them in thirty years! At sunset *Breath* headed into the Mona Passage. We gazed at the last of the island, wondering how Punta Espada (Sword Point) and Cabo Engano (Cape Trickery) had deserved those names.

When darkness fell, the beacon at the island's end began to flash, but instead of the usual white light we saw two red lights, flashing alternately, one above the other. Adrenalin vaporized my leisurely reflections. That was the hurricane warning signal!

We switched on an English-language station in Puerto Rico and didn't have to wait long before a special weather bulletin announced the coordinates of tropical storm Klaus. The persistent low south of Puerto Rico had turned into a tropical storm that threatened to become a hurricane. I plotted its position on the chart and felt the breath knocked out of me. We would be encountering storm-force winds within two hours, with a lee shore close behind and a treacherous bank beneath our keel—Banco Burgano—of which the chart warned "dangerous tidal rips and overfalls in heavy weather." I remembered all the bad things I'd heard over the years about vessels lost in the Mona Passage. Even the name had an ominous edge. Moan.

"But did you hear the announcer say it was heading northeast?" said Dorothy. "If so, it's headed away from us."

"Northeast my foot! Tropical storms always go west or northwest in these waters. The announcer made an error."

"But I heard it twice!"

"Then it was a typo from the weather service dispatch—unforgivable with people's lives on the line! It may be academic to some timeserver sitting on his fat ass at a comfortable desk well inland, but to us, trying to figure out our next move. . . . Northeast? In these latitudes? Ridiculous!"

We had to get out of the Mona Passage into open water before the storm struck. We headed south with all sail set and the engine on to help us get to windward. None of us will ever forget the wild ride that followed, as the wind rose and the seas grew. We all put on foul-weather gear and safety harnesses and watched the sky turn black with fast-moving low cloud. Soon we shut the engine off and flew in silence through the night.

The waves kept building. At one point the boat went airborne off a particularly steep sea that had no back, and she hit the trough with an impact that shuddered the rig. The old saying—"Shiver me timbers, laddy!"—came out of nowhere, and it was a relief that we didn't have to worry about breaking any ribs, springing a plank, or any of the other old wooden-boat mishaps. *Breath* was inordinately strong. It was comforting to remember that, when *Breath* was taking shape, several boatbuilders had opined stuffily that she was overbuilt. A boatyard had once offered to build Paul Johnson's boats commercially, but the builders insisted on cutting back on the amount of fiberglass. They cited computer models that calculated the stresses imposed by various wave heights, pointed out that comparably sized boats had much thinner lay-ups, and claimed they'd go broke building to such extreme specs, but Paul stuck to his guns.

Same with *Breath*. She wasn't built to make a profit, nor was she built to computer specs. She was built to container specs—that is, to survive a collision with a steel container that was floating just awash after being knocked off a ship by a storm. These dot the ocean like deadly needles in a haystack, and plunging down on one upsets a whole applecart of well-reasoned calculations.

Hitting a container or a giant log, being struck by a freighter or a whale. . . . Computer models are all very well if one plans to keep the boat in a test tank, but sailing on the high seas introduces squirrelly anomalies. When you're out there in a black night with a tropical storm coming, the notion that the only thing between you and two thousand fathoms is "overbuilt" seems grossly misguided.

A computer can calculate stress, but can it calculate fear?

After an hour of flinging over the waves and falling off their backs, the wind leveled off at about 35 to 40 knots and the seas got less turbulent. Dorothy took Santos below and out of the spray when it came time for the latest coast guard weather advisory—we kept the radio below when there was spray on deck—and soon she shouted, "New coordinates—it *is* going northeast. Listen!"

And so it was, to our huge relief and to my instruction. Never again would I make pronouncements about what a hurricane must do. A hurricane can be completely unpredictable, and to prove the point, in November 1999, 15 years later almost to the day, Hurricane Lenny did the same thing, starting south of Jamaica and tracking east right over Saba, St. Barts, and St. Maarten.

The wind swung more and more into the north, and by morning the northwest, giving us an unprecedentedly fine broad reach eastward down the coast of Puerto Rico and Vieques. We sailed into the Virgins having made 180 nautical miles in 24 hours, but our exhilaration died when we entered St. Thomas harbor and counted 60 vessels on the rocks, all driven ashore by the freak storm. They too had assumed a Caribbean storm would never go northeast.

ELEVEN

ARRIVING ON ST. JOHN

We dropped Buddy off and carried on to St. John, bypassing Cruz Bay and tacking up the north coast. We must have been preceded by ample rains, because the hills were cloaked in a halo of green and gold light that hovered as though the forest were saturated with sunshine and water and had to start shedding it back. We stood deep into Cinnamon Bay, abreast of Cinnamon Cay, and tacked smartly a hundred yards off the beach, catching a lift in the breeze that heeled the boat over, raised a satisfying stern wave at her rudder, and left seething white foam in her wake. We must have made a stirring sight with full gaff rig and tops'ls pulling. I noticed a young couple staring out from shore. This was the first place we had stayed on St. John, and we had stood in the same spot, staring at the sea and boats.

"Look Dorothy—that guy with his arm around the girl—that was us 17 years ago, longing to be out here."

"I remember," she said dreamily, then added, "Actually, I was probably imagining a little house and garden overlooking the sea." But her laugh and long gaze toward shore showed that she felt it too. For a moment Time fell away, as it does when a song comes on the radio that summons up every nuance of another time and place to the last pheromone. The sequence of events that had brought us to that beach on St. John flooded back, vivid as an unfolding dream.

* * *

Maybe because we met in an elevator on the 14th floor of a New York City office building, we had to do something different.

Dorothy was 19 years old and I was 20 in June 1966, and we both happened to have summer jobs at the Interchurch Office Center, a huge building housing the headquarters and mission-support functions of many main-line Protestant denominations. My parents were missionaries in the Philippines—where I'd grown up—and nepotism had gotten me a job as secretary's helper in the office of a church executive.

I had had a better-paying job lined up—conning poor people into buying a certain encyclopedia on installment, at an interest rate that must have violated anti-sodomy statutes, so that, as I was instructed to stress, their children would be sure to escape poverty and go to college. Since I had spent the previous year working in the Mississippi civil rights movement, the managers figured I'd handle the black slum scene well. I quit after a day, upon realizing that the whole deal was a scam playing on the desperation of the poor. A year later it was satisfying to read in the *New York Times* that the Justice Department had indicted the company for fraud.

I was not thrilled by my new employment, typing, fetching coffee, running errands, wearing a tie. It was dull work at low pay, but somehow I managed to impress the office manager as "a fine young man." She passed this intelligence on to Dorothy, her distant niece, who had gotten a job on the same floor in the same way.

"There's a nice young Dartmouth man working in my office. Would you like to meet him?"

"No thanks, Aunt Linda—Dartmouth men are animals!"

Dartmouth did have a bad reputation, and in the days before coeducation, not without cause. Its students, isolated in the north woods, after weeks or months without the society of girls, were drawn to Smith and Mt. Holyoke, top-tier women's colleges in western Massachusetts, and tended to behave badly after arrival, getting drunk and bawdy. Dorothy had spent two years at Holyoke and had had a couple of bad experiences with my classmates. Anyway, she had just managed to transfer to Oberlin College, which was co-ed and more in touch with 1960s politics.

My boss was not easily dissuaded though, and she conspired with Dorothy's boss to send us down to the cafeteria for coffee and donuts at the same time every day. Inevitably we met. I remember my first impressions of her as the elevator door closed on just the two of us. She looked up at me with confident eyes and a radiant smile—and a pleasing curve to her derriere.

We soon found that our prolonged absences fetching coffee brought no frowns from our bosses, but one of Dorothy's suitors down the hall noticed and took the opportunity to point out to her that—had she noticed?—the Dartmouth boy was wearing mismatched socks! He himself was a sharp dresser but shallow-minded, and his comment clinched my case.

With my next week's paycheck —all of $65 after taxes—I took her to dinner at a fancy steak house along the edge of Central Park.

I couldn't afford it, she protested, but I swept aside objections and ordered wine with the meal. Upon leaving the restaurant we noticed a horse-drawn carriage going by, a romantic conveyance on a balmy summer evening in the grand old park. I flagged down the next one, also against Dorothy's demurrals, and we rode through the night past the city lights. My arm was around her, she nestling tight, me getting up the nerve to kiss her. Then she moved her face close to mine, eyes half-closed as if in a swoon, eyelashes fluttering like butterflies, and we kissed. When the carriage came to a halt I ordered it on again. I had never been so happy.

By the time I put her on the bus to her suburb across the Hudson and waved good-bye, my entire week's paycheck had vaporized. Never was money so well spent!

We got married a year later, and she came back to Hanover with me and taught while I finished my undergraduate degree in history.

As graduation neared, we became the beneficiaries of an IRS error—they refunded us $900 instead of the $200 I had expected. Who were we to question professional, hard-nosed government accountants? I certainly didn't pretend to understand tax codes. For all I knew they did owe me that amount, though headline stories that the IRS shift from written records to punch cards (at the dawn of the computer age) was causing widespread errors in the refunds that year might have given pause to someone more inclined to be scrupulous. After some discussion of the morality of it, we cashed the check, packed our possessions, and drove south in our jaunty but terminal Sunbeam convertible. If an error had been made, they'd find it and bill us. In the meantime we had our ticket out.

We sold the car in Miami for airline tickets to the Virgin Islands on the advice of Dr. Bastholme, a dentist who had flown over all the West Indian islands during the war. He was a friend of Dorothy's family who put us up while we tried to sell the car. Our intention had been to head for the distant out-islands of the Bahamas to camp on a lonely pristine beach in front of a reef miles from the nearest soul. Dr. Bastholme dissuaded us.

"How will you get your water? Long hikes with heavy jugs in burning sunshine—and water's in scarce supply anyway in the out-islands. You'll be imposing on the villagers. Sandflies will eat you alive. Go to St. John instead—it's the prettiest island in the Antilles, and you can stay for free in the U.S. National Park. Safe water from a spigot. Showers. Cold beer. . . ."

As soon as the car sold, we left. Dorothy realized as the plane leveled out over the green continental shelf and left the flat of Florida behind that the day was September 16.

"Do you realize the significance of this day?" she asked me, nestling up under my arm as I stared out the window at the first rocks of the Bahamas.

"Well, we're going on a vacation—that's nice, and maybe it will be significant too."

"September 16—ring a bell?"

"Ohmigod! Our first anniversary! I completely forgot—I hope that doesn't make it our last."

She laughed and said, "I just remembered it myself . . . and this is a great way to celebrate it." That was just like Dorothy. Jewelry, restaurants, presents—none of that mattered to her. A card or a kiss, served with genuine emotion, would do fine.

We spent the night in Charlotte Amalie and early next morning made our way to the ferry dock at Red Hook, at the east end of St. Thomas, and sat on the dock gazing across four miles of sparkling water at the unblemished green mountains of St. John. It seemed impossibly beautiful. The ferry finally arrived, to no particular schedule, a jaunty wooden North Sea trawler called *The Jolly Roger* with seating for 16 people. We rode over on the foredeck, holding hands, watching the island grow bigger and greener until we entered a pretty bay surrounded by hills, coconut palms, and a few attractive houses. The ferry tied up at a sagging dock opposite a battered old wooden schooner with dramatically raked masts whose deck was almost awash with the weight of a cargo that included bundles of iron re-bar, a refrigerator, bags of cement, and bunches of bananas.

Cruz Bay was tiny back then. There was no place to get fresh vegetables, no gift shops, no dive shops, no charters, no restaurants. There was a bar though, right off the dock, with 30-cent Heinekens. We rode in the taxi-bus along the north shore road, agog at the beauty of that coast—unspoiled green hills falling to exquisite beaches, and the sea blazing forth aquamarine light—and arrived at the campground to find the place deserted. A hurricane was imminent, and what campers there were had been evacuating even as we arrived.

But the storm veered from its path and tracked far enough north to give us sparkling clear weather. We had our pick of sites and chose the prime location just off the beach in a copse of sea grape trees. From our tent we looked out across scintillating blue water towards the passages between Whistling Cay and the Narrows, where turquoise burned in the shallows. Now and then a sailboat would appear in the channel and glide down the coast, heeling to the fluky gusts and leaving clean foam tingling in its wake. I wanted one of those. I felt like Mr. Toad sitting in the road in a trance after first seeing an automobile.

Next thing we knew we were living aboard a 28-foot wooden sloop and teaching school in St. Thomas to pay for it.

I taught the first year in a junior high nicknamed "Little Vietnam" for its student fights. One of the most intense memories of that year was looking at the sea between St. Thomas and Water Island sparkling through the windows. For a moment I would blank out the pencil quarrels, hair pulling, and stifling heat and long with all my soul to be out of the classroom, afloat on that radiance.

Dorothy, on the other hand, showed a flair for teaching. When I dropped by her classroom after school I would find her, head down with a couple of her second-graders who couldn't speak English. They would be perusing a picture book and learning to say "cow" instead of "vaca." They clung to her hands as they said good-bye.

Her charisma worked with adults too. We both taught GED classes at night, mainly to down-islanders eager to advance themselves. I taught English grammar—dull stuff—but Dorothy taught biology and had enthusiastic students crowding her desk after class to debate evolution versus Creationism. She touched off a firestorm of controversy among her literal Bible believers, who could show her, right there in Genesis, black and white, incontrovertible, that God created the world and everything in it in just six days.

We stayed near our mooring at first, but as soon as we had become reasonably competent we sailed on a long weekend to St. John. The beauty of the island as experienced from the sea blew us away. We couldn't bear to leave. I called in sick, and we spent the day falling off the boat into the translucent sea and skinny-dipping in the moonlight. I would have called in sick for a week, but Dorothy insisted on getting back to her class. For the record, we were a little ashamed of ourselves and never abused sick days again.

The next two years we taught in St. John, a much smaller and more cohesive community, which we got to know via our students. Summer vacations found us cruising the nearby islands from Puerto Rico to Anegada. We also had our first child, a boy we named Rafael, who was conceived under a brilliant full moon as we swam off a secluded beach. After teaching for three years we paid off the boat, withdrew our $1,800 in retirement funds, and set off for St. Barts.

It was our first overnight at sea. By the next morning the wind had picked up, the boat's motion was lively, and so was our boy. Raffy was a year-and-a-half old, very familiar with his boat home and contemptuous of restraint. He insisted on leaving the cockpit to walk the deck, as he did daily back on the mooring in Cruz Bay. We tried to explain that he would fall into the sea. We held him close to the rail and dipped his hand in the water rushing past. It was all to no avail. His cries became screams, and finally he flung himself at the coaming that separated the cockpit from the deck. He drove us crazy with continuous shrieking. At my wit's end, I finally said, "If that's what he wants, then let's let him have it!"

Dorothy looked at me as if I was Charles Manson, but I took good nylon cord and strapped his lifejacket on tight again and again. I hooked his safety line to the cable on deck that held our own safety harnesses when we went forward, and then secured another line from his lifejacket to a stout eyebolt. It took me 20 minutes to rig him up so foolproof that even his mother acquiesced. Then I let him loose.

"Go for it kid. Walk that deck!"

Raffy gave me a suspicious look, then scrambled over the coaming onto the lee deck and started walking back and forth, scarce holding on, crowing over his freedom, a daredevil smile on his lips. Soon enough the boat lurched over a steep sea, and green water washed along the deck and swept him into the Caribbean with an astonished look on his face.

The boat was going six knots. Raffy came to the end of his safety lines in one second and dragged, upside down, head in the water, for about two seconds while we hauled him back aboard—we'd never taken our eyes off him and were pulling at the ropes the minute he hit the water. He took a gulp of air, gave a terrified squawl, and clung sobbing to mommy, but not for long. Soon he was back at his toys in the cockpit, cured. It's one thing to have mommy and daddy tell you something, but it's quite another to see for yourself while dragging upside down in 2,000 fathoms, wondering if anyone noticed.

It was Dorothy who took it hardest. Not long afterward she had the first in a series of recurring dreams in which the boat was sailing along under self-steering when baby Raffy, playing on deck, suddenly fell over. Dorothy cried out and jumped in at the same moment that I did too, and the three of us were left holding each other, treading water, watching the sloop sail steadily off until it disappeared, and we were all alone on an empty sea.

We made it into St. Barts without further incident, save for one close call at dawn the next morning when I noticed something ahead in the first grainy glimmer of light. I veered off and we sailed past a floating steel platform, two huge barrels welded together with steps going up to a railed walkway. Fifteen minutes earlier I wouldn't have seen it in the dark. I watched it go by, wondering where the hell that came from—quite possibly from some busy port in Europe a year's drift ago. That made an impression on me. When we met Paul shortly thereafter in St. Barts, his obsession with designing strong, bulletproof boats found a believer in me.

TWELVE

EAST END ANIMALS

When we sailed in to Round Bay and dropped the hook in the sheltered cove off our old house, we were finally home. It was the end of 1984, and we had been gone almost two years. *Breath* had performed her maiden voyage without a hitch. She was solid as a rock. And Santos had passed the test with flying colors too, doing his duty and proving good company . His place aboard *Breath* was assured.

His place on shore was not so assured, however. There were other animals already there—dogs, donkeys, goats, mongooses, cats—who felt they had rights. If he wanted to claim his birthright as The Dog of the people who lived there, he would have to look lively.

Fortunately, looking lively was his stock in trade.

In those days, man's hand still lay lightly on the East End peninsula. This was due to the state of the road, which, for as long as people could remember, had resembled a dry riverbed. One of its steepest grades had a surface of loose rocks like ball bearings, down which one aimed one's vehicle in a controlled skid and hoped for the best. That road was like a dam holding back the rising waters of development.

When Santos got there the road had been newly paved but was still used more by donkeys with their fluffy, wide-eyed foals than by motorists. Hours might go by without seeing a car.

Although a newcomer, Santos jumped to the top of the animal hierarchy. As the only dog of the only family in the cove, he was prince of beasts. Among the wandering herds of goats, the itinerant donkeys, the mourning doves, the bold thrushies, the stray cats and wild dogs and sly skulking mongooses, he alone had an official position, with duties and privileges to match.

Alone among these kindred he had a guaranteed subsistence: food, shelter, and, eclipsing all else, the assurance of as much fresh water as he could drink—no small thing when drought afflicted the island.

And as for his duty, why it was nothing less than to take charge, to guard the premises, to run some interlopers off the property and see to it that others toed the line while passing through. In short, he was to be the policeman. It was a job made in heaven for a schipperke, whose name means *little captain* in Flemish.

Santos had his work cut out for him, though, because many of the animals felt that the old house under the giant tamarind tree was their domain. The goats and the donkeys, especially, considered themselves aggrieved. After all, they had already been there, living around the bay *and* in the house, when we first arrived. They had a history there that went back years before Santos's arrival.

* * *

Before East End we had been living on Lovango Cay. It had given us four wonderful years, but the time had come to move on. We needed a more convenient place to build *Breath*, somewhere with electricity, phone, and some sort of access by road, even if vestigial.

While working in Coral Bay I heard from a friend about a dilapidated but potentially serviceable dwelling at the end of the road at East End. It had been lying abandoned for several years since its last tenant, an eccentric old hermit, had died. Most relevantly, it was still hooked up for phone service and electricity and had a piece of flat ground beside it, next to the water, where a boat might be built, then easily launched. In fact, boatbuilding had flourished there a century before.

So one day I borrowed a skiff, bounced out to East End, and beached the boat at the head of a deeply scalloped cove where the sea barely moved against the sand. The quiet cove shimmered a deep blue. The wind rustled the old gnarled tamarind tree softly, and one could hear the gentle clear coo of mourning doves. The house lay in the sun, sagging, its roof rusty and partly overgrown by a lime tree whose branches and fruit lay piled in the rotting gutter.

I walked into the yard and let the vibes soak in. The place was perfectly peaceful, the sunshine warm, the grass thick, the air buzzing with the distant drone of bees. I loved it right away. There were no neighbors in sight, none in the whole cove. It was ours if we wanted it.

Then a clomping sound came from within the house, a muffled thump, and out the doorway poked a gray muzzle and long fuzzy ears—a donkey. When I approached for a closer look, out burst a troop of them, hawing and snorting suspiciously, stomping their hooves, sending up little puffs of dark dust from the charcoal-saturated ground.

The house was classic West Indian, 70 years old, two rooms under an artfully framed hip roof whose rafters were routed and whose joints were all mortised and tenoned by hand. During its early years, it had been a rum shop that people entered with empty jars to fill from a barrel of transparent volatile spirits that smelled like acetone. (So much so that, years ago, when a barrel of real acetone fell off a barge and washed ashore on a small island in the Grenadines, the islanders, thinking it was some kind of high-proof spirits, broached and quaffed the barrel with fatal results. Instead of high-proof it was high-test.)

But by now the house was considered uninhabitable, rendered so by the goats and donkeys that had been living there as if it was theirs. In rainy weather the goats would scramble indoors, bleating and snorting with satisfaction, to sleep there all night in a huddle of togetherness. Donkeys shared it, clumping in noisily on the wood floors and sleeping on their feet. The landlady was ashamed to charge anything at all, but I finally prevailed upon her to take $25 a month, then got to work. Weeks of hard labor got it cleaned up, the roof repaired, doors and screens put on, guttering renewed, and the last, least trace of goat residue removed.

That last job was the biggest. We had to wash and scrub the whole house time and again with bleach and strong soap, then leave it open to air out. Then we would go inside, close all the doors and shutters, and sniff. Three times it smelled, and three times we scrubbed it again, harder, with ammonia, carbolic acid, and a thick solution of baking soda. Finally even Dorothy's exquisitely sensitive nostrils were satisfied, and we began to paint. The interior had been dark gray with a turgid maroon trim—whatever colors the hermit had been able to score for free. We painted it white, cream, and pink, and the effect was extremely pleasing.

The goats, dumb as sticks, accepted their eviction order with resignation, but the donkeys were another story—they put up a struggle that amazed us and demonstrated their considerable intelligence. They kept trooping by while we worked on the house, stomping their feet at a distance, harumphing disdainfully, and generally keeping an eye on our progress, awaiting the right moment to make their move. They must have tapped their collective unconscious for a folk memory of the Musicians of Bremen. How else to explain their inspired tactics the very first night we slept in the bedroom?

Feeling well satisfied with the smell of fresh paint faintly lingering, new screens keeping out the bugs, and our new home all scrubbed and clean, Dorothy and I drifted off to sleep in the bed I had just built.

Half an hour after our lights went out, four donkeys crept up (not an easy thing for a donkey to do) and silently gathered directly outside our screened bedroom window, their muzzles placed together not five feet from our ears. One moment we were sleeping peacefully, lulled by the sweet sounds of the East End night—a few crickets, the lap of wavelets on the beach—and the next moment an earsplitting bray, the most atrocious sound in the animal kingdom, exploded our sleep. Delivered point-blank in a unison worthy of the Tabernacle Choir, this cacophonous blast of jackass breath had the effect of a cattle prod to the crotch.

Our bodies levitated clear of the bed as every nerve and sinew clutched in simultaneous spasm. Then the source of the unmistakable sound registered, and the millisecond of sheer terror gave way in rapid succession to waves of relief, outrage, and grudging admiration, like a white-water raft bumping over fast rapids.

They continued braying at the top of their lungs until I burst out of the screen door. At that point one of them bolted off, but the other three weren't budging—a grizzled, weather-beaten old male and two of his lifelong harem. Lips wrinkled away from strong buck teeth, long ears laid flat back against their necks, they stamped at the gravel and brayed so violently I thought they must have confused their fables and meant to blow the house down.

I bellowed back, to no effect. I reached down and picked up a pebble. They ignored me. "The nerve!" I thought, and heaved the stone hard at the male's flank. It bounced, raising a little puff of dust from his thick hide. They stopped braying then but still stood there, looking at me stubbornly. I grabbed a whole handful of pebbles then and flung them, peppering the animals with low-velocity buckshot. They reared back and snorted, but obviously the pebbles hadn't made enough impact. I scrabbled around in the dirt for a larger stone, found one, and hurled it hard at the male's haunch. He flinched a little, regarded me with scorn, but cantered away as I pelted bigger rocks at their backsides.

I went back to bed less than triumphant—they were still braying just out of rock range, my hands were dirty, and my breath was agitated. But my indignation gave way to Dorothy's amusement.

"My hero!" she cried, holding her arms open for my return, and I had to laugh considering how cleverly the donkeys had timed their attack.

Nor had we won the war. Persistent campaigners, the donkeys visited us nightly for almost a month. The next night I sprang outside and scrabbled in the dirt and dark for a rock that was sufficiently big to make itself felt through those tough hides. Grabbing impulsively at a neat pile of round stones, I got a handful of fresh donkey droppings for my pains—I swear I heard a bray of derision. Score two for the donkeys, zero for the people.

Subsequently I took to caching good pelting stones in a bucket, the kind of rocks young David searched the riverbank for as he prepared to meet Goliath. I stashed my ammo by the screen door, and at the first bray I would fling open the door and start hurling; the donkeys would bolt away as fast as they could. Eventually it became a war of wits. The donkeys would bolt away as soon as they saw the screen door fly open, while I rapid-fired and crowed in triumph, feeling I had won by driving them off. Of course, they had already won every time they woke me up and got me out of bed.

After awhile the donkey mating season arrived, and the nights were full of brays from the hills and the hard clatter of hooves on the road as the dominant male chased away any horny young contender by clamping powerful teeth on the skin of its neck.

After the donkeys returned to normal—or what constituted normal for them—and foals were rounding the bellies of the mares, they discovered advantages in having us humans around. Our laundry water stood unguarded in our open-air washroom during long spells of drought, and we often discovered in the morning that a five-gallon bucket in which clothes had soaked overnight was empty—soap, bleach, and all.

At the same time, the donkeys continued to regard us as usurpers of their homestead, as did the goats, and they always tried to reoccupy the old homestead whenever we were out.

* * *

Enter Santos. When we got back to St. John and reoccupied the house, we felt that we'd finally outsmarted the barnyard animals by bringing one of their own whom we'd co-opted. Now we had a guard who would keep watch and order while we were gone. And so it

seemed. He reliably set up a great hue and cry if a goat, or most particularly a donkey, entered the yard; and often, as we arrived home,
we'd see him snapping at the heels of some hoofed intruder, threatening to maim any beast that tarried. We commended ourselves and our
high-voltage watchdog for his diligence.

But we hadn't reckoned on animal loyalty or Santos's basically
live-and-let-live attitude. After awhile it became clear that for all his
posturing when we were around, his regime was considerably less
draconian when we were gone—to say the least.

One day Dorothy baked a fresh cheesecake and left it to cool on
a countertop while we all drove to Coral Bay in our Toyota pickup
for the annual Earth Day cleanup. Now, normally Santos could recognize our return from a distance by the sound of our truck—he had
a keen ear for vehicles—but this time a friend who needed to move
some rocks borrowed our truck, and we returned home incognito in
his Suzuki, with the boys salivating over the prospect of dessert.

What did we find when we walked into the house but Santos—
asleep at his post!—while a troop of goats trampled promiscuously
over our floors and a nanny goat with bulging udders had its snout
deep in the cheesecake, inhaling it with goatish grunts while its tail
twitched obscenely in spasms of pure pleasure. We swatted them with
a broom out the doorways, and they clattered down the gravel path.
Santos, after a spate of vociferous barking, slunk away shamefaced
and disappeared for the better part of the afternoon.

Problem was, he never identified goats as a real threat. He knew
we didn't want them around the yard and when we were there did
everything in his power to please us, but when he was there alone he
didn't care if they were there or not.

His main impulse with goats was to chase them. That he loved—it
was such a rush when it worked right and they stampeded off because
he made them believe, even if just for a moment, that he was dangerous.

The goats were dumb enough to fall for it time and again. It had
to be done right. He had to appear suddenly out of nowhere—like
the time he jumped from the window of our moving truck and fell
like a clap of thunder on a herd of goats browsing by the roadside.
With an easy escape route at hand, they panicked and bolted, no goat
wanting to be the straggler who got mauled. After all, abandoned
dogs are the only predator of goats on St. John besides man. Man
is confusing because he sometimes provides water and food. Man is

like God, remote, unknowable, impossible to circumvent, but a feral dog is the traditional tribal enemy slavering at the gate. Seeing one catapult into their midst, their response was to run first and figure it out later.

When that happened, Santos was in hot pursuit of some twenty animals, all much bigger than he. They bleated and snorted, their cloven hoofs clattering over the gravel, their bodies breaking dry branches as they leaped away in headlong terror. Santos nipped at the heels of the laggards, growling in a mighty fury—absolutely loving it.

Then, after the first instinctive flight, a stinking old ramgoat with a long shaggy beard and massive horns curled back like brazen scimitars, his pendulous testicojones in a long leather sack bumping between his knees, stopped and turned with horns at the ready and stamped at the ground. Santos made a quick feint to see if it would bolt, but it was dug in and breathing fire. The diminutive dog came to a swift skidding halt and watched calculatingly, then ambled off with his tongue lolling out the side of his mouth in a self-pleased grin. He had gotten what he wanted—fun.

But it was his relationship with donkeys that showed us what was really operating between the animals. He had a passion for donkeys, a compulsion to go after them and nip at their heels and bark furiously.

A donkey could not enter our yard without Santos going berserk, springing bolt upright, his feet scrabbling in a rotary blur on the wood floor until they caught a seam or a knothole that shot him out the door. He'd charge them as they came loitering opportunistically onto the premises, looking for water or garbage. We'd watch, horrified, as Santos rushed right in under their sharp hooves. They'd snort and bray and lay their ears back flat in displeasure and give little threatening kicks, and when they saw us appear they'd grudgingly hobble off, Santos still insufferably vociferous, within an ace of instant death from a donkey's pile-driver kick. Sick with apprehension we'd implore him to come back, but he would ignore us.

Yet the funny thing was, they never actually tried to kick him. They had ample opportunity to knock him insensible, clear into the bay if they chose to. Donkeys have an extremely swift, accurate and powerful kick, like a hoofed nail gun. But they never used it on him, obnoxious though he was.

It became clear what was going on when I noticed that, as with goats, if Santos thought we were gone he paid absolutely no attention to donkeys. They could browse as they wished, could even come right into our open-air washroom and drink whatever they could find. Santos would lie snoozing, his head between his paws, and scarcely look up. It became clear that he attacked the donkeys only because he felt it was part of his job description when we were around.

But what intrigued me even more was that the donkeys concurred. They would grudgingly vacate the premises once we showed our faces, quite clearly unimpressed and even contemptuous of the little dog's absurd yapping bravado, but nonetheless respecting his right to a livelihood and not taking it personally. It was real animal solidarity.

* * *

The donkeys helped shape the East End experience. They had once been useful farm animals, beasts of burden carrying people over rough trails or toting panniers of supplies and produce up and down the hills from the gardens to the sea, but their role had passed along with the age of subsistence agriculture. Wandering about on their own recognizance, they were unfortunately destructive to the flora and horticulture of the island, being fond of whatever people grew.

They lived almost symbiotically with people, feral but not really wild, knowing there was a connection between their race and man, and that they were owed. They liked to hang around people's houses, ours especially because it had that big shady tamarind tree in our front yard to shield them from the sun, and they could browse for fallen fruit and feed off the newest leaves. Just across the road lay the most sheltered nook of water and beach in all of East End, with shady trees at the edge of the sand. They appreciated this beautiful spot as much as we did. It was on their route as they browsed and ambled the length and breadth of the peninsula, whose terrain and best views they knew better than any person.

Early one morning I met them on the high road between Francis Bay and Cinnamon Bay. Dawn was just breaking, and a lovely freshness remained in the air from a pre-dawn squall that had swept by, shaking the trees, showering down droplets, and passing on. A soft mist lay lightly about, and rainwater reflected in the hollows of the asphalt like mirrors set into the road. The donkeys' coats beaded up and sparkled. They cared nothing about the rain being wet or cold; rain meant juicy foliage and clean pools to drink from.

I got the distinct impression that the donkeys were there at dawn specifically to watch the sunrise. Smart and aware, heedless of discomfort, in closest contact with nature, they reminded me of the Spartans. The animal kingdom in the West Indies forms a continuum that starts with whales and ends with the sandfly. I'm not sure where in that continuum to put donkeys, but it's somewhere near dogs . . . and people.

THIRTEEN

A DOG'S LIFE IN THE VIRGIN ISLANDS

We spent five years at East End after returning from our maiden voyage to the States. Dorothy and I settled down to work, chartering *Breath* on daysailing and snorkeling trips to the nearby British Virgins. The boys attended school, and Santos developed his act, honing skills that he needed in this way of life and that would save his life at least twice in the years to come.

Dorothy and I slept on the boat, the boys in the house, within easy shouting distance. We would come ashore first thing in the morning and return to the boat after the boys' bedtime, and of course there were many trips back and forth during the day for whatever reason. Often Santos would find himself on shore when the action was out on the boat, or out on the boat when everyone was ashore.

It didn't take him long to realize that he could be wherever he wanted by the mere expedient of swimming, rather than barking and waiting for a ride that might be a good while coming. At first we encouraged him to jump because it saved us making an extra trip in the dinghy just to pick up a dog, but after a while we realized it was a double-edged sword. Now there was no keeping him on the boat, or for that matter on shore, against his will unless we actually tied him. But by the time we realized that, the damage had been done.

Round Bay and especially our nook offered some of the best swimming anywhere. The sea was clear and calm, with scarcely a ripple, and the bottom fell away evenly in clear, soft sand. Santos took full advantage of it and typically swam for pleasure or just to cool off a dozen times a day. He would walk into the water without a splash and swim placidly around and around in a figure-eight pattern, never even getting the hair on his back wet, much less getting salt into his sensitive nose.

The coarse outer hairs of his thick ruff were hollow and filled with air, designed for insulation against the winter's snow, like those of a husky. This layer floated out around his neck and buoyed him up like a life jacket, so that he swam with ease even in rough water. As he swam he seemed to enter a state of Zen detachment. His eyes, normally so passionate, would glaze over, and he would go into a kind of trance. In this state he could swim indefinitely.

The sea became another way of getting somewhere, and if that was the only way available he plunged right in. Given sufficient incentive, no distance would stop him.

Once we left him on *Breath* anchored in the middle of Christiansted Harbor, St. Croix, several hundred yards off Protestant Cay. When the human crew returned, no dog was on board. Protestant Cay, however, was jammin' and jumping—a hot reggae band, tables loaded with food, and quite a crowd of revelers. It didn't take a Sherlock Holmes to figure out what had happened. I took the dinghy ashore and found him in the shade near the dock. He was happy to see me but had a belly so bloated he could scarcely walk.

The dog was absolutely fearless. Another time we arrived at midnight off a darkened fishing village in Venezuela's Golfo de Santa Fe. Santos strained his nose toward a noisy convocation of local dogs ashore. After we turned in he must have leaped into the black waters, domain of hammerheads, and swum to shore, because an hour later Dorothy heard a familiar bark from far away. She woke me up to listen. "Sounds like Santos, but it's coming from shore. . . . It *is* Santos!" I had to get in the dinghy and row into a strange shore at 2 A.M. to fetch him back. He was waiting on the beach like a wayward youth ready for a designated driver to bring him home after drinking into the wee hours.

Then there was the time we anchored in Red Hook, St. Thomas, to go shopping and came back to find that the dog had swum to a beach to partake of a political fundraiser featuring chicken and hamburgers on the grill. West Indians are not delighted by stray dogs haunting a food table, and he was ordered off. He walked calmly into the sea from whence he'd come and swam a quarter-mile to the opposite shore, dodging barge traffic, the charter fleet coming back for the afternoon, and the ferries to St. John. A fuel dock attendant picked him out of the water, but before long he jumped back in and returned to the boat, where we found him circling the ladder and awaiting our return, perfectly cool.

He made a name for himself that day because so many people saw him in the process of avoiding him. People were invariably amazed to see such a little dog way out in deep water, swimming with such aplomb and obvious purpose.

He learned about surf from the boys, who headed for the north shore beaches to go body surfing when the big winter swells started rolling in. They would take him out beyond the breakers and let him swim back for shore. He'd get hurtled on the crest of a wave, roll in the ascending froth up the creamy beach, then plant his feet in the sand to keep from being sucked back. He would sneeze and snort violently for an hour afterward. Still, handling oneself in surf is an important skill to have . . . just in case. And as it turned out, Santos's surf training probably saved his life several years later on a disastrous night in Africa.

* * *

Santos made few concessions to his size, but the fact remained that if a situation got down to throwing weight around, he was inherently limited by his 11-pound mass. He just wasn't one of your 90-pound dogs. Santos got his results instead by relying on speed, agility . . . and bluff.

Santos was incredibly fast—and not just the straight-line speed of a racer, but agile-fast, quick. The sinews of his bandy little legs were strung with bow cord; he could spring backward, forward, or sideways, or turn on a dime, or feint and counterfeint in the blink of an eye. This swift, deft, rapier-like control was his main weapon— the unmistakable message of the irrevocable-as-a-bullet thrust was FEAR THIS!—that and a histrionically vicious growl.

At East End, Santos, after much practice, perfected the act and art of guerrilla blitzkrieg, the equivalent of a jungle platoon imper-sonating a battalion—mostly smoke and mirrors but convincing in the short run. His maniacal snarling projected the all-important psy-chological component, the threat that however small this animal, it was out of control, berserk. This he coupled with his flat-out, totally confident charge.

An unforgettable demonstration occurred the day I took Raff to interview for a place in the tenth-grade class of a private school in St. Thomas—a mission made necessary because St. John schools only went through ninth grade. We had to take Santos along—a hassle in the days before car ferries because most cab drivers looked down their noses at the prospect of a dog soiling their immaculate taxis.

Anyway, we tied Santos just inside the school gate and proceeded to the principal's office, where we cooled our heels while she spoke at length on the phone.

She finally received us, none too enthused at the idea of Raffy entering the tenth-grade class in the middle of the school year after having been home schooled for the better part of two years. She averred that he would have to repeat ninth grade to make sure he had an understanding of the basics. Raffy reacted unhappily, and I tried to explain that he wanted to be with his age group.

"Oh no," she cut me off imperiously, "that's putting the cart before the horse. First thing is to master the work. . . . He will be a little older than his classmates, but . . ."

"Ma'm, he'll be almost two years older due to his birthday falling late in the school year. Socially, that's a difficulty for a teenager!"

"Please!" She fixed me with a look that must have dropped generations of young malefactors to their knees. It certainly stopped me cold. "Do . . . not . . . expect . . . *me* to lower the standards of *my* institution to meet your . . . your . . . I must inform you that I have encountered this so-called home schooling," she continued, pronouncing the phrase as if tasting a mouthful of sour milk, "and I have found this home schooling to be invariably substandard. The class he wants to join is very advanced and already full and I doubt there is room even if he could meet the standards. At any rate he will have to take our entrance exams, and that will be the final arbiter. There's nothing more for you to say." She looked quite dour and altogether formidable.

"OK," I said, and left Raffy to take the tests, telling him to meet me down the street at a place where we could get lunch. I untied Santos from the gate and went to the marine store. On the way back we found ourselves in the heart of Charlotte Amalie on Back Street, a crowded one-way street congested with creeping traffic and offering scant sidewalk space or none at all. Whereas Main Street is all elegance (if you consider gift shops flogging booze and useless but costly trinkets elegant), crowded with tourists and taxis and expectant merchants, Back Street is lined with low-rent shops catering to locals, shops selling sporting goods or African fashions, deep-fry joints, and hole-in-the-wall rum shops.

We were walking close to the shop entrances, squeezed over by the traffic, Santos pulling on his leash, head down, dogged, breathing exhaust. This was definitely not his favorite place to be, and he was eager to get to the hillside park at the end of the street. We approached the entrance to a rum shop. A stoop and a doorway led into a narrow room lined by a long counter and cheap barstools—the kind of place where voluptuous Spanish-speaking women congregate toward dusk, still waking up, in sleazy shorts and half-buttoned blouses, the kind of place that features in the newspaper as the venue of a brawl or a stabbing late of nights.

This being only mid-afternoon, a group of rowdy but good-natured young West Indian men were firing shots of rum inside and lounging on the stoop drinking Guinness. You could see from their flushed countenances that they were buzzed. When they saw Santos coming they started bantering, digging each other in the ribs, pointing at him and laughing, calling out comments.

"Me son. . . .!? Wha da is? Walkin 'pon a leash like a dahg . . . buh da cyan' be no dahg!"

"Look like a *pig!*"

"A hedge hahg!"

"Yo schupid up! Dass a dahg yes!"

They appealed to me. "Mistah . . . dass a dahg fo true?"

"Yup," I answered. "He's a boat dog, bred to work on boats." I paused for a moment while they gazed at Santos, bemused, while Santos stared at the pavement, unamused, eager to be outta there. As we started to move on, one of the guys leaned down and pretended to grab at Santos's face, not in a mean way but just to get a reaction. Santos turned his head away and kept pulling. He wanted nothing to do with these noisy drunks seeking entertainment at his expense. The guy did it again, determined to have some fun, and once more the little dog flinched away—this time with a warning growl. But that only served to encourage the fellow and he feinted at Santos again.

This time, without warning, Santos went ballistic—literally. With a bloodcurdling snarl he leaped up at the guy, a blur of speed that brought his audibly snapping teeth a millimeter from the offender's hand, crotch, thigh, and ankle, all in a spectacular backward arc that was an acrobatic *tour de force.*

The dude jerked back, tripped on the step and fell onto the stoop while his buddies exploded with laughter and cheered the dog. They were all on their feet, gesticulating at the dog to wait, come back, do it again, but with a smile I waved them off and we proceeded, Santos pulling like a sledge dog. We left them laughing and rhetorically augmenting the little dog's awesome aerial assault. I could still hear them going at it animatedly, halfway down the next block.

In a cafe opposite the park, we met Raff. I asked him how he'd done.

"Alright, I guess. I like the school—the kids seem friendly—but I'm not going to attend ninth grade, Dad."

"Don't worry, we'll work something out."

We returned at the appointed hour and were ushered into the principal's office without delay. This time she put down her work and almost jumped to her feet. Gone was the dour visage. Her eyes beamed warmly as she extended her hand.

"Good to see you, Mr. Muilenburg . . . and Rafael. . . . Rafael," she murmured, purring his name, "you are a promising young man. Yes indeed, promising."

"How did he do?"

"Let us say . . . quite well."

"Well enough to get a place in the tenth grade? Because otherwise we'll have to go elsewhere."

"Oh no, not elsewhere. . . . There will be a place for him here. Oh yes, you inquired about the possibility of a scholarship on the application form. The financial aid committee has to meet, but I think, ah, you can hope for a good outcome."

I couldn't resist asking, "So, his home schooling—not as bad as you feared?" But she ignored that and bustled about with Raffy, concentrating only on him.

When she noticed me again, it was to say, "Ah, you may leave now so that we can proceed with Rafael's orientation."

She was a piece of work, that principal, but passionate about her school and her students. She focused her considerable persona on Raffy for the next two and a half years. As it turned out, she knew what she was doing, and Raff didn't let her down.

* * *

From the time we moved back in to East End, living on shore next to the road soon posed us a problem, the answer to which had far-reaching implications, though we didn't know that at first.

What it was—Santos turned out to be a car-chasing fool.

He chased cars like an avenging black streak, flat out, barking hysterically, accompanying the vehicle along the level stretch and then halfway up the hill before he would give it up. The asphalt radiated heat like a black iron skillet. Then, mission accomplished, intruder dispersed, he'd come ambling down the hill with his tongue almost touching the ground, deeply satisfied, and take a cooling swim—then resume his station, waiting for the next one.

God knows we tried our best to keep him from such a dangerous obsession, but it was hopeless. Chasing a car is as close as most dogs will ever come to harrying a zebra or a wildebeest across the African savanna. Maybe at some level of DNA encryption Santos thought he was felling a cape buffalo. Dogs need glory too, and in Santos that need verged on obsession. He was in other respects very smart, but this behavior lay beyond intellect, in the deep realm of instinct, and when instinct cracks the whip, dogs and presidents jump, regardless of consequences.

All dog-training authorities agreed that to correct inappropriate behavior we had to catch him in the disputed act and chastise him then and there, so that the animal would connect punishment with crime. It was no good waiting for him to return to his water dish and hurling a slipper and a curse from an easy chair. No, we would have to drop everything—supper, a good book, a nap, whatever—to chase after him. This created the ludicrous spectacle of a car being chased by a dog *and* a man, the dog barking and the man shouting. After nabbing him red-pawed—much easier said than done—I then had to drag him home intoning "bad dog! bad dog!," all the while resisting the urge to kick him, then solemnly tie him up and lecture him sternly about the error of his ways.

We did this several times without the slightest effect on his behavior. It was no use waging a war of wills with Santos. That was a war he always won.

I felt like a character in a "Far Side" cartoon with two frames. In the first, captioned "What we tell dogs," a man berates a dog, saying, "Ginger, you leave those cats alone! You hear me Ginger? Do *not* chase cats, Ginger, you hear? No!!" In the second frame, entitled "What dogs hear," the picture is the same but the word bubble says, "Ginger, blah blah blah! Blah, Ginger, blah Ginger, blah blah blah."

Santos was so strong-willed that to keep him from chasing cars meant we'd have to tie him up 24 hours a day and give him walks morning and night on a leash. But imprisoning him within a fence or making him an indoor lap dog would do violence to his nature. He was the polar opposite of a lap dog. He was more than just our pet—he was a passionate, audacious fellow soul who deserved scope to pursue life to the hilt, not to be stifled.

Of course, if we took him into town or were walking along a highway, then we leashed him. But the East End road wasn't an eight-lane interstate, and other dogs in the area ran unleashed without coming to grief. We had to decide how he was going to live. Would he be free to fulfill himself while incurring a certain level of risk, or would he lead a much more circumscribed but safer life? *His* wishes were never in doubt. It was up to us.

We decided we had to give him his head, then watched him live the exuberant life of a jolly young dog, going where he pleased to sniff and explore, making his own circle of friends, going for a swim, taking mid-afternoon naps on the cool tile floor of the governor's retreat. We also resigned ourselves to his chasing cars and hoped for the best.

Santos spent a lot of time lying in wait for cars, not only to bark them through his territory but to play a daredevil's game. Sometimes an hour might go by without a vehicle, and then he would hide between the roots of a tree by the beach and listen to the sounds of the cove. The mourning doves made a wonderfully serene sound as they called and answered while picking up seeds from the dry forest floor. Tiny hummingbirds shot from blossom to blossom, the short swift throb of their wings a sound you could feel as well as hear, like the single pluck of a cello string. The sea chuckled and sighed on the sand. Below the surface the silent explosive lunge of a mackerel into a cloud of fry would send hundreds of them jumping into the air, their re-entry a marvelously textured sound, like a passing ripple of rain. Sometimes the sea boiled as a school of blue runners joined the fray, slashing the surface into froth, forcing the fry to the surface while a bridal canopy of white terns fluttered overhead, crying out a wild, delicate excitement as they dipped and dropped like soft stones, while pelicans plummeted into the water like salvos of cannonballs.

But when a car came by, he'd spring into action and really take it to the limit. During tourist season rental cars went by slowly, husband driving, wife riding shotgun, kids in back, taking in the surrounds. Santos figured out how to stop them—he'd run along the side of the road a little in front of the jeep and veer tentatively into its path. If the driver slowed down, he'd veer even more in front of the car, causing the wife to scream and the man to slam on the brakes.

Of course, if the car didn't slow down he'd have to dart back to the side smartly. The game required speed, agility, and split-second judgment—it reminded me of Theseus and the Athenians jumping the bulls in the Cretan court at Knossos. I just had to hope that no minotaur lurked in the wings.

One day I was working in my shop, which was next to the road but screened from it by a tamarind tree and bushes. A rental jeep drove by and slowed down to take in the view. Santos bolted out of somnolence and raced up to the jeep barking. When it slowed down he did his number, edging in front of the wheels cautiously.

There followed the predictable chorus of screams.

"Harry, stop! Watch out for that little animal!" I heard the sudden screech of brakes and looked out, screened by the foliage, to see the jeep with husband, wife, and two kids in the back. The car was stopped, and Santos was sitting in the road in front of it looking pleased with himself.

"What the dickens is that? A wild boar?"

"No, it must be a little dog."

"Oddest looking dog I ever saw. Where's its tail? Looks more like a Tasmanian devil or a baby wolverine."

All eyes upon him, Santos pranced up to the shotgun seat, ears back in affable greeting, his fox face deft and silky, and proceeded to beg shamelessly, like a tiny Yellowstone bear. He got up on his hind legs, pawed the air, and gave a winning little growl. An exclamation of delight rang out.

"I told you it was a dog!"

"Wolverine?! You think we're in Michigan? This is the Virgin Islands, Dad!"

Five minutes went by as he worked his audience. They took a picture of him taking a chip ever so gently from each child's hand. They patted him, praised him, and finally drove off up the hill. Santos resumed his post.

* * *

Whether we knew it then or not, the decision to let the dog run free was more than just about the dog. It was about our own choices as well, about the kind of risk we were willing to accept in our own lives. There was no lack of message, from relatives and society at large, that it was high time for us to come down to earth, out of our blue-water paradise, and accept reality—in other words, to get a proper job with its restrictions and its benefits.

In a nutshell, to trade freedom for security.

The dog was a proxy for us, a stalking horse. Santos could be kept on a leash, always on hand to guard the premises and likely to live longer, or he could be allowed to wander, freer but more at risk. Correspondingly, we could give up the sailing life for insurance, a career ladder, and a pension, but we'd have to stay behind the fence and wear the leash. We'd have to put work before roaming.

It was a constant debate. What was life for? Experience, love, and adventure? Or responsibility, substance, and security? It was hard to have both, yet they were not necessarily mutually exclusive. We all seek the balance that suits our natures, and it behooves us to know what is lost and what gained, without illusions, as choice after choice is made. The trouble is, it is hard to assess in process. Hindsight is so much clearer.

By watching a dog's life, maybe we could get a perspective on our own—while there was still time.

FOURTEEN

SANTOS AND RASPUTIN

From his throne on the top step of the doorway to our old West Indian house, Santos could survey all traffic passing through his domain. Goats, donkeys, fowl, and most vehicles he tolerated with lordly ennui so long as they kept their distance from the house. Cats and mongooses he ran off as a matter of course. But what really got him frantic was a beige Toyota pickup in the back of which rode a huge rottweiler named Rasputin.

Rasputin was an expensive animal of distinguished pedigree who had received a good education at a dog school in Miami. Phlegmatic, to all appearances dumb as a stick, obedient to a fault, he was the opposite of Santos in every way. He had been trained to be his owner's personal bodyguard. In town he sat in the cab to guard its occupant and his money. Amory's restaurant was thriving, and he thought a big dog would be better all-around protection than a pistol.

Amory was a neighbor who, fairly or not, many people considered arrogant and supercilious. We had no complaint about him—he was always good for a ride if our truck was broken down, and his conversation was informed. He did hold himself aloof though, and visibly prided himself on his possession of the finer things in life, such as pure-bred guard dogs and classic yachts. Ironically it was these that brought him ridicule. Amory wrecked his new boat on the Anegada reef during its maiden voyage, a total loss. His dog lasted longer but met a similarly undeserved fate.

Rasputin's job was to intimidate people, but he didn't intimidate Santos. Every morning and evening the beige truck drove by with Rasputin seated dutifully in the back, looking out lugubriously over the tailgate. Santos could recognize its engine long before any of us could even hear it. He might be snoozing or even eating, but the instant he heard that sound he'd drop everything and sprint toward the road, barking at the top of his lungs. He tried to meet the truck and chase it through and out of his territory. His bandy legs pelted the blacktop, his muzzle wrinkled back in hate, and he bared his teeth, snarling and barking hysterically. The virulence of the 11-pound dog was awesome. Meanwhile, 120-pound Rasputin, with jaws the size of Santos's torso, would occasionally incline his head bemusedly over the tailgate, take in this absurd display, and give one deep-throated, resonant "woof!"

Amory hated our little dog for making such a public spectacle of his daily passage—and no doubt it *was* a little humiliating to have such frenzy attend one's every appearance. It cast one as fall guy in a farce, the foil to a comically brash egocentric. When he heard that maniacal barking, Amory would grimace and gun the engine hard, and Santos would give it even more, going past in a blur, a shriek with a Doppler effect—then come trotting back, exhausted but deeply fulfilled, his spent body still emitting occasional reflexive yelps like hiccups.

This display repeated itself twice a day, upon Amory's going and his coming. Santos lived for it, and lay waiting for the sound of the engine. Probably because Rasputin was the biggest dog on East End and Santos the smallest, Santos especially had to prove himself. His outsized ego could shrink from nothing. He had to beard the lion; there was no choice to be made. Every day the big dog intruded, and every day Santos went head to head with him, instantly and ferociously.

Even if Rasputin weren't in the truck, Santos attacked it with no less fervor—the truck was Rasputin's symbol, maybe even the source of his power. Who knows what goes on in the mind of a dog? Certainly vehicles held an aura of the divine for Santos, who reveled in riding them. His favorite place—the only place that would do—was the front seat. He would invariably worm his way into one's lap and stand with his head out the window, thrusting his muscular hind legs restlessly against one's groin as he eagerly strained ever farther out the window. He had to be firmly restrained from jumping out of the moving vehicle when we passed other animals.

To fully convey Santos's passionate dispute with Amory's truck, it is necessary to recount the first time Santos broke his leg. We were walking by Haulover Bay in the late afternoon, about a mile from home, when the Lieutenant Governor drove up, stopped to chat, and then drove off. Santos, who had been investigating the underbrush for a mongoose, impetuously dashed after his car in full paean and disappeared around a curve. We called frequently as we walked home, but he didn't appear, nor was he back at the house.

We were ready for bed before he came back—limping severely—and crawled surreptitiously into a dark corner. Dorothy tried to examine him, but he growled at her, an unprecedented thing. He wanted to be left alone. In the morning we found him ashen with pain. His leg had been broken in two and was hanging by mere skin. We were amazed to think of him fighting off shock as he forced himself back, over steep hills, up the porch steps, all the while dragging that poor dangling leg.

We rushed him to Dr. Andy Williamson's clinic in St. Thomas, where the good vet operated immediately and pinned the bones together with a stainless steel bolt. Three days later Santos came home with his rear right limb in a cast, which he carried well off the ground as he hobbled around on three legs. At 500 bucks the repairs were a great bargain, but the most we'd ever shelled out for an animal. In fact, we hadn't spent that much on our own medical needs in years. Then again, we never chased cars.

As he slept under the table his first morning home, we were savoring breakfast and discussing his mishap. "Well at least the experience will finally persuade him not to chase cars again," I declared with conviction.

No sooner had the words left my mouth than Amory's truck crested the hill. Santos's ears pricked up and he scrabbled to his feet and shot out the door like a jet catapulted off a carrier's deck. "Santos! Stop! Come! Damn!" I bellowed, to no avail. I chased after him in time to see the truck fishtail around a bend, tires screeching, hotly pursued by a three-legged dog stumping frantically down the road, his right rear leg in a cast held high. We finally had to tie Santos up mornings and evenings until Amory had passed by in order to protect our investment in that leg while it healed. And when it did, East End's David and Goliath show resumed unabated.

* * *

Santos's great moment came one sultry day in September when a hurricane was heading for the Virgins. We got in the pickup and drove over to Princess Creek, where we had anchored *Breath*, to check on her and put out another anchor. The "creek" was a pool of deep water with a sandy mud bottom bordered by mangroves and landlocked within green hills. There were four such coves, known collectively as Hurricane Hole, and they offered the best refuge in the islands against severe weather. Princess Creek had the additional advantage of a paved road running by its shore, so that when a storm was in the area, boat owners who lived or worked ashore could leave their boats anchored there and get back and forth while waiting to see whether the storm would hit.

Amory had recently replaced his wrecked boat with a sleek and pricey Swan, which was anchored at Princess Creek, and he happened to be aboard it with Rasputin. His truck was parked next to the dinghy landing, a break in the thick mangroves that lined the shore. We parked just behind his vehicle.

So it was that Santos came upon the opportunity of a lifetime, the stuff of dog dreams. For the first time ever, Rasputin's truck was parked . . . and unattended!

The little dog instantly took it all in. He wasted no time. Trembling with excitement, his hackles raised so that he looked like a black porcupine, he approached the beige truck on stiff legs, growling low. Very deliberately he lifted his leg on the right rear tire, changed his mind, lifted his other leg, shifted and fidgeted until he found the precise pose and exact angle of fire—then gave it a long squirt that left an unmistakable trail down the dusty rim. After sniffing it carefully and finding that it was good, Santos marked each tire in turn, painstakingly, then went around once again for good measure, totally absorbed in his work.

Then turning toward the bay, Santos gave an insufferably triumphant bark. Right away a deep-throated and unprecedentedly agitated "woof woof woof!" rolled back over the water like thunder. The normally imperturbable Rasputin sensed that shame had been brought to his ride, and he was balanced precariously at the edge of Amory's fine yacht, about to fall in, looking anxiously shoreward— much to Amory's annoyance.

Sad to say, not long thereafter and much to Santos's regret, poor Rasputin met an untimely end due to no fault of his own. Amory, aristocrat of dog owners, one day absent-mindedly left his expensive animal locked in the cab of his truck, parked full in the noonday sun with the windows rolled tightly up. Since it was a new Toyota and thus airtight, poor Rasputin asphyxiated or died of heat stroke, a cruel and undeserved death.

He wasn't forgotten, though. For years after Rasputin's death,

Santos continued to chase Rasputin's truck with undiminished fury. The image of the big dog, the great adversary, lived on in Santos's mind until the very day Amory sold the truck and departed the island. And who knows, perhaps even until the end of Santos's days, whenever the old schipperke whimpered in a dream and his legs jerked, he was seeing Rasputin peering over the tailgate and hearing his deep woof.

FIFTEEN

DAYSAIL DOG

Most people work because they have to. What they work at is not usually what they would choose to do had they unlimited options. Dogs are different. Their duty is their delight, and they do it with a passion. They herd sheep, hunt foxes, retrieve pheasants, track convicts, pull sledges, and guard flocks with tireless devotion, giving an altogether different meaning to the old expression "to work like a dog." From medieval times, Santos's ancestors had been bred for service afloat, and he was born ready and eager. He didn't have days off during which it "wasn't his job," or sick days, or personal leave or emergency family obligations. He didn't get depressed or suffer a midlife crisis. Keeping watch, warding off, and sounding the alarm—work was his reason for being.

Santos's workday started at the crack of dawn, at least during laughing gull season.

Visitors from the north say we have no seasons in the Caribbean, but one sure sign of our spring is the return of the laughing gulls. These East Caribbean gulls are nothing like their drab, lumpish northern cousins, those flying rats with predatory eyes who scavenge dumps fifty miles inland. Laughing gulls are small and pristine, crisp studies in black and white with bellies of fresh snow, heads of jet black, and uppers of nimbus gray. They are seafarers and migratory wanderers; northern-hemisphere winters being too much for them, even in the balmy Virgin Islands, they fly south to Brazil for their winter bivouac. Then, after a six-month silence, early on an April morning, a familiar raucous cry registers through the fleeting fog of sleep, and we know the laughing gulls are back.

For a few days or a week, only the loners straggle in, outriders and scouts; and then suddenly the whole laughing gull nation appears en masse, and for the next half year the wild, sea-free sound of their lunatic laughter pervades the harbor. They take up their usual posts on buoys, rocks, and especially unused boats—including dinghies—which they soon foul with their droppings.

A charter boat cannot have dung in its dinghy, and Santos's first order of business was to keep ours free of gulls.

We would wake up in the morning to a low growl directly above us on the afterdeck. Santos knew not to bark before we rose unless the situation were dire and immediate, and he also knew that mere barking wouldn't do the job—the gulls were brazen and canny and wouldn't move until they had to, the dinghy normally being tied too far astern for him to reach—so he would wait, lying on the afterdeck next to the tiller arm, his head between his paws, watching intently, keeping up a sputtering, muted, whimsical growl until a shift in the fitful harbor breeze brought the dinghy close enough for him to suddenly spring up, snarling in triumph, feigning a leap. The gulls would shriek, their open beaks showing their startlingly scarlet throats, and take to the air, albeit grudgingly.

Santos rarely actually jumped into the dinghy, because then he would be stuck in it, bobbing around, marginalized, until someone lifted him back up.

* * *

Had *Breath* been a bulldozer we might have graded roads for a living. Instead when we got back to the Virgin Islands we entered the charter business, taking tourists out for a day of sailing and snorkeling—a day that Santos dominated. *Breath* was clearly his boat, and by the end of the afternoon people would take leave of him with a certain awe.

A lot of the charter business is social, and in this the little dog easily equaled any human crew. One of the first and most important jobs of the day was breaking the ice among the guests, who were often complete strangers to one another.

Early one morning a full boatload of passengers was congregated on the narrow, antiquated Coral Bay dock, waiting. I was in a jam because, on the way in to fetch them, the outboard had given a sodden cough, stopped, and now wouldn't start—water in the carburetor. The tourists were getting fidgety, having risen from their beds early and missed breakfast in order to arrive by 8 A.M., only to wait while the captain tinkered. If this was the state of the dinghy, what might be expected of the boat? Many of our guests were upscale yuppies, convinced that the best was their birthright. They hated being made to wait; their time was precious—*quality* time—and being herded together like sheep in a chute didn't make them happy either.

Santos saved the day. He had been doing his morning rounds— making his mark afresh, checking at Skinny Legs for scraps, policing the other animals. He ran back to catch the dinghy, saw that departure wasn't imminent, and peeled off with a flurry of good-natured barking after a rooster. With an ill-tempered squawking, it flapped up into a tree as the swift little dog swept below it, snapping theatrically.

Having gotten everybody's attention, Santos moved to his main act, a furious charge at a troop of peacefully grazing donkeys, barking insolently as if he had the king's commission in his pocket to disperse this rabble at once. These were the same donkeys who regularly browsed through the dock environs, keeping an eye on things, and they'd seen this absurd show more than once—many times more than once. A young one might snort and stamp its hoof, another might lift its leg disdainfully as if avoiding something unsanitary underfoot, but the rest ignored him, their body language emoting a wearied, scornful *"whatever . . . !"* Santos's nose was about six inches from their rear hocks as he barked, and his now mesmerized audience of waiting passengers gasped with apprehension until he turned and, with all eyes upon him, made his triumphal entrance onto the dock.

Until they saw his face, most of the passengers weren't sure he was a dog; from a distance he looked like a coked-up hedgehog or some offbeat cross between a Tasmanian devil and an Amazonas peccary. But the moment he danced up to the dock, alert, savvy, confident, with his ears laid back in affable greeting and his tongue lolling, he was unmistakably a dog.

He was moving from guest to guest, giving each of them a cursory inspection, when two large young mongrels loped up eagerly to share the attention and started badgering Santos to play, knocking him clumsily with their uncontrollably wagging hips and tails. At first he bore it testily, in the manner of one who suffers a fool. They kept it up, almost edging him off the dock, ignoring his warning growls— until suddenly he exploded like a letter bomb in their faces, a black tornado with a blood-curdling snarl and a blur of snapping teeth. It so startled the two big dogs that they sprang backward and landed in the drink. While they floundered through the shallows back to shore, Santos calmly resumed his greetings.

The tourists all started talking at once..

"Didya see that? This little dog? Just ran those two big guys right off the dock!"

"Unbelievable. . . . Talk about force of character!"

"Awesome snarl, like a wolverine on bad acid!" By now they were all laughing together.

His next act was dinghy jumping, negotiating the usual congestion of small craft at the dock by leaping from dinghy to dinghy with impeccable balance until he got to our skiff and strode its foredeck—on station, ready to ride. By this time the guests were delighted to learn that this was a ship's dog, belonging to the very boat they were booked on. Much mollified, they peppered me with questions about Santos's breed while I cleaned the plugs and drained the float chamber, and when the machine once again fired up, we all ferried out to *Breath* anticipating the best. Santos as always rode in the prow, reaching a forepaw out toward the boat as if guiding the way. People loved that.

And in fact there was no leaving him behind, even if we wanted to. We tried it once when a guest wrinkled up her nose at the sight of Santos and proclaimed that she was allergic to dogs. Now, being allergic to cat hair is common and more or less unremarkable, but being allergic to dogs is more unusual and, sometimes, the telltale mark of a problem personality. This lady gave every appearance of being a high-maintenance, readily upset pain in the derriere. The other couple had already taken to Santos, so her husband tried to persuade her.

"I don't think this breed would bother you, dear. His hair is kind of coarse, not fine and wispy like those other dogs." He stroked Santos's coat to show her.

"I really don't want to take the chance. I'm sorry . . . I just wouldn't enjoy the day with it on board, up close. A boat is a confined space, and you know how claustrophobic I can be." The husband ducked his head either in assent or from a desire not to meet anyone's eyes just then. I too didn't want to meet anyone's eyes just then, because mine were rolling with disdain.

"Do you mind?" asked the husband.

"Not at all!" Dorothy replied. "It's a good day for him to have his monthly flea bath, because our oldest son has a day off from school."

"Santos, you have to stay . . . stay," she told him firmly, holding him by the ruff. Santos looked uncomprehendingly at her and at the dinghy. As soon as she stopped petting him he leaped into the bow and stood there pleading, his ears back along his head, the fine hairs of his face emphasizing the intensity in his eyes.

"Aw, look at the little feller—really wants to come along," said the other woman. But I picked him up and set him on the sand, saying, "No boy, you have to stay and have a *bath . . . a bath.*"

"Why Peter, shame on you!" exclaimed Dorothy, suppressing a giggle while trying to hold the dog as he lunged for the dinghy again, desperation in his eyes. He wriggled out of her grip and jumped up, this time crouching down in a posture of supplication. His ears were in constant motion and extremely expressive—they'd lie back flat against his head as he pleaded, then flick upright as his eyes brimmed with hope for a second, then go back in abject disappointment. He was a hard one to refuse.

When the skiff set out for *Breath*, Santos immediately swam after it. Our guests boarded, milady making a predictable scene about how she needed a better ladder. Santos reached the boat and swam in circles at the boarding point. Still we were adamant, and left the rail, paying him no attention. But the other husband, George, was fascinated.

"He's quite a swimmer, eh? Look Judith, he's circling the whole boat now. I've never seen such a good swimmer. What kind of breed is he anyhow? How long will he keep it up?"

"He's a schipperke, a Belgian barge dog . . . and we'll find out when I cast off the mooring line." After twenty minutes of stowing bags and getting them back out for suntan lotion and passports, warming up the engine and taking off the sail covers, we cast off and motored out, taking care not to hit Santos. He gave a stricken look as we motored past and started swimming after us, absolutely unwavering.

"What are you going to do?" asked George, while his wife Judith never took her eyes off the dog. I shrugged. Judith turned to Dorothy.

"He's still coming. What will happen to him? We've got to go back!"

"No, he'll be all right. He'll get the idea and turn back any minute now," Dorothy said, while I went slower than usual because I wasn't sure just what the little maniac would or wouldn't do.

"Judith, hand me the binoculars—they're in the leather pack."

Now George battened his gaze on Santos as if the dog were a man overboard on the high seas and George the would-be rescuer detailed to keep the swimmer continuously in view.

The dog kept coming steadily, the black speck that was his head still visible in the water quite a distance from shore. I looked at Dorothy and could see she was upset. Would Santos swim to Tortola or meet us at Norman Island? He knew the way. We were a quarter-mile gone and around the point, out of sight of Santos—and about to turn back—when the allergic lady herself begged us to return and pick up the dog.

"I wouldn't want his death on my conscience," she said. "I'll be fine. I'm not that allergic anyway, just squeamish about dogs, but this one is different. Please go back for him."

So we did—he was still coming, even though we'd gone out of his sight—and even the allergic lady got fond of him as the day wore on. And I found some good points about her, too.

Santos was up on the bow that afternoon as we came home. We ghosted in past Pelican Rock, then a wind gust heeled the boat over in the flat water, her wake seething like champagne. As she approached our cove the long gust died, and the air that wafted from shore— his sphere of influence by any standard—bore a scent that Santos sniffed with growing displeasure. Something was amiss on the land. The dog's coat bristled; he began to make his warning noise, a low, suspicious "rrruff . . . rrruff."

By the time the boat eased up to its mooring, Santos was beside himself. Four donkeys were wading in the water right on the little sandy beach in the corner of our bay where the dinghy had to land, taking the sun and acting as if the place belonged to them.

The vehemence of each bark lifted him stiff-legged off the deck, his spiky black mane flaring, and as the boat stopped to pick up the mooring buoy he gave us a look of sheer disbelief that we weren't going to steam full ahead and plow a furrow up the beach.

But his own duty was crystal clear. He gave a sharp yelp, his going AWOL yelp, and flung himself off the bow. He surfaced emitting a strangled, gargling bark—he had been barking underwater. His four paws pulled urgently for shore, and he left a discernible wake, widening behind him in the flat blue water.

The donkeys looked up as he neared shore. The closer he got, emitting erratic growls and yelps, the more alert they became, and a little skittish. Perhaps the sight of the black head and the flashing jaws stirred a vestigial warning neuron in the donkeys' brains, a remnant primeval memory of black caimans in an ancient Abyssinian waterhole . The donkeys stamped nervously and—just in case—moved back onto the beach enough to get their hooves out of the water.

Santos's feet finally touched bottom, scrabbled for traction, caught against the gravel, and shot him out of the water like a sub-launched cruise missile. With his hair wet and clinging, he resembled a bedraggled big-eared rat, but his mad charge strongly intimated rabies. Whatever the reason—maybe they were visitors from another part of the island, encountering this dervish for the first time—the donkeys suddenly stampeded for the bush.

An unmistakable gloating note laced Santos's victory cry as he plunged into the undergrowth, hot as a poker on their heels. It looked like TV footage from the Serengeti—a herd of fleeing Abyssinian asses pursued by a Napoleonic peccary about to wrestle down the hindmost and rip its throat out.

Then something happened in the bush where we couldn't see. We heard an outraged braying, a prodigious stamping and quaking of foliage, and suddenly they reappeared in reverse order, Santos first with his ears flat back, streaking for dear life across the beach, with the male donkey hot in pursuit, livid with rage, his ears laid flat back along the bulging chords of his neck, his massive buck teeth clenched in hatred, braying an apoplectic curse.

Our hearts in our mouths, we watched the little daredevil leap into the water and swim to safety, just ahead of the donkey's gnashing teeth. The pursuer reared up short at the water's edge, and Santos, knowing he was safe, swam back to defiantly badmouth his adversary. Finally the donkey gave it up as a bad job and trotted off with his harem.

Back on the boat we fell to the deck with laughter. As we came ashore he swam out to greet the dinghy. We lifted him in and he shook himself all over our guests, who kept exclaiming that they'd never, ever, in all their life seen such a dog. Shortly they said good-bye to us, but George couldn't bear to leave the dog. As they drove off he kept saying, "What an amazing little dog!"

* * *

Santos assessed the guests every morning, visiting each one briefly until he found a willing lap where he could lie on his back, his eyes closed in supreme languor, his rear leg occasionally pawing the air as she scratched his belly, a little Roman emperor awash in pleasure.

Yet part of him remained ever on guard; when he sensed a power-boat penetrating the no-go zone that surrounded *Breath*—breaching the sacred circle!—he would convulsively wrench himself away and bound onto the deck with bristling mane to peal out his warning—a warning to the transgressing boat as well as to us.

Nothing—no caress, emolument, nor delicacy—came between him and his duty. It was unthinkable that any boat, especially a fast runabout, should pass unheralded or unchallenged.

A good breeze is normal in the Sir Francis Drake Channel, and *Breath* would customarily arrive at Roadtown with a wake boiling out from under her rudder and her charter guests looking forward to a day of sailing and snorkeling. Santos knew he wasn't allowed on shore and would wait patiently for us to go clear Customs and Immigration, but he would jump up to "secure the perimeter" when he saw us returning—that is, to bark first off the stern, then off the bow, then from the starboard side, and finally greet us on the port side, standing to attention as we arrived. Thus were we "piped" aboard. Where and how he picked up this ancient military ritual, I'll never know. Maybe people learned it from dogs.

From Roadtown the boat would surge along on a beam reach past green islands and over turquoise shoals where the bottom can easily be seen. After passing close to the tip of Peter Island, *Breath* would head for The Indians, where the guests could plunge into 50 feet of gin-clear water near rocky pinnacles that rise sheer from the bottom covered with colorful sponges and delicately traced lavender sea fans. Snorkeling over lavish, healthy coral gardens, through an underwater arch and between the rocks, people lose track of time, immersed in the psychedelic sea, with hundreds of silvery fish hanging in a gauzy veil about the rocks. Sudden pulsating schools of bonito flash by and are gone.

But each day when the guests took out their snorkeling gear, Santos tried desperately to herd everybody away from the rail where, from previous experience, he knew they would wind up overboard. Every splash elicited a hysterical protest, his bark taking on the distinctive timbre he reserved for Man Overboard! The urgency of his inbred responsibility had not diminished a whit over the centuries.

Despite having seen thousands of people, hundreds of children, jump into the water, Santos unfailingly went ballistic. He even started barking at jumpers on neighboring boats.

He took himself and his responsibilities very, *very* seriously.

We usually stopped at the Bight in Norman Island and ferried our guests over to the *William Thornton* for lunch. This vessel (a.k.a. the "Willie T") was one of Santos's all-time favorite establishments. Most so-called floating restaurants are merely a barge bolted to a city wharf in water no one would ever eat fish from, but the Willie T was a 100-year-old 90-foot Baltic trader moored to a 7,000-pound anchor in 30 feet of water that was as blue as sky. Looking down was like looking through glass; in the depths were revealed the immaculately rippled sandy bottom, a giant, somnolent barracuda named Barry, a school of big blue runners, sergeant majors, fat needlefish, and opportunistic remora, all of whom (except the barracuda, lost in torpor) made the surface churn every time a plate was scraped over the side.

On board, things often got pretty lively. In season a steady stream of skiffs, dinghies, and rental runabouts disembarked goodtime revelers, scantily dressed, who clustered at the bar, danced on the afterdeck, and jumped off the upper deck—sometimes topless, sometimes even naked. Not for nothing was the Willie T's "house" drink the potent Painkiller (Pusser's dark rum, cream of coconut, pineapple juice, and orange juice)—a lot of people, by the time they'd been there awhile, weren't feeling any. Mighty splashes accompanied by screams and bursts of laughter reached Santos's keen senses, as did the smell of burgers and ribs on the grill.

There was no keeping him aboard short of locking him below. He would clog the boarding gate and implore with heartrending pathos to be included—the emotion his eyes could generate was overwhelming—while we sternly told him his all-time, flat-out, hands-down *least* favorite word, "stay." When we left he would climb up on the caprail and teeter there, looking at us, looking down at the water, barking. He hated to jump because he disliked salt water in his ears and nose, but he absolutely had to be where the action was, and in the Bight that decidedly meant the Willie T. No matter how choppy it was or how far away we had anchored, Santos jumped—99 times out of a hundred. As time went on he even developed a proper dive, holding his forepaws out and entering head first.

Dorothy and I knew without looking the exact moment he would hit the water, because our guests would almost capsize the dinghy with laughter while the people on the Thornton, looking across the water, would suddenly call out in alarm.

"Oh my God, the poor little baby fell off the boat! Harry, do something!" Santos's diminutive size convinced people he was vulnerable, that his splash into the sea was accidental. Occasionally Harry would actually plunge in to effect a rescue, or get into his dinghy, which, by the time he started it, was usually too late, for Santos had no need of rescuers; he swam unwaveringly for the floating dock, where someone would invariably be waiting on their knees to fish him out of the water. He typically received a hero's welcome, acknowledged it briefly by shaking on his benefactor and briefly nosing the people on the dock, then dashed wet and dripping through the bar, headed for the tables, nose to the deck in search of hamburger or chicken bits. The crew of the Willy T called him "the sweeper," and for a long time tacked up on their bulletin board, right next to pictures of naked girls jumping off the top deck, a reprint of the *Reader's Digest* article about his hairbreadth escape from drowning five miles off the coast of Venezuela—a story soon to be told.

SIXTEEN

SANTOS AND THE ELEPHANT

Santos lived well for just a dog. "Just a dog...." It's funny that the expression "a dog's life" is synonymous with misery, and that "work like a dog" means spending long, hard hours chained to your job. Historically, of course, that *has* been a dog's lot—dependent on man and often abused. Even today, in the impoverished Third World, the average dog's life is tough. Reach out your hand to one and it shies away, more accustomed to being struck than stroked. Worse yet, in the Far East it's as liable to be eaten as fed. Elsewhere it is tolerated, remanded to the barest of margins, where it skulks around abjectly, anticipating a kick.

But times change and language changes accordingly. In our afflu-ent, pet-prone country, leading "a dog's life" is coming to mean hav-ing it "made in the shade."

Take Santos. How wide a gap yawned between his experience and that of a pariah dog in the slums of Calcutta! His life was far more threatened by excess than by deprivation. Not only was he a First World dog, he was a charter boat dog, inhabiting one of the cushiest sinecures of dogdom. He was a star, playing to boatload after boatload of bemused guests. There was always someone aboard who found him irresistible, cuddled him, and fed him morsels from their plate, and Santos made it his business at the start of each day to find that individual.

For his drink he frequently had iced water cupped in someone's palms from the ice chest; and as for his meals . . . suffice it to say he supped from the table of the gods—*his* gods at any rate—which is to say, he got our leftovers. At the end of a day's charter, I often shook my head and thought, there's a dog that has it made.

Yet never did Santos have it so good as in the five blissful weeks he spent cosseted in the company of two prepubescent girls. Kim and Lindsay devoted themselves to him one summer while we sailed down the island chain from St. Maarten to Venezuela. They spoiled him so extravagantly we feared we'd never get a sensible animal back when they left.

But just when he'd been most pampered and indulged, the little dog faced the challenge of a lifetime on a beach in St. Lucia and met it with a spirit as keen and tempered as a Toledo blade. Like Horatio, Santos was not fortune's fool; he stayed true to himself, come what may.

Breath was tied close to shore to attract the interest of tourists driving by. Often they would slow down to look, but one morning I heard an exclamation and the screech of brakes, then the sound of a jeep backing up. Out jumped a tall, athletic man with prematurely white hair, followed by a very shapely brunette and two little girls. He admired the boat, asked me a few questions, and promptly chartered it for a weekend trip to Peter Island. Dispatch in decision-making was typical of U. T. Thompson III.

We enjoyed an idyllic sail that weekend, the kind that persuades people to buy boats. The weather was exceptionally clear and the air pure and luminous, so that we could even see the ravines on the peak of Virgin Gorda. The tips of distant islands, warped by refraction, seemed to lift off the horizon.

Breath sailed up the Sir Francis Drake Channel, tacking into radiant bays between long, rocky ridges where the hardy foliage soaked up sunlight like a solar sponge and glowed it back just beyond the edge of human sight. Gusts fell down the hills to fill *Breath*'s sails and make her rigging hum, playing her like a stringed wind instrument, her hull a sounding box for the sea.

We reached Deadman's Bay at the far end of Peter Island by mid-afternoon with the sun at our back. It set the pool of blue water alight, reflected off the flawless sand, and glistened on a thousand rustling fronds in the grove of coconut palms ashore. After striking the tops'l and stays'l we stood into the bay, turned her bow into the wind, dropped jib and then main, glided to a standstill, and let go the anchor.

Santos hit the beach sprinting and raced like a streak to its end and back for the sheer joy of it. The kids pelted after him and he led them a merry chase, which ended when all four of them plunged into the water. Then Diego took the girls out in the skiff, he proudly at the throttle, the girls demure on the center thwart, Santos poised as always on the prow. They came back glowing.

We had supper in the cockpit as the sun sank beneath the western rim and sent up broad spokes of gold and lavender high into the sky. No swell, no bugs, and the stars shone like a magnificent testament to God's good taste. It was prime. The family was sold on sailing, on *Breath*, on Diego . . . and they *loved* the dog.

Tom was a native Californian attorney who'd made lots of money in the California real estate boom in the early '80s. His family lived in the lap of luxury, which he was proud to provide, but he also feared that he was spoiling his women—that his girls would grow up soft, habituated to the ease of affluence. He admired the way we lived in an old West Indian cottage, short on amenities but long on beauty. By the end of the sail, Tom had proposed an extended summer cruise down the Lesser Antilles, from St. Maarten to Venezuela.

"A long cruise on *Breath* is just the thing to toughen up my girls," he told me.

"Is that an insult?"

He laughed. "It's a tribute to your lifestyle . . . your values. There's just one stipulation."

"What is it?"

"You have to bring Diego and Santos as crew."

* * *

Santos knew what to expect when he saw the dinghy raised on deck and lashed down while a Force 6 easterly was making the rigging thrum and the boat creak at its anchor rode even in the flat water of Gorda Sound. The sea-wary skip became noticeably glum. He wanted none of what was to come. Me neither, but we faced that worst of seagoing strictures—a deadline. We'd been waiting day after day for the weather to improve, but the wind only wore itself into a steadier groove and raised a bigger sea. Now we had two days to get across the Anegada Passage to St. Maarten to meet the Thompsons.

"Sorry, Doggus," I told him. "It's going to be tough, but that's what you are. Right?" I frazzled his ears jovially, and he, sensing mockery, withdrew stonily.

One never knows what attitude the Anegada Passage will cop. The northeast entrance to the Caribbean can be brutal. Though I have enjoyed balmy crossings with not a drop of spray on deck, my defining memory is of the time my old wooden boat broke six oak ribs while slamming across the current-wracked Saba Banks.

Sure enough, as soon as we left the protection of the last point a steep swell broke with a resounding thump against the topsides and toppled its crest into the cockpit, dousing Santos where he lay.

The dog huddled in the cockpit and glared at me. He knew who to blame.

Soon we switched on the engine, dropped the jib, strapped main, mizzen, and stays'l in tight, and motorsailed shamelessly to windward against steep 8- to 10-foot seas made surly by the interference of banks, tides, and islands. Hour after hour we took constant spray. Santos would shake his fur out and plead from the top step of the companionway for a lift down into the warmth and dryness of the cabin, but for reasons of toiletry he had to remain on deck.

That top step was protected by the closed hatch cover from the worst of the spray. There he would lie, his head hanging down as far as possible, trying to get eye contact with somebody. When he did, a burst of pathos would stream from his eyes, accompanied by the whimper of a long-suffering, oh so *worthy* animal in need of compassion. If you wavered, he would pour it on.

We might dodge "the look," but there was no escaping his voice. Santos couldn't actually talk, but he spoke in tongues with all the fervor of a snake-juggling hillbilly Baptist thrashing around on the floor of a backwoods church.

He began like any other dog casting about for pity, working your standard whimpers and whines. After warming up, however, he would become more insistent and in due course desperate. He implored with yelps, yips, sighs, groans, and moans. Eventually he plumbed the depths of despair, descended histrionically into the pit of hell, and lay there on its icy slab, groaning. And growling. Most dogs growl in anger or fear, but Santos growled freeform; it was another rich mode of expression, like a singer using falsetto.

Such a repertoire of sound nobody aboard had ever heard from a dog. Seated at the navigation desk just below the companionway steps, I could barely restrain myself from laughing aloud.

I felt for him, but rules are rules. We had to draw the line somewhere. We were people and he was just a dog, no matter how he tried to blur the distinction.

Dogs like Santos express so many recognizably human emotions that one is impelled to ask, what is the defining difference between dog and man? I gave this question a lot of thought and finally decided that 95% of life we experience in common—we fear, love, mate, eat, play, rejoice, and mourn. Our difference lies in the other 5%, which boils down to something like this: On a fresh summer morning, when wildflowers bloom riotously in the meadows, a dog on a jaunt with his exquisitely sensitive nose alive to all the fragrances of creation would rather roll in rotten fish liver than sniff the most fragrant rose.

Santos's pleadings were finally answered by the sight of Terre Basse Point, the long, low beach that lines the western tip of St. Maarten. It appeared shining in the early sun after a dark train of dawn squalls blew down the Anguilla Channel. In the calm that followed, he smelled land. With mounting excitement he watched it go by, his nose whiffing sporadically as we worked up the coast. By mid-afternoon we anchored off the beach where Philipsburg lies on a narrow strand between the sea and a large salt pond.

Here the Thompson family was comfortably ensconced in the best hotel on the beach, and here ended Santos's ordeal. He had paid his dues and now came into his reward, like a martyred Saracen transported to Paradise. The girls immediately seized him and took turns nuzzling his face, scratching his ears, hugging him like a baby. Santos basked in their arms, occasionally coming out of his reverie to heave a sigh of deep satisfaction. With his pink tongue tip protruding from his muzzle, he was the avatar of teddy bears. Kim and Lindsay, 11 and 9, adored furry animals and brimmed over with unfocused love. Santos happily became the focus, a lightning rod for love; he took the full charge and wanted more.

Then they walked him along Philipsburg's cosmopolitan streets, past Indian shops crammed with duty-free electronics, past Chinese restaurants and Indonesian bungalows, American taverns and glass-fronted Dutch hotels whose opening doors let out welcome swirls of cold air, where Santos would call an abrupt halt and sit down on the cool flagstone in the middle of the sidewalk. From there they proceeded to the ice cream shop, where the children ordered sundaes and Santos, under the table, received mouthfuls straight from the spoon. No doubt he remembered the previous day's misery, now past, and reflected on life's ups and downs.

* * *

The sail from St. Maarten to St. Barthelemy was the usual lumpy slog past dangerous rocks until we gained the flat water of St. Barts' lee and saw the bottom flash up through thirty feet of bright water. One minute we were becalmed, the wind blocked by the steep spine of the island. Then, with *Breath* dead in the water, a gust would suddenly spill over and hit her like a drop-hammer, pushing her over until water gushed in at the scuppers. Then she'd slip out from under the wind's weight and start to move, her wake emerging from its

stupor, chuckling, then bubbling, then seething, past the Rockefell-
ers' beach at Colombier, past green hillsides dotted with prosperous
red roofs, past the fishing village of Corrosol to the mouth of the
harbor.

Gustavia was a picturesque port, its tiny teacup harbor almost
landlocked by hills, the town built all around the harbor. Back in the
old days, St. Barts was the main port of supply for West Indian smugglers. Its small quay always had an island sloop or schooner loading a
cargo of rum, scotch, and brandy to be off-loaded on dark nights in
remote coves from Venezuela to Puerto Rico.

Every morning, just after first light, Diego rowed through the
anchored fleet and made for the bakery accompanied by Santos, who
strained at the leash, pulling uphill, until he choked. Diego and the
dog would share the first warm croissant and then return in triumph
with fresh bread and baguettes for breakfast. We consumed them on
deck while the air was still cool and the baguettes still warm, with
butter and honey, soft cheeses, pate, and good, strong, black coffee.

In just three days there, Santos became a persistent beggar for
Camembert cheese. Admittedly we gave him mixed signals about
begging. The Official Line (Dorothy) frowned on any people-food
treats because it led to begging, but I occasionally subverted it by
giving him a treat. After all, provided they don't make a nuisance of
themselves, dogs have a license to beg, a grandfather clause that harks
back to times immemorial. Dogs do live at people's service, work for
them, and depend on them for food. Since, in the millennia prior to
Purina, dogs have been mostly fed on scraps, often flung backward
from the trencher table to waiting hounds, there is a fine line between
culpable begging and attentive waiting.

Some people take offense at a begging dog, while others find
him amusing. The Thompsons fell decidedly in the latter category,
especially when the dog was someone else's. And, as a beggar, Santos
had irresistible style. He would approach circumspectly and lock his
gaze on the food. He stood there, ready as a nocked arrow, still yet
hopeful, reminding one that—in the event there were to be a share
for him—he was there. And whenever something was given him he
would take it with exquisite delicacy and finesse, his eyes checking
yours time and again to be sure that it was OK, then run off to eat it
on the foredeck so that he wouldn't make a mess.

The girls would hold out a cracker loaded with Camembert or
pate de foie gras and say, "Santos, sit!" His butt would hit the deck

before the word was out of their mouths. "Lie down!," and he'd flop onto his belly instantly, never taking his eyes off the prize. At "roll over" he would wriggle onto his back. Soon, at the command to sit, he would sit, lie down, and roll over all in one fluid movement.

I had my reservations about all this luxury—he was definitely getting spoiled—but figured, what the hell, let him live large while he's got the opportunity.

Then it was off to tour the island by car, Santos standing on a willing lap with his head thrust eagerly out the window, his nose acquiring information about dogs and denizens while we gazed at old stone walls, neat fields, quaint houses, and stunning views. For lunch he had his own hot dog and French fries at a chic beach club, and supper found him behaving exceptionally well under the table of a fine French restaurant on the waterfront as the girls slipped him forkfuls of filet sautéed in an elegant sauce. Diego and I weren't parting with a bite.

* * *

A great breeze swept us 40 miles south southwest to St. Eustatius and St. Christopher. We passed between them, leaving Statia's perfect volcanic cone to starboard and the smooth rise of St. Kitts' canefields to port. The green velvet uplands ascended evenly until Mt. Misery broke through with a rugged violence suiting its name to tower in the perpetual cloud cap. We passed close below Brimstone Hill, bristling with battlements and fortifications, then into the dead lee below the 4,000-foot height of St. Kitts, where only occasional eddies of wind reached around the mountains. The lights on shore winked on by the time we reached the Narrows between St. Kitts and Nevis. An untrammeled breeze laid our rail over and released our wake as the dark silhouette of Nevis blocked out stars ever higher and wider in the southeast.

We landed the next morning near a great weathered log that lay half buried in the long expanse of amber sand. There wasn't a soul around. Nevis hadn't been discovered yet—there were no fancy hotels, no chic vacation villas, just the endless beach backed by miles of coconut grove. Behind and above lay the mountain, the powerful backdrop dominating every vista of Nevis.

Tom got his wish for his women when we left Nevis. Once we rounded the last protective corner of the island, the wind blasted the boat with surprising force. Committed to going, everything well stowed below and the dinghy lashed on deck, we laid the boat on her ear and thundered to windward. The weather, already Force 5, deteriorated to Force 6-7. A layer of fast-moving clouds raced low overhead. We heard later over the Coast Guard weather broadcast that an area of disturbed weather had pushed 35 knots of wind through the Leewards. We staggered on, getting pounded and set way to leeward. Montserrat, our destination, appeared hazy and hopelessly out of reach to windward, so we gritted our teeth and carried on instead to Guadeloupe, finally motorsailing through big cross-seas that came around both sides of the island and met 15 miles off its northwest coast in some of the roughest and most confused water I've seen.

* * *

Tom's women adapted beautifully to good weather and bad. They had good stomachs and good attitudes. Lindsay occasionally lost it, but with matchless aplomb. "I'm fine," she'd say, flashing a wry smile as she ran back below to whatever game they were playing. That impressed me, that and the way Judy pumped out great meals regardless of difficulties in the heeled-over, hot, thrashing boat. She'd emerge sweaty and frazzled but cheerful and eager for Tom's approval. "Have I passed the test yet?" she'd ask. The standing joke: this trip was her trial by ordeal, which, if passed, gave her unlimited shopping rights.

Judy would arrive with suitcases bulging with clothes. While we normally urged guests to pack light, we happily made an exception for Judy because at the end of the trip she gave us most of the clothes so as to justify a shopping binge in Caracas or Constantinople—wherever we were when the cruise ended and they checked into the local Hilton. In Turkey, which has great leather goods, she even gave us their suitcases, claiming they were old and beat—a lie even by Beverly Hills standards. For years after one of their visits I would wear tailored shirts from the best stores in California, Gucci jeans—stuff I would never buy. But they *were* nice clothes.

Late one afternoon we arrived off the bold sea into a wide, calm bay. On three sides of us rose wonderfully green mountains, whole hillsides planted in glossy broad-leafed bananas that shimmered in the wind. Misty rain came through the high pass. Dominica, the island of 365 rivers, lived up to its reputation.

Tom rented a car and Santos got to keep his head out the window as much as he wanted. In fact, he was getting as much as he wanted of just about anything. For one thing, he had never had so many walks in his life. Wherever Kim and Lindsay went, they took the dog. Being picky eaters, they took more delight in feeding him than themselves and gave him the choicest pieces from their plates. They cradled and kissed him like a baby. They brushed him at least three times a day. When they went swimming, they paddled him around on the surfboard. They loved to dress him up with a bright bandana around his neck, a beret on his head, and dark glasses atop his muzzle. They even did his nails, putting shiny red nail polish—with glitter!—on his jet-black claws, and dubbed him "Santi-Wanti," a name that stuck.

That bothered Diego . . . and me too. What's in a name? More than we had realized, apparently. On the surface it was amusing and harmless, but at a deeper level it blunted what we most liked in the dog—his passion, his machismo. We both thought he looked ridiculous and expected him to knock the glasses off and rub the silly glitter against a rock, but he didn't. He wandered around looking like an effeminate beatnik, the shades hanging at a deranged angle.

It reminded me of a merengue singer who put out a brilliantly original first album that was a huge hit throughout the Spanish-speaking Caribbean. The cover pictured an earnest young man dressed in a plain dark jacket and tie, looking self-conscious, expectant, and vital. When his eagerly awaited next album came out it was a dud, totally derivative. On the cover, "the Star" lounged in a satin velvet jumpsuit, mirror shades, gold chain, and flashy rings, a pathetic example of talent kneecapped by fame.

Santos in his flashy getup looked like that singer, and his promiscuous begging, his lolling around all day, being fattened and caressed, stroked and fawned over—well, it made Diego and me distinctly uncomfortable. We felt that our dog was being seduced away from us by ease and affluence. Perhaps Diego was feeling overshadowed by the sophisticated, strong-willed girls, and I was a bit insecure next to Tom with all his money. We felt a bit like hicks, and it seemed like our prized dog, our symbol, was losing his edge—going over to the tapestried tents of the Sybarites and leaving us plain-spun Spartans behind.

We should have known better.

Visible from far at sea, Petit Piton is St. Lucia's most famous landmark, a massive rock spire that dominates the coast. Its peak floats in clouds 2,000 feet above the sea. When we got to St. Lucia we anchored in Jalousie Bay, directly beneath the cliffs of the Piton.

The anchorage was very deep, the bottom an underwater mountainside. We anchored and tied stern-to the shore. Below our keel the bottom tumbled down a steep slope studded with rocks, golden coral heads, and lavender sponges, all clearly visible as through blue glass.

The cove was stunning. The flight of sheer rock stopped the breath. It soared up like the fang of a saber-toothed tiger, crowned with glowing foliage and backlit by clouds of silver fleece. Everything at its base served to set it off—a sea of blue crystal, a beach of fine black sand, groves of palms shining on the slopes. Close to shore a shapely skiff turned in the zephyrs; on its stern was stenciled "One Love." Next to it tiny minnows leaped out of the sea, their wet bodies flashing an arc of quicksilver.

Even before we anchored, something out of the ordinary was compelling Santos to shore. He danced with agitation at the bow, scrabbling halfway out the bowsprit as we motored slowly toward shore with the anchor lowered. When it caught and the stern swung around to face the beach, he raced back and scrambled out onto the rudderhead, where he balanced precariously on three feet and beckoned to shore with the remaining forepaw. He trembled and yelped in the prow of the skiff, and even before the stem grated on the shore, Santos had jumped into the surf, run up the sand, put his nose to the ground, and started following a trail through the lush grass.

Going from tree to tree and sniffing assiduously, keenly intent, of a sudden he heard the cackle of poultry. He broke off his research, dashed down the surf line, then veered up across the sand and into the grass to home in like a low-flying scud missile on a flock of chickens. Hens and chicks exploded away from him like minnows from a marauding mackerel.

For a moment he stood there, Santos the Terrible, panting triumphantly, his pink tongue hanging out in good-natured exuberance.

Resuming his quest, he disappeared into the tall grass, where presently we heard excited barking and indignant squeals. The grass shook as something big passed rapidly through, and then out burst a 250-pound sow, running for her life with Santos exultant at her heels. We marveled at the disparity. Seeing us laughing, she caught herself, drew fiercely to a halt, and, with a flare of fury in her piggish eyes, turned upon the detestable little rodent that had shamed her.

Now pursuer and pursued were reversed, the sow charging with grim intent, fast in the short run, packing impressive mass and momentum—and gaining steadily. She would make mincemeat of him with her sharp hooves.

Santos ran flat out, ears back, glancing over his shoulder to gauge her approach. The girls screamed in alarm, and even I had a sinking feeling, but there was nothing anybody could do. Our hearts in our mouths, we watched as the raging sow bore down on him, saw Santos look back a last time—laughing!—and adroitly dodge aside while the pig went thundering past like a runaway train, helpless to alter her course. It was bull versus toreador—Santos the elegant, deft, agile tormentor.

Relief for the sow came in the most unexpected form. To the amazement of all, out from the undergrowth and into the clearing stepped—an elephant! A real, live, full-grown Indian elephant. Santos stopped dead in his tracks, dumbstruck with awe. The defining moment of his life had just stepped out of the bush! An incredible—a miraculous!—opportunity had just been handed him. He had to act—all his life had been leading up to this. There was only one possible response. ATTACK!

Barking his ear-piercing war cry, he hurled himself flat out, straight at the mastodon. Santos versus the king of the jungle!

The elephant reacted as if Santos were a rabid rat. It reared back, flared its huge ears, and trumpeted a scream of alarm. Santos snapped at an ankle as big as a tree trunk, and then at another. The elephant freaked with revulsion, as if a cockroach had crawled up its trunk. It brought its feet down in a stamp that shook the earth, but the lightning-quick little dog had already dodged out from under, then deftly sidestepped the resounding thwack! of the elephant's trunk raising dust right where he had been.

Dashing just out of range, Santos wheeled and braved his adversary. The dog was more pumped up than we'd ever seen him, barking hysterically and utterly deaf to me. Time after time Santos rushed in underfoot to count coup, weaving, darting, and dodging, erratic as a butterfly, swift as a bee, as the ponderous creature tried to stomp or smack him.

Santos's frenzied barking and the elephant's piercing trumpet calls brought everyone running. Laborers, millionaires, mariners, and hair braiders all stood in an arc around the combatants. The absurdity of this David and Goliath show—the manic daring of the dog and the ludicrous agitation of the elephant—had people helpless with laughter, holding their sides, tears streaming from their eyes.

It was Santos's finest hour. One on one, head to head against the largest animal on earth, and the elephant freaked!

Santos was tireless, but the elephant became increasingly upset. Its keeper, between sobs of merriment, finally decided to stop the show before the elephant ran amok. We managed to collar Santos on one of his dashes, no easy feat—he gave me a wide berth but a stranger from the next yacht nabbed him. I took him back out to *Breath*, keeping an adamant grip on his collar until I dropped him aboard. As soon as I started back he jumped the rail and left a wake, his eyes shifting from me to the shore. I finally had to tie him in the cockpit.

The elephant was a mild and pleasant beast under normal circumstances. Its keeper showed off its tricks. With a little coaxing it would put its foot on top of a coconut and, with an easy shifting of its weight, crack the thing open to get at its milk and meat. I shuddered to think of what could have happened had Santos miscalculated. Although sometimes I wonder . . . because the very next morning the dog and the elephant met up again and acted like old chums, walking at the shore together, Santos only inches away from the mastodon's huge foot.

A multimillionaire English brewery owner had imported it from India to be an elaborate prop for a New Year's party on Mustique. Mustique is the exclusive island in the Grenadines where the international jet set have their magnificent villas. This party had the British Raj as its theme, giving all the guests—rock stars, models, wastrel nobility, assorted super rich, and their sycophants—a chance to wear their biggest diamonds and dress sleazy, as belly dancers, maharajahs, and concubines.

After the party the elephant was put to pasture at the coconut plantation beneath the Petit Piton, which the beer magnate also owned. There it was looked after by the same young man who'd been dressed as its keeper in the party—he had the pictures to prove it. For a number of years it amazed yachtsmen who put into the anchorage and saw, after a couple of martinis, an elephant wandering the shore. Was this Africa or the Antilles?

Later I heard that it had died prematurely, and I wasn't surprised.

Elephants are sociable beasts, and being uprooted from home and kindred and cast into lonely exile in a strange land, a one-time party prop and an ostentatious curiosity thereafter, must have done for it.

Before we left I went up to visit the beast in its stall, to give it some peanuts, but it never noticed me. It was lost in a private misery, pacing one step forward and one step back in an endless, nervous rhythm. It was an eerie and depressing thing to see, and I left the peanuts on the floor.

SEVENTEEN

PUERTO AZUL BEACH BREAK

Our trip with the Thompsons ended in Isla Margarita, a large, mountainous island near the Venezuelan mainland. Diego, Santos, and I were on our own for a few days until Dorothy flew down to join us. When she arrived, we decided to haul the boat at a yard in Cumana, about a day's sail away, before heading back to the Virgins. The cost of a haulout in Venezuela would be half what it would be in the Virgins, and in Venezuela the yard would do the work, whereas up in St. Thomas *we* would have to do it all ourselves. As Judy Thompson would have said, it was a no-brainer.

In Venezuela, anyone who can afford to own a boat need not work on it, especially not hot, grubby work like sanding toxic bottom paint in the broiling sun—the heat on that coast has been infamous for centuries. The boatyard was not set up for live-aboard owners, and so, due to the crudity of the yard's facilities and its lack of clean restrooms or a shower, we stayed in a pleasant hotel that cost us just $10 a night. Our room looked out on the town park with its grand old trees and its gardens and fountains, but the management frowned on animals, so Santos had to stay with the boat—not a bad idea anyway considering the possibility of theft always present on the coast. The boatyard was patrolled by a grim-faced security guard who carried an Uzi strapped to his back, and its walls were topped by broken glass, but one never knows.

We'd return each morning, and before we reached the gate of the boatyard we could hear Santos barking from up in the cockpit at whoever came near the boat. I tried to apologize several times but got blank looks in return, and finally gathered that nobody took the slightest offense at his constant vigilance. Instead they admired his spirit and diligence. Venezuela is another country that appreciates a good watchdog. What surprised them was his size. Guard dogs down

137

there are big, chosen for their deep barks and the threat they pose to any intruder. The workers couldn't get over how small he was yet how tough he acted. They were constantly calling to him, egging him on, laughing over his martial antics.

In particular they delighted in seeing him run off bigger dogs. During the day he lay in the shade of the hull, where he could keep an eye on the entrance. Other dogs were always wandering by, coming in through the open gate to see what was happening. Whenever one got too close, Santos would assault it with the most extreme language and often as not run it off the property with its tail tucked between its legs. These other dogs were five times Santos's size, but they were the kind that slink around expecting the worst; he dominated them with sheer bravado and innate confidence.

The boatyard workers would shout with delight to see the little guy win—maybe there was an element of social criticism there. They ended up giving him a new name—"Perrito Macho"—which translates loosely as "Little Dog With Big Balls." Ever afterward that was our favorite nickname for the pooch. It described him well, almost on a par with the most apt and witty remark ever made about Santos, by Gregg Rochlin, who called him "a hamster masquerading as a wolf."

Our experience at the boatyard in Cumana was so favorable that we began to plan our haulouts for Venezuela. If we didn't have a charter, we ofttimes sailed down anyway during hurricane season to avoid tropical storms, which favor the upper Caribbean, and to cruise. The Venezuelan coast is a marvelous place for a boat. Where else can you dive in crystal-clear water on mile after mile of barrier reef, or gaze at 10,000-foot sierras lofting out of the sea, or watch flocks of parrots flash overhead, or see hundreds of scarlet ibis settle into a small mangrove islet for the night and turn it into a blooming poinsettia?

We must have sailed down to Venezuela a dozen times over the years, and wherever *Breath* went, Santos went. He was too useful to leave behind. Not only was he an impeccable watchdog, but as an entertainer he drew conversation after him like a following sea. The few times the boat left without him, Dorothy said he spent a great part of every day at the governor's place, lying on the cool tile beneath the porch roof and looking out to sea, watching for *Breath*'s return. The boat was his true home, his puppyhood den and nexus, the constant center from which he encountered the shifting world.

After a charter, the guests' goodbyes to the dog were often more prolonged than their farewells to the captain.

* * *

If Santos were telling this story, he'd remember one of *Breath*'s haulouts in Venezuela as constituting one of his most miserable experiences. The oppressive heat of the Caribbean coast suffocated him in his thick black coat, and he was bored. There was nobody to romp with and nobody to slip him morsels from the galley porthole, because Dorothy and the boys were back in St. John, 500 miles to the north. Worst of all, he was imprisoned on the boat day in and day out, with never a chance to visit a tree or shrub or even a patch of fragrant earth.

Breath sat high and dry on a soulless slab of concrete in a boatyard, hemmed about by other boats. The harsh noise of grinders and sanders assailed his ears; clouds of noxious dust and fumes drifted over the deck. Santos and I had just finished a three-week charter along the coast and offshore islands, and I had decided to try Puerto Azul's boatyard. Then Dorothy and the boys would fly down—tickets were cheap in those days—and help me sail the boat home.

It seemed a good idea to me, but it must have seemed a damn poor idea to the dog. Not that Puerto Azul lacked attractions. Venezuela's biggest country club/marina boasted wonderfully green lawns and winding walkways shaded by giant hardwoods. Santos, lying disconsolately under the awning, could see, smell, and hear an open-air restaurant perfect for begging, a big swimming pool filled with shrieking kids, and best of all a long, smooth beach.

But the club was strictly off-limits to dogs.

Every time I climbed on or off the boat to get sandpaper or some tool, the poor dog attended me at the rail with imploring eyes, hopeful, desperate, and so sad . . . and every time I steeled myself to ignore him. I felt guilty, but my hands were tied. I had specifically agreed to keep him on board, and numerous guards patrolled the area. The only way to give him some liberty was to take him by dinghy outside the entire Puerto Azul complex, which included everything protected by the breakwater—the cove itself, the docks, beaches, and condo buildings.

I tried that the first day of the haulout, dutifully hand carrying him to the dinghy in which we set off looking for a safe landing place—not easy to find on that bold coast. Beyond the breakwater the sea broke roughly on the shore, an unbroken mountain wall that towers up to 9,000 feet, its peaks covered in clouds and its slopes mantled in thick jungle. So sheer is the ascent from the sea that in many places the coastal road had to be dynamited out from the base of the cliffs.

Rising and falling in the swell, we looked in vain for a break in the rock-studded shoreline until we came to a small, steep beach. Surf foamed up the sand, but I judged we could make it, and anyway we had come too far to turn back. I waited for a slack interval in the waves, gunned the motor, and rode a swell to the beach. We hit the sand with a jolt. As I hopped out, the ebb tore the dinghy out of my grip, then the next wave flung it back at me sideways. I ducked aside just in time, the dingy half swamped, and Santos found himself tumbling upside down to shore. We got back to the boat soaking wet and I vowed never again! Santos would just have to suffer.

After a few days, however, his luck turned when he managed to attract the notice of Elena, an Israeli girl living with John, an American on a small cruising boat in the harbor. John had noticed the seaworthy lines of *Breath* as they walked through the yard, and had stopped to talk. He was fascinated by Colin Archers and gaff rigs and plied me with questions about the boat and its construction. Elena grew visibly restive—the finer points of fiberglass lay-ups held scant appeal for her. Just then, Santos put his head and paws over the caprail, looked down, and whimpered. Elena looked up and fell in love. Her wild black ringlets bounced as she ascended the ladder and, with earth mother emotion, scooped Santos into her arms, exclaiming passionately in Hebrew how adorable he was. Santos was young in those days, his coat shiny black, his fox face sleek and sensitive. He looked ardently into Elena's eyes and quivered with affection, knowing intuitively that here was his prime chance for a woman's care.

From that day forward, every day when Elena and John came ashore she would come by the boat, perfunctorily greet me, and ascend the ladder to spend up to an hour with Santos, feeding him leftovers, playing games, cuddling him like a baby. Santos lived for her visits, and from the comparative lethargy of his dull times with me, he would incandesce when he heard Elena's voice at the foot of the ladder, wiggling and bouncing with anticipation.

Eventually Santos and I were invited out to their boat for dinner and to meet their animals. Like a number of yachties cruising Venezuela, they had acquired a conure, a kind of half-sized green parrot with a red ring around each eye, a cheerful, lively little thing that did constant acrobatics on the swings in its cage. I had seen a similar bird on the streets of Caracas, telling fortunes. An old man had it in a large cage set up on a cart that he pushed around the parks. Under the cage was a drawer with folded slips of paper, each inscribed with a fortune. For a quarter the bird would open its door, hop down to the drawer, and pick out a slip with its beak and give it to you— an ancient link to the avian augury of Rome.

They also had a very old, fat, bad-tempered Pekinese. This decrepit dog waddled around with its hair in its face, glaring petulantly, in fact looking slightly deranged. I tried to pat it on the head and it snapped at me. After that I gave it a wide berth, and so did Santos at first, but eventually they started playing together.

When I asked if their dog had a litter box on deck, Elena said that she always took the Peke to the beach ashore.

"I thought that was strictly forbidden."

"Oh, the guards are my friends," she smiled. "She's just a little thing. They let me take her to the very end of the beach where there are no condos. Let's go—we'll bring Santos too."

"Are you sure?" I asked dubiously, wondering what outrage Santos might commit if set down on the long beach after days of being cooped up.

"Don't worry—I take Alexandra in every day. They're used to us. One more little dog. . . . they'll look so cute playing together on the beach. I'll bring my camera."

He might be little, I thought, but he was explosive compared to the old, fat Peke. Still, perhaps the guards would intimidate him and he'd be on his best behavior. I brought a leash for him just in case.

We motored in to the far end of the beach, away from the side with the lounge chairs under the palm trees where members—plump matrons in string bikinis with diamond rings sparkling from languid hands—draped themselves in the sun. This beach was part of Puerto Azul, and security was tight. A high concrete wall topped with broken glass sealed off the grounds, and to get to the outside one had to pass through two well-manned checkpoints, showing ID to guards protected by bulletproof glass. The social order in Venezuela is not exactly stable nor based on consensus.

When the two beach guards saw us they came to inspect the dingy. Elena jumped out as it grated on the sand, holding her long skirt halfway up her shapely thighs to avoid wetting its hem. She was charming—tossing her glossy ringlets, fluttering her long curly lashes, presenting her ample breasts against the thin cotton of her T-shirt. No wonder both guards were in the habit of meeting the dinghy with big smiles.

Elena put Alexandra on the ground, but the dog just stood there and begged to be carried again, then hobbled reluctantly about as if its feet were bound and abruptly squatted and peed, sopping her long belly hair. It was a pathetic animal.

Elena then indicated Santos, waiting eagerly in the dingy, and asked for permission for the other "perrito chiquito" (cute doggie) to come ashore. Most Venezuelans love dogs, and the guards were duly fascinated by Santos's unusual appearance, his alert ears, silky muzzle, and soulful eyes. "Precioso!" they said admiringly.

While I got out to pull the dinghy higher on the beach I had told Santos in the sternest of tones to sit and stay, and so he did, albeit in an agony of anticipation, quivering and keening with desire to get his paws into the sand. But when one of the guards, the young skinny one with a shock of black hair beneath his cap, whistled to him, the dam of Santos's self-control broke. He leaped off the bow, hit the beach at full sprint, whipped around the two startled guards, and shot down the strand—straight for the chaise lounges where Venezuela's well-oiled elite basted in the sun.

The swiftness of the dog stunned the guards. They looked bewilderedly at the Peke, still dribbling into the sand, then back at Santos streaking down the beach, barking madly, already halfway to the first beach chair, whose occupant was looking up in alarm.

The guards took off running, looking like the Keystone Cops with their patent leather shoes kicking up puffs of sand as they tried to accelerate on the yielding beach, clutching their hats to their heads and holding their dangling billy clubs away from their thighs.

Mortified, I called my dog, but it was hopeless; with a bit in his teeth he was gone, free, in his element, feet flying over the sand, the sea sparkling at his side, the wind of pure speed in his face. He barked his joyous war cry, alerting the world to a formidable presence hurtling like an asteroid onto the scene.

He bared his teeth and growled as he feinted by the first chaise lounge. The matron jerked up her feet convulsively and toppled off the chair with a cry of alarm. Santos shot past a couple more surprised people, screeched to a halt at a coconut palm nicely painted white around its base, and lifted his leg on it, letting fly a short staccato stream—then scampered off to the next tree to do the same. This was virgin ground, unmarked by any other dog. Santos was the prime canine of Puerto Azul.

He was being patted by a crooning lady and her delighted children when he looked up from his reverie to see the guards charging him red-faced, out of breath, and extremely agitated. Even from a hundred yards away I could see the funlight go on in Santos's eyes as his stance changed to his "catch me if you can" posture—crouched down in front with his forepaws low and his hindquarters high, poised to spring. This was a familiar game, one he loved and excelled in. He awaited the rush and darted in, easily dodging the young skinny guard. He ran straight toward the older, heavier one, stopped almost within reach, feinted left, then right, then left again—and the man went down with crossed legs.

I was apoplectic with calling him before finally he decided to hear me and ran up sheepishly. Elena scooped up her dog and I collared mine and we launched the dingy as if evacuating Dunkirk. The guards were down the beach explaining mightily, and I did not want to be there when they got back. I hope they weren't fired.

For what it's worth, they learned that not all little dogs are created equal.

* * *

Back in the Virgin Islands that winter we worked hard, all of us at our allotted tasks. By now the dog was in his prime, adept at his social responsibilities, a dog for all seasons (of people). He fascinated little children and kept them entertained so their parents could snorkel, and, as we sailed, enjoy the serenity, the interplay of boat between air and ocean. He cuddled in ladies' laps and gave them soulful looks. He played fetch with boys or contested ownership of a towel with a mock ferocity that delighted onlookers. He presented his ears to men for a scratch in silent camaraderie, and always when there was food he worked the crowd and did his tricks.

I often remarked that if we didn't own him we'd have to hire him—it appeared that on an average day, some 30% of the conversation aboard revolved around him.

Raffy, now a senior in high school, had to rise every morning before dawn, get his breakfast, collect his books, jump on his motor cycle, and drive the entire length of the island to Cruz Bay, where he caught the ferry to St. Thomas and then the safari bus to Charlotte Amalie. There he walked the last stretch up a winding street lined with colonial-era villas and past a house of ill repute and a church to get to his school.

We were doing well but certainly didn't have enough money saved to send Raff to college the next year. We pinned our hopes on a scholarship. He was at the top of his class every year, but in a small school in a territorial backwater. It remained to be seen how his academic accomplishments would stack up to stateside competition. A lot was riding on how he did on the SATs, the standardized college entrance exams. The Virgin Islands didn't have any courses coaching students in how to take the test, so we stayed up late and helped him review vocabulary.

He worked a lot harder on his physical training than on his studies. He breezed through his textbooks and absorbed their contents almost nonchalantly, on the ferry or in study hall or after supper. We didn't see him study much, but working out!—that took first priority as soon as he got home. He set up his weights in the abandoned house next door, where he'd strip to his swim suit and pump iron and do sit-ups and push-ups, glistening with sweat, heedless of the mosquitoes that clustered around him. He was absolutely determined to bulk out and buck up. Diego often attended to hand him weights or to sit on his legs when he did sit-ups.

Intellectually, what he loved best were long, passionate discussions late at night about politics, history, or religion. Eventually his mother would row herself out to the boat in the dinghy, leaving me the skiff to follow when we finished.

When the time came for the test, Raff and I sailed *Breath* over to Cruz Bay so that he could catch the first ferry in the morning. We spent a quiet night talking things over and doing a little last-minute vocabulary work, and then retired. I sat in the cockpit thinking. Tomorrow was going to be a big test for Raff, to see how he measured up to stateside standards.

I realized that it was a test for us, his parents, as well. Had we shortchanged our children or enriched their lives by pursuing an unorthodox path, off the cuff, perennially short of money? Instead of building up equity and IRAs, we'd always taken any accrual of cash and gone cruising. On the one hand, their experiences sailing through the Caribbean, learning Spanish, and interacting in multi-racial cultures were invaluable. But on the other hand, had we compromised the boys' chances of fitting in to U.S. society? Should we have long ago returned to the States and plugged ourselves into proper careers and a settled way of life?

Various relatives had offered ideas and help, obviously concerned as the years went by and we got older but no richer. Religiously inclined, they nevertheless seemed to ignore Jesus's advice to give all you have to the poor, take no care for worldly things, and look at the lilies of the field (which neither spin nor toil). Instead their text was from Proverbs, about the foolish grasshopper who lived for today and the industrious ant who stored up supplies for the morrow.

The boat creaked placidly at her anchor, wavelets slapped against her waterline, the breeze wafted tension off my skin. Overhead the stars wheeled slowly, clouds came to cover them, and I fell asleep in the cockpit.

In the afternoon Raff came back from the day's tests and said he'd done alright. I didn't grill him. It would be some months before he got the results.

EIGHTEEN

HELD FOR RANSOM AT PUERTO CABELLO

In the summer of 1988 we sailed back down to Venezuela to escape hurricane season, and after spending glorious days diving the reefs of Las Aves, 90 miles offshore, proceeded to Puerto Cabello, the main town on the coast of the Golfo Triste.

When we dropped anchor the first thing we heard was, "Watch your dinghy like a hawk!" In the last month three dinghies had been stolen and none recovered.

The thieves' modus operandi was bold and simple. One of them swam out at night and cut the painter to the most expensive inflatable with the shiniest new outboard, and swam it silently to the town beach. There he and his gang heaved it onto the bed of a truck and drove off into the impenetrable maze of the old colonial city. The whole operation took three minutes. No matter if the outboard were through-bolted to the transom. The thieves weren't dismantling it on the beach with a flashlight and a hacksaw—they did that at their leisure in the safety of a warehouse.

Every night the yachts took defensive measures. They fastened their dinghies with steel cables and locks or hoisted them out of the water with the main halyard to hang there next to the mother ship all night. Someone even painted a skull that glowed in the dark on his outboard cover with the inscription, "You t'ief you die."

We had the least to fear. Our dingy didn't appear worth stealing. It was battered; the whole thing needed paint except for the small outboard, onto which we'd purposely dripped paint the day we bought it. It was not a "sex boat," but still a very serviceable skiff that we'd hate to lose.

Our ace in the hole was Santos. Here he was in his element, with his particular talents in hot demand. Vigilant to a fault, he exulted in his office. Nothing could come near our boat, not even a fish splash, without him letting the whole harbor know. This could not be lost on the thieves. He always slept on deck, his ears and nose keeping sub-liminal watch. The dog hated to come below, even in rain. With his water-repellent coat glistening, he'd stand at the companionway and refuse all offers to come inside. Down below it was too close, whereas on deck the cool evening air drifting down from the mountains brought heady aromas—other dogs, sun-ripened scraps, street corner grills, and wood smoke laced with the scent of night blossoms.

The focal point of the anchorage was the beach, which filled to capacity on weekends, jammed with people and dogs. Santos stood longingly on the bow, whimpering piteously. Accordingly, when we took a slip at the marina, we tied the boat far enough out from the dock to discourage leaping ashore, even though it made our own transits more difficult.

Saturday morning Raffy and Diego left for Merida to see the magnificent snow-capped Venezuelan Andes and hopefully to meet some college girls. I was up the mast replacing the strop to the peak block, Dorothy was at the market shopping for vegetables, and San-tos was on the bow, staring wistfully across to the town beach, giving subdued little yelps.

Who could blame him? Half the town was on the beach. Families were picnicking, throwing chicken bones over their shoulder where scrawny dogs vied for the remains. Kids raced along the sand and hurled themselves into the water with shrieks and splashes. Young women in string bikinis displayed their charms on beach blankets, while young men flexed and roared as they played pickup soccer along the water's edge. A man with an enormous beer belly sat in the sea with a parrot perched on his shoulder.

It was a scene! Definitely the place to be on this Saturday after-noon. Santos finally could stand it no longer. He waited at the stern until a gust of breeze moved it closer to the dock, gave a mighty, impassioned leap—and made it.

When Dorothy came back to the boat, she busied herself put-ting groceries away and then letting me down the mast. A couple of hours passed while we assumed that the dog was asleep behind the mainmast, burrowed beneath the topsail bag, or sheltered in the cool cave under the overturned dingy on deck. We only realized what had happened when she started cooking and called Santos to the galley porthole to take a bone. No dog. Again.

We inquired among the boats. Our next-door neighbor, avid observer of all happenings on the dock, remembered seeing him poised attentively at our stern for quite awhile. She had noted his concentration and assumed he was giving a rat or a cat the evil eye. Instead he had been gauging the distance, awaiting his chance until the boat moved just close enough. We checked at the gate, and the guard remembered very well a small black animal, a dog or a dwarf peccary, streaking down the dock and out under the gate. He threw up his hands at the thought of catching an animal that small and swift—impo-*sible!*

Dorothy got on her walking shoes and hurried through the park fronting the bay and past the old cannons and anchors, carefully inspecting the beach. The afternoon was late and most of the action gone. A few people remained, mostly inebriated, and a few curs picking through the sand. She asked around in her broken Spanish and was answered in the truncated argot of the fishing coast that even Spaniards find incomprehensible. Hopeless.

Next morning we passed the word along the dock. Our neighbors predicted jovially that he'd be "perro caliente" in some waterfront cafe. They were cat people though, and ignorant of the local culture—to my knowledge Venezuelans didn't eat dogs. In China it would be another matter.

Dorothy wasn't taking any chances though, and when Santos failed to show up by noon she took to the streets calling and whistling for her dog. She walked through the old colonial district, down its cobblestoned streets past iron grillwork windows and doorways that glimpsed into courtyards with fountains and gardens. She asked parrots, hung in cages from trees and archways, shimmering green like treetops in a breeze. She even asked the imperious maitre d's standing outside their restaurants, red napkins draped from their forearms, luring passers-by.

Nobody had seen hide nor hair of a small black dog.

Toward the newer part of town a string of open-air restaurants with names like the Mermaid, the Lighthouse, or the Captain's Table always had tables crowded with beer bottles and seamen from the ships in port, who caroused with women dressed in revealing clothes and then hailed taxis to nearby apartments overlooking the sea. Down this street, just adjacent to the beach, my pretty wife walked slowly, looking around hopefully, whistling. In short order two Filipino sailors called to her. When they realized their mistake the two men gamely joined the search for awhile, looking down alleyways and questioning young boys. But all in vain.

She continued deeper into the city, where the streets got narrow and the buildings grew shabbier, with rubble on the corners and graffitti on the walls. As she whistled and called, people looked at her as if she were addled, until one old lady warned her to go back, that it was "peligroso." So she came back empty-handed. Santos had been swallowed up by the concrete warren.

The only dogs she had seen were mangy, gaunt scavengers who cringed and ran if anyone took notice of them. It seemed a hard place for a dog to be lost, but on the other hand, as I reassured her, an animal like Santos was so different in looks and temperament that he was bound to draw attention.

That night the boys got home and Raffy declared, "We've got to do something!" as vehemently as if his brother had been kidnapped. We finally remembered a radio station near the waterfront.

Next morning I entered the station, a new stucco building of two stories, and found the manager. He was a young man with slicked-back hair and a degree in broadcasting from the local college. He and I arranged the details, but we had to wait for the announcer, the star, the man with The Voice.

While we waited for him to appear I talked to the manager's sister, a heavily made up bleached blonde with glinting eyes and a suety body crammed into skintight pants. She asked flattering questions but didn't listen to the answers, and when she thought I was distracted stared at me speculatively, like a cat eying a caged bird. She presented me the bill with a fake smile and a burst of Spanish that almost deflected my attention from the total, which came to twice what I'd agreed with her brother. When I objected she was by turns insulted, then hurt, then effusive with apologies and bantering laughter—her obsidian eyes darting in a chalky mask, with lipstick as scarlet and glossy as a maraschino cherry. What a piece of work she was.

The announcer strode into the room with grandeur, yet he was pleasant, a well-fleshed man in a shiny suit with a veritable bow wave of pomaded hair above his brow. When he opened his mouth, one heard why he was so deferred to. He had a remarkably rich, commanding baritone.

Back at the dock we tuned the radio to the station and sure enough, our plea for the dog and the promise of a US$15 reward—ransom for a child in gritty Puerto Cabello—came on as agreed. The DJ described Santos and how he lived on a boat and was an important member of the crew. When he spoke of the reward, his voice swelled with excitement at this unparalleled opportunity, a windfall of quick, easy money just for keeping one's eyes peeled right here in Puerto Cabello—and doing a good deed in the bargain by reuniting a family with its loved one. He almost brought tears to my eyes, his emotive pipes rising and falling on a beautiful tide of Spanish.

We were feeling encouraged—people came down the dock to tell us they had heard the ad. The marina personnel kept the office radio blaring and shouted "Perrito!" in our direction whenever the ad came on. Toward mid-afternoon the young station manager came for a visit to inform us that the spot was definitely working. They had received several calls from people who had seen Santos. Apparently a teenager had taken him home from the beach. No doubt at all that he would hear of his good fortune before the day was out.

Fifteen dollars was considerable money in Venezuela where, though the rich are loaded, many people work for days to amass such a sum. It would buy a hundred gallons of gas (yup, 100), or five meals at a restaurant, or fifty glasses of beer at the local dive, or feed a family for a week.

Sure thing, the next morning a call came through to the marina saying that the dog had been found. Bring the reward! I was out, so Dorothy jumped up in delight and took the money to the station, where the sister received it, saying she would drive to where the dog was being held and give the boy his reward. Dorothy wanted to ride with her, to give the reward personally and find out what had happened, but the sister fobbed her off with an incomprehensible excuse and went off to fetch the dog.

So Dorothy waited in the office with the manager, who served her sweetened coffee. After a few minutes she thought she heard Santos's bark, muffled, seemingly close by, but the manager assured her that his sister couldn't be back yet.

After a long wait the sister dramatically flung open the door and appeared—empty-handed. Where was the dog? inquired Dorothy, alarmed. Don't worry, he's safe, assured the sister. But there was a small problem. She needed more money. Another $15. The boy had taken the dog to a rival radio station and its dishonest manager had kept the dog and insisted on two rewards—$15 for the boy and $15 for the radio station. So what could she do? She had paid *out of her own purse* the extra $15, and now she insisted that Dorothy pay her back before she handed over the dog.

Dorothy didn't know what to say. She didn't have any more

money. Besides, now she suspected she *had* heard the dog in the next room, and this song and dance was an attempt to extort a bit more fat out of the rich and demonstrably stupid gringos, who were wasting good money on a runaway dog.

Playing to their prejudice, Dorothy agreed that, of course, if dishonest people had perpetrated this fraud the sister should not be penalized and as soon as I arrived back aboard I would march right down with pockets full of superfluous money, pay whatever she asked, and probably tip her handsomely to boot. But could she just see the dog?

The sister, at her brother's urging, reluctantly acquiesced, went outside and came back with Santos tied to a string. Dorothy rushed to enfold him and Santos pranced on his bandy legs to touch his nose repeatedly to her face in deft, delicate kisses, with his ears laid back along his head in pure pleasure. There was no decent way to part them. Dorothy exited with the dog, promising to send me right away.

When I heard the story I knew it was an extortion attempt, albeit a weak one since they had given us back the dog. I stalked into the office somberly. The smiles faltered . . . clearly I hadn't come there to gratefully disgorge funds. Stonily I asked, what was the problem? We paid for the ad, we paid the reward, we got the dog back. Where was the hitch in this straightforward sequence? The brother visibly cringed—he was not the brazen one. But game to the bitter end, his sister started an animated recital of how she had paid $15 extra to the radio station on the other side of town.

I cut her short. My wife had distinctly heard the dog bark. I did not believe the story about the crooked radio station and wanted to confront the alleged scoundrel myself before I handed over so much as a bolivar extra. She folded. She had probably already cheated the kid who found the dog out of his reward and was now just going for the gravy.

* * *

A few days later, Dorothy rose early in the morning to cook a breakfast of French toast and sausage, then with tears in her eyes and a proud smile on her face, hugged her elder son goodbye. Raff and I took a cab to the transport center, then joined a group taxi to Caracas, checked into a hotel, took hot-water showers for the first time in months, and went out to dinner at a rather nice restaurant. In the morning we got to the international airport on the coast at Maiquetia, where I saw him off on a plane to the States and then returned to

Puerto Cabello. The big moment had arrived—he was off to college. Raff had left the nest.

A lot had happened since the Saturday morning when Raff had taken the ferry to St. Thomas to take the SAT exams. A couple of months after, in the spring, I had taken a charter across the Anegada Passage to the northern Leeward Islands. We had a great trip, visiting five islands in four days, then sailed home before a brisk northeaster, making great time.

We had scarcely picked up the mooring at Round Bay when Dorothy appeared at the beach in her swimming suit, waving. She plunged in and swam nonstop out to the boat. When she got to *Breath*'s side she clung to a rope, her face aglow from more than just the swim.

"Guess what?" she said, even before greeting me or my guests.

"What?"

"Raffy got his SAT results back today."

"And . . . ?" I said, instinctively bracing myself.

"And he got 1570 out of a possible 1600! Isn't that wonderful?"

I breathed a sigh that had been bated for years. Our worries were over. With SATs like that he was in, wherever. Then he won a National Merit Scholarship and the Presidential Scholar award. For the latter I accompanied him to Washington, D.C. to see him awarded a gold medal. Later that year he was accepted at every college he applied to. Princeton and Stanford offered him prestigious scholarships. Dartmouth, where I had gone, flew him up for a long weekend and then offered him their Presidential Scholarship.

And who was proudest at this stellar showing? Certainly not Raff, who exhibited an easygoing skepticism about all the hoopla. Dorothy and I couldn't have been any more delighted, and the grandparents told anyone who would listen. But none of the family had half the gift for crowing that the principal of his school possessed. She was in perpetual and mortal competition with another, much better funded private school in St. Thomas, and Raff's prestigious award was the equivalent of a tactical nuke in her arsenal, which she brandished at every opportunity . She exhibited Raffy like a prize bull.

We sailed out of Puerto Cabello, headed back for the pristine offshore reef archipelagoes, missing our oldest son but very glad to have our dog back. We never suspected that the most dramatic adventure of his life so far was just around the corner.

NINETEEN

LOST AT SEA OFF THE SPANISH MAIN

"Hey, where's Santos?" asked Diego, holding the last bag of Doritos that he had just been given permission to open. The dog's nose picked up one part per billion of Dorito olfactory essence in the air, and his ears were exquisitely attuned to the sound of a bag being opened. Normally there was no escaping his immediate attendance upon even the slightest crackling of plastic.

Where *was* Santos, anyway? With a familiar trepidation starting in the pits of our stomachs, we began to look around and call him.

We'd been out at the Islas des Aves, seagirt mangrove cays surrounded by extensive reefs that lie 80 miles off the Venezuelan coast. There we had spent a week anchored behind a ten-mile-long reef that broke the sea and offered a calm lee. Every day we went free diving, looking for wrecks and artifacts on the great reef.

In the late afternoons we'd take Santos to one of the low sandy cays, where he raced down the beach and charged through the shrubbery to flush out birds, which wheeled overhead, screaming in protest. Then he'd slip into the smooth sea for a soothing paddle, often attended by several outraged gulls dive-bombing his head. We feared they would peck at his eyes, but although they threatened to, they never did.

Everything considered, Santos distinctly preferred the mainland to the reefs and shoals of the offshore islands. When we got up our anchors and picked our way clear of the reefs, he saw the last of the mangroves sink below the horizon without regret and started anticipating the beach bars and dogs of the coastal towns.

All night, all day, and all the following night we sailed, with no sight of land or any other boat, but by sunrise we saw the coastal sierras looming up five miles ahead, a wall of mountains reaching 9,000 feet swathed in unbroken jungle. The early sun cast horizontal rays that glowed on the dense green ridges and left the folds and valleys dark with shadows. It lit up the peaks trimmed with ermine of fleecy cumulus.

We gazed in awe at the sight, and noticed that Santos was equally smitten. He was as far out on the bow as he could get, two feet on the knighthead and the other two on the bowsprit, none too stable, straddling thin air with the sea directly below. He stretched his nose toward land and moaned.

"Santos, get back here!" Dorothy called. The little dog barely acknowledged her, and didn't budge. When she went forward to collar him she found him in a feverish state, shaking in his limbs and giving little involuntary yelps, overwhelmed with desire to be ashore. She took him back to the cockpit, but when she went down to make a cup of tea he ran back to the same spot. I too had to physically remove him —he was back in his trance. If he could have spoken, he would have croaked out "Tierra! Tierra!" like some desperate castaway 20 days adrift.

He waited until I tied the wheel and went down to check our position on the chart, and then must have run back to that reckless, untenable perch and fallen in. Or jumped. If he fell in, it was the only time in his life that he did. He who barked furiously at the merest hint of danger to others made not a sound as the hull swept by and left him swimming steadily in its wake. We were about five miles offshore in four- to six-foot seas and about 500 fathoms of water.

We figured this out later. At the time I noticed nothing. The dog was not on the bowsprit, good. I assumed he was sleeping under the upside-down dinghy to get away from the ascending sun. We didn't miss him until we arrived in Puerto Azul and dropped the anchor. I took the topsail halyard to the bow of the dinghy and heaved it up over the lifelines, with Dorothy and Diego guiding it into the water without banging our topsides, and that done, the deck was clear,

That's when Diego noticed the dog's absence. It was unlike him to be absent when the dinghy was being readied for a trip ashore—in fact, unheard of. His station then was underfoot, giving undivided attentiveness to every detail pertaining, even peripherally, to the process of going ashore.

Dorothy and I exchanged glances—we both had a sinking feeling within. We looked and called to no avail. Still no dog. Unequivocally gone.

"What'll we do? Poor Santos! He'll drown. . . . Sharks will get him!" Diego quavered.

"Wait a second," I said with an optimism I didn't feel. "We don't know where he went over. Maybe he jumped when we got close to the breakwater. He might be on the beach right now."

"Better go notify the port captain, then—they have signs forbidding pets anywhere ashore," Dorothy suggested, and that's what we did, leaving our son aboard, anxious but hopeful.

"Do you really think he went over so near?" she asked.

"Hell no . . . but I didn't want to see him cry. Santos is his best friend."

"You're putting off the moment of truth. It might be worse later."

"Yeah . . . but it isn't later yet."

The port captain's office was in a raised lighthouse built over the bar, a nautical affectation appropriate to this lavish country club/ marina for the rich of Caracas. He was busy talking to employees and giving orders over the phone, but he hand-signaled us to sit down and finally attended to us.

"So sorry—today is very busy—we have a fishing tournament, our biggest, for marlin." He pointed out the window to the banners proclaiming the Johnny Walker Scotch fishing tournament and to the large blackboard with the names of all the boats participating, with space to record their catches called in by radio so that people ashore could follow the progress of their favorites. He listened sympathetically to our request that if an exhausted little black dog should show up wet and bedraggled on the premises, we be notified—that his employees not take it to the pound, if there was a pound.

"Of course! We will keep a sharp lookout for your dog—I will instruct my workers. Listen," and he picked up the PA mike from his desk and broadcast the announcement that any employee seeing a small black dog answering to Santos should bring it immediately to the office. He offered us the use of the marina's facilities, then received a call on the VHF, and so we went down to the lighthouse bar overlooking the sea and thought about what to tell our son.

"Want a beer?" I asked my wife.

"It's not even noon yet."

"Would you rather go back to the boat?"

"No . . . not yet."

"Let's have a beer and see if the little guy shows up on the breakwater."

"Yeah, I guess so."

Neither of us had much desire to rush back to the boat empty-handed and confront Diego's anxious face. This would be a sad blow. He'd already been missing his big brother, and Santos had taken up a lot of the emotional slack, being always ready for a tussle or a snuggle. To the boys he was more than just a pet. They loved him, but even more they were proud of him, especially his daring spirit—he projected a quality any boy could well aspire to. Especially to Diego, who was young and small for his age, Santos embodied the primacy of attitude over size. It would be a shame if this positive example turned into a depressing memory—more than a shame, it would be tragic. To have him lost, drowned . . . it would break our unit and call into question our whole way of life.

* * *

We took a turn around the grounds, hoping to see him on the beach, checking the kids' pool where the splashing and screaming would have attracted him. Then we walked out along the breakwater to its end, looking out to sea for a black head and surveying the dock and slips built along its inside. Nothing.

Finally it sank in—we could put it off no longer. I hadn't come up with any answers for my son, and now my wife was close to tears.

" Oh well," I consoled Dorothy, "with his temperament we were lucky to have him as long as we did." She nodded.

"And now we won't have to always be cleaning up after him." Schipperkes shed a lot, and ours was sloppy. We would find bits of food and the occasional "mistakes" on the deck.

Still silent.

"And no more hair-trigger barking," I continued. His bark had made us enemies more than once, usually alcoholics in nearby slips whose late-morning hangovers his shrill bark had penetrated like a hot poker.

Dorothy's eyes brimmed. "I just keep remembering the good things—how he took food from my fingers so gently, and always thanked me. He was such a dear little dog. To think of him out there all alone . . . the boat sailing off . . . just like in my dream!" Tears started flowing down her cheeks.

What else could I say? Our little captain was gone. Wretched at heart, I paid for the drinks and we walked back to the dingy. I was casting off when we heard a shout. The port captain came hurrying down the steps from his office with a big grin on his face.

"You won't believe it. I was just calling the boats on VHF radio to tally their midday standings for the scoreboard. . . ." He paused, out of breath.

"And . . . ?" we gasped.

"And the last boat said they caught nothing . . . except a little black dog! There couldn't be two of them swimming around out there!"

We were at the dock at 5 P.M. when the *Nena II* pulled in. In true Latin style, the whole family was on board, infant to grandmother, including the maid. The boat captain's mother was the one who had spotted Santos, rising and falling on the swell as the boat sped to the favored fishing grounds. She insisted that her son turn the boat around and take a closer look, marlin or no marlin. They scooped him out with a handnet and by the end of the day were sorry to part with him. They did have salvage rights, after all.

Back on *Breath* he received lots of attention and got his very own helping of the family supper, but his eyes were glazed, as if they'd seen the whole of his life pass before them in the hour of swimming with his death. Right after supper he crashed. When I drifted off later, I thought about what a charmed life he led, and that maybe this experience would make a more sensible animal of him.

That fantasy died at dawn, when a flurry of barking awoke us. A fisherman had dared to pass within 150 feet of our boat. A few hours later, seeing some kids playing with a German shepherd on the beach, Santos jumped into the dingy, then into the sea, and headed for the action. The first we heard of it was a knock on the hull.

"Hello, is this your dog? We found him swimming past our boat."

"Yup," said I, "that's our dog."

TWENTY

TRANSATLANTIC CROSSING

In May of '89 we set out across the North Atlantic ocean. We couldn't really afford to, but that is always a paltry excuse not to pursue a dream. If people waited until they were "ready" to have a baby, the world's population would have guttered out long ago. If we waited until we were in every way ready, we'd never leave. We relied on the theory—the faith, the hope—that things would work out along the way. A job would come up, some opportunity would present itself, help would appear. Nothing "happens" for those who travel within the silk cocoon of money—why should anyone help those who have no need of it? Traveling on the edge, one experiences a culture and its people in a different way than when one buys and pays his way from place to place. Instead of being treated as a tourist, a source of income, one is seen to be a co-struggler, one who can use a favor or inside advice or a local's discount—one to whom a kindness done will reflect a plus in one's eternal ledger book.

Having said that, virtually everybody would prefer to travel with plenty of money, given the choice. Not having that choice we went anyway and put our faith in providence. If we ran short we could teach English wherever we holed up for the winter, and the next summer pick up some charters in the Med.

Raff was absorbed in his freshman year at Dartmouth, so there were only five of us on the crew roster when *Breath* got ready to jump off from a marina on the French side of St. Martin—Dorothy, Diego, my dad, me, and Santos. And Santos had gone AWOL.

We had finished topping up water and fuel and had bought a selection of emergency equipment—sail needles and spare sailcloth, a powerful flashlight, more batteries, rolls of duct tape, epoxy. We had packed the ice chest with block ice, taken on extra water in jugs that we lashed to the cabin side, and finally pulled the dinghy out of the water and lashed it down securely.

"I think we're ready," said Diego.

"As we'll ever be," I agreed.

"OK, Dorothy, start the engine. Dad, you stand by to receive the docklines, starting in the bow. Diego, you start letting 'em go from the shore . . . bow first, then the spring lines. We're outta here!"

"Does anybody know where the dog is?" came Dorothy's voice from below, and everything ground to a halt while Diego went on a search of the marina premises. He found him, predictably, at the snack bar, under a table where a family with two young children were eating hamburgers. When he heard Diego's voice Santos tried to look inconspicuous, but Diego knew exactly where to look, and with apologies to the tourists he snagged the dog from underneath their table.

"I'm sorry. I hope he wasn't begging or bothering you."

"As a matter of fact he *was* begging, and very successfully too. My kids have fed him most of their hamburgers, I think. Great little dog. . . . Is it yours?"

"He belongs to our boat, and we're about to leave . . . but he doesn't want to go. He hates long trips away from land."

"Oh really. Where to? Anguilla?" He gestured at the long, low gray line across the channel.

"Spain." Diego said, and left with the dog tucked firmly under his arm. The tourists called after him, "Spain? Which . . . you mean in Europe?!"

* * *

One thinks of crossing an ocean as getting away from all the hassles of civilization. Alone on the big blue, emptied by the vastness of the sea, a high-seas passage is like a month-long meditation that stills the brain from the petty chattering of shore and its discontents.

That's true most of the time, but in this day and age, trouble from shore can find you just about anywhere.

Breath motored out of St. Martin in a calm, picked up the reinforced trades just north of Anguilla, and drove hard to the north northeast for days, marching up the degrees of latitude until, at 27° north, the wind began to flag ever so slowly, eventually leaving her becalmed in a gentle swell. From there past Bermuda, the breeze was light and fitful. We flew all our light-air sails for days on end— the oversize jib, the reaching staysail, the main topsail, and the flying jib.

As we entered our eighth night out, we were 300 miles east of Bermuda, ghosting along before a languid westerly breeze that had wafted up after sunset. The night was dark and clear, and we hadn't seen a ship in days.

After dropping the flying jib and topsail for the night, I turned the watch over to Diego and went below to join Dorothy and Dad for supper. My wife had cooked beans and rice with scraps of sausage and lots of onion and garlic—good sea fare—and I was halfway through a bowl when Diego called down with a tinge of worry in his tone. "Pops! You better come up here. I think I see port and starboard lights coming pretty fast."

Diego had just turned 12 but had stood watches alone since he was six, and he was dead serious about his duty. If he had a concern, I took it seriously, even if it meant leaving a good supper and a glass of wine.

Only when a vessel is headed straight for you can you see both sidelights—red *and* green—at once. This is a crystal-clear, unambiguous danger signal—collision is a distinct possibility. And of all the potential hazards on the high seas, being run down by a big ship is the likeliest cause of untoward death. I put my bowl down and mounted the companionway ladder.

Diego sat with the binoculars glued to his eyes, with Santos bristling and sniffing the air beside him, alerted to trouble and poised to sound the alarm—if he could figure out what it was. I took the binoculars. The sharp vision of the "night glasses" showed both red and green lights to the east, apparently moving rapidly toward us. I had never seen sidelights grow brighter so fast. Could it be one of those new high-speed freighters capable of making 40 knots—a ship that could go from hull down and invisible to impact, cutting you in half, in just over ten minutes? People had talked about it as a new hazard for boats not keeping the sharpest of watches. Whatever it was, it was coming fast. I went below, turned on the engine, cranked the proper pitch into the prop and then looked again at the oncoming lights.

My heart jumped into my throat! The lights were much brighter, racing at us, in fact almost upon us! As I looked I could see them start to rise in elevation, a sign that the bow was close enough to start making us look *up* at the lights.

I shouted to Diego, "Full throttle! Hard to starboard! Turn, turn!" then bellowed down the hatch, "Get up on deck! We're about to be rammed! Get lifejackets!"

Diego, pale and tense, spun the wheel and rammed the throttle full blast. *Breath* started to respond to the power of the 120-horsepower Ford diesel even as those 120 horses stampeded; she turned and gathered way—her stern sucked down, a stern wave starting to build—but it wasn't fast enough. The lights were rising, looming, almost overhead. Dorothy bolted up the companionway with Dad right behind her, pulling on a lifejacket. I strained my eyes into the dark for the giant steel cutwater, the high, curling bow waves, and braced for impact . . . and the lights made an impossibly swift, sharp turn and veered off to the south. Simultaneously we caught the loud wash of sound—the roar of aircraft engines flying 50 feet off the water, rapidly receding.

"Oh my God!" Diego gasped in relief, while I gaped at the single green light fading. The joints in my knees quivered with a surfeit of adrenaline.

"What the hell are they playing at, those bastards!" I said, forgetting the old missionary's reverend ears. He didn't blink an eye. In fact he weighed in.

"A damnable outrage! Abominable!"

"What's going on?" asked Dorothy.

Good question. Who would play such an irresponsible trick on us, and why? I got a shiver of doubt as I realized how vulnerable we were, all alone out there. I called the plane on VHF but got no response.

Eventually we settled down and returned below, but an hour later, with Dorothy newly on watch, she called, "Peter, there's a big ship close off our stern—and it doesn't have any lights."

What, no lights? I came rapidly on deck and sure enough, off our stern—close!—hung a blacked-out ship with military lines, an inkblot silhouetted by the western stars. Why on earth should it be blacked out? We watched it awhile as it got within a couple hundred yards of our stern.

While I was on deck, Dorothy switched on the VHF and scanned the frequencies.

"Peter, I hear a transmission, American voices. They sound military. Why don't you try to talk to them?"

I removed the transmitter from its hook. "Vessel blacked out off our stern, this is the sailing vessel *Breath*. Do you read me? Over." Nothing. I tried again. "Hey guys, it's a bit unsettling for a 40-footer to be played footsie with by a 400-footer. What's up? You want us to move, we're on your piece of ocean, just say so." But no answer came back. We'd spoken with a freighter bound for Trinidad two days previously and had carried a range of ten miles easily. Nothing was wrong with the radio.

I got fed up.

"Yo! Butthead! Yeah, you—yukking it up around the radio! It shows a gross lack of seamanship to harass a small boat with a big ship out here in the middle of the ocean. Do something useful to justify burning up the taxpayers' money. Rescue somebody, attack Russia . . . . But get off my ass!" Dead silence.

I assumed it was military, but why would the U.S. Navy be harassing us? Or any navy? A scary possibility occurred—was it smugglers who were supposed to offload cocaine or heroin here? Plutonium? Genetically engineered anthrax? Would they run us down when they discovered they had the wrong boat? The radio news had recently reported the wholesale murder of everyone in a Miami apartment, infant to grandmother, who had been innocent witnesses to some drug deal.

The middle of the ocean suddenly felt pretty vulnerable—but after an hour of being tailed without incident, we got used to it. As the night progressed, the ship came and went.

Dad came on watch at midnight and slipped *Hamlet* into the Walkman. He listened on headphones while steering for a star, and was hearing the ghost of Hamlet's father beckon the prince to the fearful precipice when, in an instant, brilliant light flooded our boat and the surrounding sea. Asleep below, with the engine on, none of us had heard the approach of a helicopter. Now it was directly overhead, its clatter and the downdraft unmistakable as we rushed up on deck. Looking up, we were blinded by floodlights.

Then, as suddenly as they appeared, the lights cut out, the noise clattered away, and we were left in peace, finally for good. We were too amazed to complain. When we got to the Azores I met a delivery captain with many years of experience in all oceans who'd had a similar experience. He'd been harassed by aircraft and naval ships in the western approaches to the Straits of Gibraltar. After a day they went away, and a sub surfaced nearby, waved, threw something into the sea, then resubmerged. It was a wine bottle with "Thanks!" written on it in magic marker. Apparently he had been an unwitting participant in a war game, the sub hiding under the yacht so that attacking planes and ships could not claim a kill.

"Well Dad, for a minute there, did you think you were going

to ascend to heaven in a staircase of celestial light, like the prophet Isaiah?"

"That was Elijah," he chuckled, and clicked back on his tape.

* * *

My father was 77 years old but fit as a fiddle. The day he'd arrived I was flat on my back, having thrown it out the day before pulling a dinghy out of the surf. We needed gas for the outboard, so he took the six-gallon tank to the gas station, and when he couldn't find a cab he lugged it back, full, a quarter-mile to the dinghy.

He was an enthusiastic sailor. When I was a boy, he had taught me how to sail in Manila Bay on a 25-foot Folkboat, and years later, when he retired, he bought a 32-foot Golden Hind and sailed it with my mother from England to Greece, then across the Atlantic to the West Indies and eventually back to their retirement home in Florida. My mother proclaimed it "the best three years of my life, and I never want to sail anywhere again!" But Dad leaped at the chance to join us for another ocean passage. When my mom questioned whether it was taking too great a risk with his heart condition, he replied, "If I'm going to die, there couldn't be a better time or place than out on God's ocean."

He'd been tireless on this trip, regularly overstaying his watch to give extra rest to one of us who seemed to need it. He did lots of dishes, standing braced at the sink—doing my share for me because I had to navigate (I was still using a sextant), pitching in for Dorothy because she did most of the cooking, and helping out Diego because the boy hated doing dishes.

I had to beg him to stay off the bowsprit when I went to change the jib in squally weather. He protested but agreed to stay on the foredeck. With his full suit of foul-weather gear on, hooked to the lifelines by his safety harness, he sat on the wet heaving deck, pulling at the jib as I unhanked it, stuffing the sail into the sail bag as the wind hurled spray and rain. He loved rough weather and big seas. It was like a show he was privileged to see—with front row tickets.

We had rough and calm and everything in between. The first few days going to windward in the reinforced trades put Dorothy and Diego under the weather. Dorothy was used to it, expected it, dealt with it. I chalked up mentally the increasing debt I owed her for every day of seasickness. Someday I would have to make a big payment. That debt grew noticeably when the full tank of diesel we'd taken on in St. Martin sprang a leak—thankfully in the vent hose leading out of the top. Once we discovered the pinhole, the leak was easy to fix, but all members of the crew were nauseated for a day before the air down below was fit to breathe again.

Every day in the afternoon, Diego, under Dorothy's tutelage, baked bread. He took it out of the oven, steaming hot and golden brown, and we each had a slice or two with butter and honey. By this time the ice was gone, and most of our packaged snacks as well as our fresh vegetables were gone too. Fresh bread was like ice cream out there.

Santos would hang out near the galley ports while the bread was baking, frequently poking his head through the porthole over the stove, and even snooze that way with his head inside the cabin, nose twitching beatifically. The highlight of his day came with his scrap of fresh bread, though we thought the hour of anticipation he enjoyed with that powerful nose probably brought him more satisfaction.

The only living creature he could relate to was a shearwater that adopted us for several days. The seabird kept company with the boat, flying in huge arcs and figure-eights around *Breath*, then landing in the water just ahead of the boat's course so that we could see with what beautiful precision it came to rest, braking with its wings while its feet paddled the surface, easing itself down without a splash. As we ghosted by under full sail, it bobbed in the gentle wash of the hull, regarding all of us but especially Santos quite confidently, heedless of the dog's low growl.

* * *

Santos's senses stood us in good stead as we approached the Azores. The weather had been idyllic for a week, with clear skies, smooth seas, and a steady 15-knot wind from the southwest to which we raised every bit of sail the boat could carry. Under this cloud of canvas we slipped along at a good clip with a gentle motion, delighting in the sound of our wash, which was soothing and fresh and tingly clean, not a roaring, overburdened cataract the way it sometimes got in heavy weather. "This is as good as it gets," Dad proclaimed. "There is absolutely no place I'd rather be."

Once that was said, of course, the weather started to change. The wind died down until we were making only two knots. High cloud materialized to dilute the sun into a smoky flare, and then low clouds rolled in from the south—big, dense, moist charcoal clouds. They were unusually low, actually resting on the sea's surface, and very slow moving. We were enveloped by them for an hour at a time, in calm and drizzly mist.

In the morning of the next day, with the weather the same, Santos suddenly got up from gnawing at his old coconut husk, went to the stern, and peered behind us into the mist. He stayed there, stiff legged, and started to whuff the air with his nose. In a while he started his suspicious low growling, a low "Rrrrr rrrr rrruff rruff."

"What's up boy?" said Diego, putting his hand on the dog's back. "People are sleeping, hush." But Santos kept it up, giving Diego a guilty but defiant look until the boy turned to check behind the boat. Nothing . . . *Breath* was in the clear, though there were several large clouds lying on the water—from which a ship emerged as he watched.

That was a shock—one didn't think to blow the foghorn and ring the bell way out on the vastness of the North Atlantic ocean, but the incident was a reminder that as we approached the Azores we were entering a shipping lane—much transatlantic traffic converges on those islands.

Late in the afternoon we were enveloped in a long gray cloud when Santos started the same routine. Dorothy, on watch, called Diego and handed him the queen helmet shell. He could sound it better than any of us. He gave three long blasts, Santos broke into loud barking, and from close at hand in the murk came the deep answering blast of a ship's whistle.

That got us all up on deck, agitated.

"Blow the horn again, Diego, so he can know where we are," I said, and he did. Another answering blast came back more to the side of us than before. We could hear the rumble of massive engines now.

"He must have radar," said Dorothy, and she switched on the VHF to Channel 16 to hear a voice in heavily accented English saying, " . . .repeat, passing 300 yards to your port side. . . . Have you very clear on radar. . . . Good voyage to you."

"Thank you, thanks much, good voyage to you also," I replied.

Santos stood there at attention, still growling toward the sound of the engines as it passed.

"We should have called you Radar," said Diego. as he ruffled up the dog's mane with both hands.

"What a worthy little beast you are, Santos. You're getting a treat for being such a good . . . lookout? Sniffout?" Dorothy kissed his muzzle, then ducked down and came up with a smidgeon of sausage, which she gave him.

"Sausage? I thought we were out. You said . . ." Diego expostulated.

"Did I say that? Well if I did it was to keep certain unscrupulous persons from consuming it on night watch with their sherry." She gave me an arch look. "It will be the end of it tonight when I put the rest of it into our supper."

"Oh boy, meat! I'm sick and tired of tuna fish!" the boy sang out, and his grandfather laughed.

A couple of hours after midnight Santos gave the warning again. Visibility was terrible, the night black. Dorothy called below for help, and Dad went up and took over the helm. Santos kept growling . . . and scratching. Scratching? She soon found he was trying to recover one of his rawhide toys that had gotten stuck where he couldn't reach it.

* * *

All in all, long passages were not Santos's first choice for a good time. He liked the constant contact with his people but apart from that pined for shore. He missed the excitement of riding in the truck and having the fulsome earth under his feet. The salty sea was a boring place for any animal who lived in the world of scent—here was only astringent brine and empty air devoid of sign.

Diego felt somewhat the same. He was the only young person on board and still too small to be a lot of use when it came to hard physical jobs, though he tried hard. That dispirited him. He and Santos commiserated on the long night watches, the dog lying in Diego's lap and placing his muzzle in the boy's palm with a short sigh of comfort. Or he would wedge his head between Diego's arm and torso and fall asleep. When it was raining he wormed his way underneath the skirt of Diego's jacket and lay quite dry, pressed up against his thigh. He was good company then, as good as any person.

With great hope and joy he confirmed my sextant sights when he finally scented land late in the afternoon of our twenty-second day at sea. Even though we were taking spray in a rising easterly gale, he stood mesmerized with eagerness, nose into the wind, sniffing and whimpering, willing it closer. By late afternoon we could all see it, the southwest promontory of Faial, the tumble of a long high ridge whose lee we gained just after dark.

By the time we got close enough under the ridge to get a respite from the open sea, we were glad of it. An easterly gale was blowing full force, the seas were building to match, and we were down to reefed mizzen, deeply reefed main, and staysail. Getting to the east side of the island, where the port of Horta lay, was impossible. Fortunately the west side, where we were, took the form of a deep V-shaped bay, wide open to the prevailing westerlies but perfect for sheltering from an easterly blow. We worked our way to the head of it in the dark, knowing that the coastal cliffs drop into the sea and keep on plunging.

That virtue became a problem when we tried to find a bottom we could anchor on. The chart showed a shelf at the very head of the inner bay, but in the dark it looked dangerously narrow. If the wind should shift we'd be put ashore on that rockbound coast. We edged in as close as we dared, sounding with the lead, and finally found bottom in 50 feet of water. We dropped the hook, paid out the chain, and stared at the lights of the village high up the ridge. The wind rushed down the slopes in gusts of cold rain and heeled the boat over but showed no sign of shifting around and putting us on the rocks. So, with trepidation, we retired after drinking hot cocoa fortified with a tot of rum.

By midnight the gusts were so bad they were almost laying the gunwales into the water, first one side and then the other. Just after 1 A.M. I awoke to the feeling that something had changed—the wind no longer came in the hatch the same way, and a chop rocked the boat where earlier there had been none. A quick glance out the hatch told all. We had dragged anchor off the shelf and drifted a hundred yards out. One hundred fifty feet of half-inch chain with anchor had to be cranked up in the pelting rain, and then we tried again—this time setting two anchors, one well onto the shelf and another at its outer edge to keep us off the rocks should the wind suddenly shift. And we set an anchor watch. This time she held, and we slept, even as the gale tore veils of spume off the bay and roared overhead like a runaway freight.

In the morning, we woke to find Santos standing at the rail, transfixed by the sight and smell of the island—and so were we all. Our senses had been purged and honed by 23 days of confinement on the great salt void, and they avidly took in form and color. Black rock ridges fell to a sullen sea, but above the seaside cliffs, vivid green covered the land. Meadows, crops, and orchards all radiated their particular hues of living green. The hillsides were awash in blue flowers, and above us a village of red tile roofs looked down on the boat. In lulls between gusts we could distinctly hear a tractor—and dogs barking. Santos moaned and made toward the caprail.

"Stay boy!" Diego was quick to caution. He'd taken the anchor watch and had been restraining the dog since dawn. Santos turned to Dorothy with a pleading so intense it hurt. He whimpered heartbreakingly, his little soul imploring us for a touch, a taste of land.

We had heard that Portuguese customs officers were unforgiving of lapses, but given the circumstance of the gale, surely . . . if we avoided the village . . . we could set foot on shore? Santos watched us discuss the matter, his eyes shifting from speaker to speaker. When we agreed, Diego turned to him and said, "Santos, let's launch the *dinghy*." When he heard that word, joy leaped into his eyes—had he heard right?

"Where's your *leash*, Santos . . . *leash!*" asked Diego. The dog's eyes shot lasers, and he danced on his hind legs in a fever of anticipation.

"Here come our *shoes*," said Dorothy and threw them up with a showy clump! clump! on deck. He dashed around the mast at top speed and came to a screeching stop with a volley of high-spirited barks. Hope was about to unhinge him.

We launched the dinghy and took him to what passed for a beach. He leaped off the prow and shot down the sandy patches, and came back tongue lolling—but something was missing. The rock was slippery, the sand sparse and black and mined with flotsam. The spot was surrounded by crags, remote from man or dog—in short, as far as he was concerned, it was land, but barely. It belonged as much to the tempestuous sea.

Two days later the seas went down and we finally made it into Horta. From well out in the approaches Santos recognized this to be a proper landfall with people, restaurants, and dogs. Docking the boat in the crowded harbor took concentration and communication, but Santos was so worked up, we had to tie him in the cockpit. There he flung against the leash with such force and groaning that it was impossible to think. We had to chuck him below, from whence came his frantic lament. What a passion that dog had!

But here his fondest fantasies of land came gloriously true. For dog or man the Azores made an unsurpassed midocean rest stop. Horta was filled with delightful parks and flower gardens and handsome buildings and stately trees. Traffic was slow, the streets were still cobblestoned, and dogs ran free. Few of the inhabitants had ever seen Santos's like, and everyday a score of passersby—from toddlers to schoolgirls to white-haired pensioners clad in berets and tweed jackets, clenching pipes in their teeth and walking their own pets—would stop to stroke him, admire his looks, and inquire as to his breed.

The Azores have a 500-year history of resuscitating sailors who have run out of food and water returning to Europe from the Americas and the East Indies. Ships would struggle into port with their crews incapacitated by scurvy, out of water, reduced to eating rats and boiling up their belts, and the Azores, also known as the hospital islands, would transport the sick ashore to breezy rooms with flowers in the windows and views of green hills and feed them just-picked oranges and grapefruits to cure the scurvy,

Our health was fine, but we desperately needed wine and olives, both of which were immediately supplied at a sidewalk cafe from where we could gaze over *Breath*'s masts and on across the channel to the spectacular mountain cone of Pico, 8,000 feet high. Santos sat at our feet contentedly and ate the scraps of sausage we fed him while we savored a nicely chilled white wine and then ordered another bottle

TWENTY-ONE

AZORES, GALICIA, AND ALGARVE

We spent a happy month in the Azores, cruising from island to island, taking pleasure in the people and the flowers. At what other port would you be visited one bright morning by the mayor and the summer festival queen, who presented each boat with a bouquet of flowers and a good bottle of local wine?

Reluctantly we shaped a course for Galicia, the northwest corner of Spain, where we arrived at the height of their summer celebrations. Every morning fireworks shot off into the sky to announce the fiesta of some town or village—often several towns at a time—there being only 90 days to the summer and hundreds of towns and villages eager to have their day. They staged boat races, bands played on the waterfront, processions wound their way through the ancient streets, and free food and drink were laid out.

Santos had no fonder memories than those of Muros. We cast anchor off this ancient town in the fullness of summer, when blackberry bushes hung heavy with fruit, spilling out of empty lots and overhanging medieval walls of cut stone. Every day Santos accompanied Diego for hours while the boy wandered the alleys and backstreets of the town, eating blackberries until his stomach was swollen and filling a bag with the rest.

All over town posters announced Muros' summer festival. When the appointed weekend arrived, the town set out long tables groaning with bottles of wine and trenchers of paella, chicken, fish, and fruit. And mussels by the ton. Muros was a mussel cultivation center, so there could be and would be no shortage of mussels. A touring Russian cultural troupe took the stage for two nights and put on a phenomenal, absolutely world-class show featuring gorgeously costumed traditional dancers, cossacks walking tight wires, a baritone from the Bolshoi, a virtuoso violinist, and a man who could mimic birdcalls with such humor that he turned the audience into a helplessly heav-

ing sea of laughter. It was the summer of 1989, just before
the USSR unraveled. The place was packed, wine flowed freely, the
food kept coming, and the town pulled out all the stops—fireworks,
rock bands, dancing on the quay—while the weekend unfolded in the
heart of the port.

This was a venue made in heaven for dogs. The Galicians were
feasting and drinking and wonderfully disposed toward the world,
especially toward small black dogs who had sailed an ocean to join
in their revelries. Santos had his pick of sweetmeats, not to mention
being hand-fed mussels shelled for him by feel-no-pain celebrants
who thought he was a part of the Russian act, a miniature dancing
bear on the loose, when they saw him prance on his hind legs. We
tried to leave him on the boat the second night for fear of his being
trampled or stolen, but he would have none of that. Diego spotted
him, his fur still damp from his swim, and went to pick him up, but
upon hearing his name called, Santos scurried away through the
crowd to one of the block-long tables under which he could travel
at speed the length of the party without fear of being stopped or
stepped on. He operated happily on his own recognizance until much
later in the evening, when the crowds had thinned and we found him
waiting at the dinghy with a distended belly and a happy smile. Dogs
do smile.

* * *

We hated to leave Muros, but other delights were calling and
the weather, so pleasant in the summer, was bound to turn rainy and
pestered with gales by fall. So we worked our way down the rias of
Galicia, then entered Portugal and port hopped down its coast.

On the Algarve, anchored off a magical stretch of coast where
the sea and wind have carved the soft sandstone cliffs into slots and
pocket coves and hidden beaches, suddenly Santos jumped in from
the bow and made a beeline for a nearby beach. We called and called
him to no avail.

"Oh well, I feel like a swim," said Diego, and he dove in and
swam steadily without looking up after the dog. Diego swam to the
edge of the sand, shook his hair back, took a look around—and froze.
Every soul on the beach but him was stark, bare-ass naked. He had
stumbled onto a nude beach.

Diego called the dog, trying to sound casual, as if maybe he
wanted to share a cookie with him, above all not letting him know

that this was embarrassing and his attendance was urgently required right now dammit!

But the little dog had complex arrays of ESP antennas devoted to picking up just such signals, so now he dashed away barking, then dashed back close to Diego, growling provocatively and rearing up like a frisky warhorse, all the while staying just out of reach, playing catch me if you can with a vengeance while Diego expected any moment to be evicted or severely ordered to remove his trunks and hand them over to the bailiff.

At that point help appeared in the form of a young woman who grabbed Santos as he was going by. She cradled the dog between two voluptuous teutonic breasts with rosy aureoles and distinct nipples that jutted out like bullets, and returned him thus to Diego. The boy had gotten an eyeful that imprinted itself on his genetic code. I was watching his progress with the waterproof binoculars.

"What's on shore that's so interesting?" asked my wife, who hadn't brought her glasses.

"Oh, nothing. . . . Somebody's talking to Diego."

TWENTY-TWO

SANTOS IN SEVILLA

By the time we got to Andalusia the weather had become a concern. With the dangerous gales of the fall equinox approaching, and we in unfamiliar waters, it was time to find a spot to winter over.

This posed a problem.

We'd be spending half a year in close quarters, tied up to a dock, sandwiched between other boats. In the Caribbean we'd never lived that way for more than a few days at a time. It ran against the whole purpose of living afloat. Why pay to live in a floating trailer park when you could swing free to the wind in clean water, away from the constraints of land and immediate neighbors?

The crux of the problem was Santos. His barking could create difficulties in close quarters. I remembered my first encounter with a schipperke, at a dock in Nassau while delivering a boat to Miami. The dog barked piercingly every time someone set foot on the dock, and there must have been twenty yachts berthed there, with people coming and going all the time. The little beast was maddening, and its owners, two smug yuppies, did nothing to quell it. Childless, they doted on their dog. Everybody else within earshot hated it.

As it turned out, I had grounds for concern. Santos's hair trigger bark did embroil us in acrimony more than once that winter. But the few who took offense, well . . . each of them was a troubled character, to say the least. And for every enemy Santos made, he made ten staunch friends. Everything considered, by springtime, when we finally left for the Aegean, he had made his mark.

* * *

We had heard good things about Seville: that it was well protected, had a mild winter and a good marina, and was an interesting city. And it housed the famous Archives of the Indies, where I could pursue research on early West Indian history. We decided to give it a try.

Seville lies 55 miles up the Guadalquivir River, down which, 470 years before, Ferdinand Magellan had traveled by rowed galley to meet his fleet of five ships at San Lúcar for the voyage that would cost him his life and render him immortal. We entered the river mouth just after dawn, motoring over a sea of smoky yellow glass that reflected the ochre sunrise sky, following for miles the long stark line of blackened posts that marked the channel through notoriously shifting sandbars.

Once we were within the compass of land, the breeze lifted its head and began to blow—softly at first, in fitful cats-paws over the water, then in steadier, widening ruffles with noticeable intent. We raised full sail, and by the time the topsail was pulling 15 minutes later, *Breath* was heeled over on a beam reach, a stern wave riding her rudder, her wake burbling like early-morning bird song. Soon she was bending to her work in earnest as the breeze became a wind and continued to freshen. The trees started to sway, the tall grass on the banks rippled with wind. We dropped the topsail and still the boat heeled enough to take water through her scuppers. Stronger gusts turned the river surface white. What was going on?

By midmorning the boat was reaming the narrowing river, the wind had reached gale force, and we were deep reefed and flying, the stressed wake boiling up behind her as we passed lush meadows where noble steeds grazed and black bulls with upswept horns surveyed herds of plump cows. People on the bank stared as we swept past. Eventually we dropped the main altogether and proceeded under headsails and mizzen, staggering along, caught by our first levanter, the violent easterly gale that can stop traffic in the Straits of Gibraltar.

We finally dropped anchor in Seville near a graceful cut-stone bridge arching over the river. Directly ashore, a cobblestoned wharf with beautifully riveted iron cranes from a bygone era bore a sign that read "Muelle de las Delicias"—dock of delights. Just beyond the dock lay the green lawns of a long riverside park above whose tree-tops showed ancient towers and spires. Santos gazed at the green and whiffed the air with anticipation. So did we all.

Sevilla turned out to be a terrific place to spend the winter, but it wasn't without drawbacks. It rained a hundred-year record that winter. The marina was a makeshift affair whose facilities were barely adequate and grew worse as stragglers arrived. Worst of all, we had to play musical chairs with the electrical outlets—there were only 11 to supply 12 boats, and we all depended on electrical heaters to keep warm.

We lay stern-to a floating dock by the riverbank. A shady tree overhung our stern, and just ashore was a pleasant glade with benches around a fireplace. Across the street started a park, whose footpaths led past monuments, gardens, and fountains to the edge of the city's old quarter, where medieval battlements enclosed a labyrinth of narrow winding streets.

Around each corner of the old city lay another delight, perhaps a tiny plaza spilling over with flowers, a cathedral with wonderfully carved stone doorways, an 11th-century tower, or tapas bars sunken with time three feet below street level where we ate enormous purple olives with wine drawn from casks that might have served Cervantes.

But Santos loved Seville for its park, where we happily took him for long and frequent walks. And truly, that was one marvelous park, a huge botanical garden planted with an unusually wide climatic range of trees and shrubs, enhanced by wrought-iron benches and marble sculptures commemorating the worthy or the wealthy. Bike paths ran past manicured lawns; beautiful coaches made of varnished wood, gold inlay, and polished leather and drawn by Andalusian steeds trotted by on the gravel tracks. In the middle of it lay a lovely pond inhabited by amusing ducks, with an island accessed by a fairy tale bridge. On the park's south border stood architecturally dazzling buildings, fantasies of castles and palaces, with moats and archways and Moorish columns, domes and spires and richly worked facades, surrounded by assiduously tended flower gardens. Built for the 1929 World Expo that never happened, they now housed archaeological, cultural, and art museums.

All classes of Sevilla's citizens came to enjoy the park, especially on weekend afternoons. Joggers struggling against the paunch that accompanies the good life panted past the museums and flower gardens, sweatbands around their brows, Reeboks on their feet. Old people scattered peanuts to pigeons, toddlers learned to run, older children learned to bike or roller skate.

And the youth of the city! In love en masse, they entwined on every bench, stretched out on the grass, leaned against statuary, and sat in little alcoves let into a long wall that overlooked the river. They gazed deep into each other's eyes under orange tree blossoms, oblivious to the world, while people of sober years watched life on the far bank and the swallows wheeling over the water at sunset.

Spaniards are dog fanciers, and the park attracted everything from St. Bernards to chihuahuas—it was olfactory heaven for Santos. And he was the only schipperke. Nobody had seen his like before. We couldn't take him for even a brief walk without attracting the interest of teenage girls or the curiosity of dignified pensioners strolling a much larger dog on a leash. "Que raza es?"(What race of dog is it?). We must have answered that question a hundred times that winter.

We soon heard of another American boy about Diego's age who was attending eighth grade in the nearby Spanish public school, and Diego decided he'd like to do the same instead of spending the whole winter embalmed in the boat doing home schooling. Accordingly we enrolled him—the Spanish authorities made it easy—and every morning he trudged off early across the dewy park to his school in the old part of town.

Soon he discovered the ducks in the pond and took to leaving fifteen minutes early every morning with a loaf of yesterday's stale bread under his arm. Even on weekends he would get up early, off to feed the ducks. We wondered what it was about these ducks that would get him up so early on a day when he could sleep later, and so one morning Dorothy went with him to watch. She expected to see placid ducks cruising the pond, self-contained, somewhat remote, more or less part of the scenery, but they were anything but placid. They were hungry first thing in the morning—ravenous would be a better word. As soon as they saw Diego with the long loaves under his arm, there rose a tremendous quacking and honking as the whole flock paddled post haste over to cluster at his feet at the edge of the bank, beaks expectantly in the air, flapping their wings in an agony of anticipation, their beady begging eyes locked on the bread.

He slowly tore off a fragment of bread while the flock groaned with anticipation. He feinted it this way and that, and the flock lurched and recoiled, fifty orange bills on long white necks magnetized, poised and swaying to every movement of his arm—then he hurled it to a far corner of the pond. With a manic quacking that crescendoed into a shriek, they took off as if for the Oklahoma land rush, necks outstretched, beaks low and pointing for the prize, their rumps elevated by their legs' frantic paddling. How they poured it on! What a racket! It was the funniest thing Dorothy had seen in years. She laughed so hard she dropped the leash and Santos leaped into the pond and dogpaddled after the ducks. He went round and round trying to catch up with the ducks, but they, outraged, hissed and made pecking slashes in the air with their bills until he gave it up and went for a run in the luxuriant grass lawns. The ducks immediately reconvened, and the show resumed.

* * *

But more than just a nice place, Seville represented the apex of Santos's watchdog career. There he was the first line of defense not just for our boat but for all the vessels wintering over at the floating dock. He had responsibilities, and the threat was real.

Justly famous throughout Spain for its history, architecture, and flair, Seville was also *in*famous for its thieves. All the way down the coast, when people heard we were headed for Seville, they cautioned us against "chorizos," thieves, particularly purse snatchers mounted on motorbikes, operating in pairs, one driving and the other snatching. Chorizo translates literally as "sausage," which made no sense until I saw the police frisking a punk on a motor scooter. With his flashy clothes, pomaded hair, and disrespectful smirk, he was as greasy as a cheap salami.

Seville was also a traditional gypsy haven. Their plastic-and-cardboard encampments could suddenly appear against an old wall in an abandoned lot near the marina, here today, gone tomorrow. Wandering over the bridge, they could case the whole dock. We were cautious about buying in to the "gypsies are thieves" stereotype, but common knowledge swore to it—and to see little gypsy children left with a showy sore and sad eyes to beg at the head of a busy bridge made one less inclined to give their adults the benefit of the doubt.

The other boats had all been equally warned as they approached the fabled city. Already a bicycle had been stolen from the premises, a stainless steel, folding, made-for-boats—that is to say, *expensive*—model. So when Santos arrived he filled a unanimously felt need for a good watchdog. And since there were no other dogs aboard, he also filled the role of marina mascot. Inevitably, though, he attracted controversy.

He kept strict watch, enough to please even the most paranoid property owner. And he barked for many reasons that sometimes included hard causes such as a cat, a rat, or someone, anyone entering the dock area. But he also barked on general principle; it was the time-hallowed duty of his breed to voice warnings. Our security was his responsibility, and like an Israeli general he was determined to err on the side of caution. He would take no chances. He would not be hushed. And he made it clear that he obeyed a higher law than his master's say-so.

Most of our neighbors appreciated his contribution. The first to react was Marikka, the Dutch girlfriend of a young Italian doctor on a 50-foot pilothouse ketch. She was a bouncy good-looking blonde who had wrinkled up her pretty nose when she heard we were Americans.

"Americans . . ." she said with an obvious lack of enthusiasm. "I hope you won't anchor too close to us." But when she saw Santos, her face lit up. She was starved for a pet, loved dogs, and fell for Santos's affable fox face. She soon became a friend and warned us that the gratuitous racism and fatuous bragging of the two Americans already there had stereotyped our nation as being populated by right-wing, loudmouthed boors, smug about money. I qualified as a signal exception on all three counts, being left-wing, self-conscious, and broke.

Santos became the mascot of the dock, the recipient of carefully wrapped bags of bones, gristle, and skin that otherwise would have gone to the garbage. It helped that being a small dog and a fastidious one, he could eat chicken bones without danger of choking. At the Sunday potlucks he was beckoned from bench to bench to do his tricks for scraps.

However, three of our dockmates made it abundantly clear that he was not welcome around them. They were two besotted Englishmen and an old John Bircher with a lecherous smirk who had sailed from California, and what a piece of work each was! We got to know them all too well.

The trouble of course was his bark—not when we were around, because we rode tight herd on him, physically restraining him or taking him down below where he never barked. But three days a week, Dorothy went off to work in the Spanish shipyard at 6:45, then Diego went to school, and I went to the Archives to read 16th-century governors' letters from Cumana. From 8 A.M. until 3 P.M. on those days, nobody was home except the doggus, and he was bored and pent up.

Unfortunately, a redheaded Briton with a temper lived on the boat next door. He wasn't a bad sort, just irascible and opinionated. Typical of a certain segment of frustrated English sailors squeezed for cash, he harbored a residual prejudice against American yachtsmen, whom it comforted him to characterize as rich dilettantes with expensive cocktail yachts. He was put out by the fact that we actually had the most traditional boat at the dock, had put in the most sea miles, and had built it ourselves.

Short and wiry with a pointy beard, he puffed up visibly when I told him he reminded me of Sir Francis Drake. British naval glory was his passion, and he would hold forth on it in a highly opinionated way. His central thesis, to which he quickly came around, contrasted the incompetence of the French and American navies with the naval genius of Britons, in his humble opinion the only true seamen. He would begin his discourse mildly, as dispassionate and objective as Socrates, proposing only to discern truth, and all was well so long as you kept agreeing with what he said. But he made some extremely debatable assumptions, and at the first objection he would glower, at the second would get noticeably ugly, and by the third would launch a tirade against the sheer historical ignorance of any opposing view. I tried my best to understand world maritime history from his point of view, but it was hopeless. He thrived on confrontation and would propound more and more extreme opinions until he got what he wanted. He saw fools everywhere about him, and feared nothing to expose them.

Once I realized there was no pleasing him, he became entertaining. I enjoyed hearing him come home from work to find that his electrical cord had been detached from its outlet and another one plugged into its place. Most people dealt with this inconvenience nonchalantly—unplugging someone who was gone and replugging their own. But when Firebeard saw that he'd been pulled, he'd bellow with rage, then thunderously denounce the *vile scum* who had the nerve to detach him while he was out working for a living while they, the *rich sods*, lolled about in idle luxury, and if he *ever* caught one of them in the act he would bloody well *punch the slimy bilge rat right off the dock!* Having thus vented, he'd yank a fistful of cords out and replace his. People in their boats would hear him rant, feel their heaters fade, and come topsides to rehook.

Firebeard stayed up late of nights drinking rotgut red wine packaged in a paper box—it was cheap, and he was poor. Not surprisingly, he slept late many mornings, nursing his head. Invariably, then it was that a stray dog, a loitering, malingering ill-bred cur, would wander casually onto the bridge and insolently peer down and give Santos whatever passes for the canine equivalent of the finger. Never one to bear slights meekly, Santos would bristle like a porcupine and peal out an all-points alarm, thereby jabbing a hot poker into the Brit's sensitized brain.

It didn't take Firebeard long to confront me: "That sod of a dog! Not even a proper dog, a . . . a bloody rodent! A felonious nuisance! He barks all day long at people on the dock, at rats on the bank, at people walking on the bridge! He even barks at the fucking aeroplanes!"

He had a valid point, but fortunately we were able to ignore it because the next boat down, a big steel ketch, held a very different view. Pierre and Toni were affable Dutch burghers, Toni plump and cute with shy but dancing eyes, Pierre lean and sinewy with a tall brush cut of gray hair. He had been a pilot in a big Dutch port and spoke any number of languages including fluent English. As opinionated as Firebeard, he liked Santos just the way he was—*especially* his barking.

"Don't hush the dog—he's a fine watchdog, he protects the whole dock. Let him bark so much he can! Good boy!" he'd say, and reward him with something saved from supper.

Pierre was quite concerned about thievery—it was his bicycle that had been stolen, and his beamy 48-foot boat was loaded with expensive electronics, a new outboard, and brand-new gear. He blamed the bike's loss on gypsies. He'd bought another bike, even more expensive, and had chained it to a tree on the bank and was always chasing off boys who wandered near the dock without good reason, especially if they were swarthy.

No love was lost between Pierre and Firebeard. Pierre thought the Englishman a cantankerous runt, and Firebeard thought Pierre a moral weakling because he lived in such a comfortable boat. He despised people in boats bigger than his own 25-foot, no-standing-headroom cutter. The only way to go to sea that showed competence and mettle was in small boats—small wooden boats, in fact. Steel or fiberglass were for the unskilled and cowardly. When Pierre heard that, he burst out laughing.

Santos added fuel to the fire between them. That became apparent one afternoon when I came back early to the boat. I heard Santos raise the alarm to a suspicious rustling on the bank, then heard Firebeard bellow a curse, "Shut the fuck *up*, you sod!," hard followed by Pierre's exuberant shout, "Good dog! Bark, Santos, bark!"

Around November, the word came down from the port authority that the new bridge under construction just a couple hundred yards downriver was going to be welded shut. It was to be a draw bridge but wouldn't open until early spring. The boaters were officially warned that anyone who didn't leave immediately would effectively be locked in for the winter, unless they wanted to pull out their masts.

Firebeard fretted, fumed, and finally left. One afternoon his boat was gone. His job renovating a house had ended. We heard he went to Cadiz, where he had friends and work. Almost a year later we heard that his boat had been lost at sea en route back to England. I hoped silently it wasn't Santos that had driven him to his fate.

A few spaces down the dock lived another of Santos's detractors, Roger, a friend of Firebeard. He too was British, a wooden-boat purist exhibiting problems with alcohol—in fact, poor Roger was a suicidal alcoholic. We visited him on his boat once and watched him methodically smoke two pipes of hashish while downing tumbler after tumbler of the raw box wine guaranteed to produce a splitting headache.

He was thin and pallid, with wispy strands of sandy hair combed over the top of his head. His weak eyes blinking through horn-rimmed glasses made him look a bit like an owl—and like an owl, he shunned daylight. He'd go out at night to find a different venue for his drinking, and come staggering back in the wee hours, his great coat hugged tight, a deathly pallor on his face, his eyes concentric whorls of dizziness. He'd collapse in his cockpit and, eventually, retch over the side. At 3 A.M. the river was silent as a sepulcher, and water carries sound. The agonized spasms of Roger's body getting rid of self-inflicted poison must have reached all the way to the second bridge.

Roger had some source of income—his upper-crust accent suggested a "remittance man" paid by a respectable family to be disreputable somewhere far from home—but he needed money and hoped to sell his boat, a handsome, well-built 34-foot wood sloop that had once been owned by a famous yachtsman. Even from a distance, though, any prospective buyer could see signs of egregious neglect. The varnish had peeled off the mast, dirt and mold backfilled the corners of the deck, and every scupper hole had its streak running down the hull. Down below was gloomy, dark wood and dirty velvet, roaches crawling over unwashed dishes, and empty wine cartons. An unsettling odor clung to the interior, perhaps sewage leaked from the head or swamp gas emitted by the bilge or a dribble of overlooked spew. Guests couldn't wait to get back topsides for a deep draught of clean winter air.

Like Firebeard, Roger extolled wood boats over fiberglass—"plastic" boats were just so many clorox bottles littering the sea—and also liked to complain that there were no "real seamen" left these days. He would look around the dock, disdain on his face as he pined for the company of true-grit skippers. We Americans were inherently undeserving of consideration, even though each of us had crossed an ocean to get there. And the French! Nothing they did was of any merit.

Yet when one begged for details of his own sea experience he had to admit that he hadn't even brought his boat across the English Channel—a friend had skippered the boat across. Now there was a real stalwart! And he would wax euphoric about the gales that worthy had weathered, the vessels delivered, the emergencies surmounted. "There is the real thing!" he'd say grandly. "This lot. . . . Pretenders!" he muttered scornfully, offended by the mediocrity that surrounded him.

And he sided with Firebeard about the dog. At the potluck, as Santos made his rounds checking for scraps, Roger would start away from the little dog as though it were a sewer rat. "Nasty little beast! Infernal nuisance!" His Irish girlfriend, Sara, always looked a little torn. She clearly liked animals and had a nurturing nature, which must have been the only reason she stayed with Roger, who certainly needed help.

At any rate the dog did not lack for scraps or cuddling at the convivial potlucks. He was generally recognized to be an asset to the little community. Not only was he a top-notch watchdog, he was also—perhaps more importantly—a world-class pre-emptive ratter. Before we arrived, rats had vandalized a couple of the yachts in their nasty, profligate way. With a trumpet flourish of satisfaction, Pierre had proclaimed that a schipperke's chief duty on the medieval grain barges was To Guard Against Rats. Being Dutch, he was presumed to know.

Rats are a scourge afloat—smart, disgusting, incredibly destructive, and with a million hiding places. One rat can ruin a whole bin of vegetables in a night, never sating itself with one carrot or peach but sampling widely and defecating freely. During the day, hunkered down in the far recesses of the boat, they gnaw on electric insulation and engine hose, causing unforeseeable failures.

While others installed elaborate rat guards, we relied on Santos. He fully understood that rats were unquestioned hereditary enemies who needed constant surveillance and intimidation, the which he eagerly provided. Alert, restless, avid for distinction, he convinced them that, at all costs, they must not be found in his domain.

To this end Santos spent hours every day worrying an old coconut husk that had stayed with us across the Atlantic. Its stiff hairlike fibers made a perfect rat effigy, and Santos ostentatiously savaged it, gnawing, growling, whining, holding it between his forepaws, tearing at it with his jaws low to the deck, his rump high, poised to leap. He especially loved to shake it back and forth in a blur—trying to break its neck—then toss it up and leap upon it with a bloodcurdling snarl and a snap, catching it before it came to rest. He would work it all the way down the deck and back in a frenzy, totally absorbed in dismembering this infinitely hated other.

Any rats on the bank could not fail to see their death being practiced by this slavering killer whose great hope in life was to get his jaws on a live rat. They watched bleakly from their rat holes, their beady eyes weighing opportunity versus risk, while he dared them to make his day.

At any rate, we never got a rat aboard, and neither did our neighbors. Santos's aggressive patrolling must have sent them elsewhere. Pierre made much of this at the Sunday potlucks, calling him over for pats and holding out a bit of gristle from his plate, getting him worked up until he was prancing and jumping eagerly—then he would toss it away shouting, "Rat, Santos! Rat!" and Santos would shoot off like a bolt from a crossbow, his acceleration a wonder to behold.

Santos made two other friends who stood him in good stead. The son and daughter of the marina owners came twice a week to our boat to learn English from Dorothy in exchange for a reduction of our monthly dockage fee. Both of them vied for the attentions of the dog as they waited for Dorothy to receive them. "Precioso!" was the favorite comment of Carmen, 13, as she gently stroked his thick mane. Carmen was going to be a beauty and a fine person too . . . kind, studious, and very appealing with grave, luminous dark eyes and glossy black hair drawn neatly back over an alabaster brow. Santos would snuggle into her lap and lie in bliss while she cuddled him.

Jaime was older but, to his chagrin, shorter and younger looking, and the complete opposite of his sister. He ignored his studies, was full of jokes and pranks, constantly fidgeted in class, and had eyes that danced with mischief. He loved to tease and fight with Santos to get him worked up. Santos, ever disposed to be martial, would instantly oblige. They would contest ownership of a towel, Santos digging his paws in and clamping his jaws shut so tightly that Jaime could lift him off the deck and swing him around, the dog growling all the while like the Nemean lion. Then Jaime would mockingly try to grab parts of the dog's body while Santos defended himself with lightning quick snaps, Jaime egging the dog on until he was on the verge of losing control, of forgetting it was a game. He was fascinated by Santos's blood-curdling snarl and by his intense machismo despite his small size. He called the dog "cinco kilos."

Santos was a great prop for Dorothy's English lessons. These started with Jaime and Carmen but soon expanded through word of mouth and would have become a full-time occupation had we stayed any longer. The dog acted as greeter when students arrived at the boat and entertained them if they had to wait for another lesson to finish. One of Santos's favorites was Isabela, a medical student, who always arrived a little early to give Santos a treat.

Then there was the patrician lady of Dorothy's own age who lived in an elegant apartment and received her and Santos for lessons with tea and pastries. She spoke no English at all and made scant progress, but she greatly enjoyed the lessons and questioned Dorothy in Spanish and French about life on the boat and in the Caribbean. Dorothy and her unusual dog were a breath of sea-air and spice from exotic lands in that immaculate, richly furnished, tastefully decorated top-floor penthouse. Her husband was head of the famous Seville shipyard and spoke good English. When he arrived home early enough one day to inquire after his wife's progress, Dorothy somewhat worriedly confided that, well . . . actually. . . . But the husband put up his hand to stop her from saying any more. With a broad smile he declared, "Very good—she loves the lessons!"

Jerry was the last of the triumvirate who took offense at Santos presence in the marina. He was an American, about 60, with white hair in a long crew cut and a somewhat weaselly cast to his pinched features. He made a bad first impression, and a few minutes of conversation was enough to reveal him as a shocking misogynist and racist.

It turned out Jerry had a thing about appearing to be Don Juan. He would meet women at the language school, generally decent middle-aged women, and invite them to see his boat, always timing his entrance for the Sunday potluck so everybody could see him with his supposed conquest. He'd introduce them briefly, take them to his boat for an hour or two, and then leave with a conspicuous smirk. From the agitated, let-me-outta-here reactions of the women as they left, one gathered things had not gone well. We never saw the same lady twice.

The less said about Jerry the better. Though Jerry and I were polite, we avoided each other until Santos sparked a confrontation.

Having come late to Seville, we were tied up to the end of the dock closest to the bridge—not a good berth. Noise and dust from passing vehicles drifted down, and occasionally a bad boy might throw an orange and run away laughing. But by far the worst of it was the nearby traffic light that made a sound so invasive we could scarcely bear it. It was harsh, metallic, jarring, like the sound of a cash register mixed with a car grinding its gears. Loud on calm nights, it was even audible in rain and wind, going "whirr . . . chuk! . . . whirr . . . chuk!" day and night without cease.

So when the chance came to move to a better space, we would have jumped at it except that it was between Jerry and Roger. And sure enough, at the Sunday potluck when I mentioned the possibility of our moving, Jerry strode over to confront me.

"You bring that goddamn black beast next to my boat it's war between us, buster. You'll be sorry."

Everyone fell silent at this unseemly breach of good feeling. Jerry stalked off to his boat.

Roger kept his peace until most people had gone back to their conversations, then he came up, reasonably sober, and said with the utmost intensity, shaking slightly, "You can't be serious about moving alongside with that horrid little dog. It would be unconscionable . . . criminal!" Sara, his girlfriend, wouldn't meet my eyes.

Jerry's bluntness tempted me to defy him, but Roger's relatively polite Oxbridge plea made me admit that if one didn't like dogs, having a Santos close by could be unpleasant. So we gave up the idea. None of the other boats would have objected to our moving alongside. They accepted Santos as a useful and amusing member of the community and were willing to make allowances. Then again, they weren't next door to him.

* * *

Things came to a head and Santos came into his own in the early spring when the "agua y luz" demonstration took place. We finally found out why the facilities at the dock were so poor. All winter we had shared one spigot for fresh water, and it was often dry. There was only one shower, housed in a drafty cinderblock shack, never finished and on the verge of collapse, whose cement floor was lethally slippery with moss and whose cracked light switch gave off sharp tingles of electricity. To get hot water you had to put a match to an ancient rusted gas blower, which ignited with a roar and an upward whoosh of flame that boded no good.

When we complained we always got a profuse apology and a runaround from Jorge and Maria—and now it became clear why. The marina lived on borrowed time. It had been set up at a disused city dock, but the authorities now wanted the space back for the upcoming World Expo. Jorge wasn't giving up without a fight, and he had some legal claim involving an escrow account that they wanted to give back to him but he refused to accept. The result was an impasse, so to pressure him the port authority decided to pressure us, his customers, by making difficulties about the supply of water and electricity. In a word, they cut us off. Whereas before we had been sharing outlets and making do, now there was no electricity at all. Presumably their idea was to get the marina tenants to move out, but because the bridge was welded shut for the foreseeable future and the only other marina was located a half hour out of town on a dull, grassy plain, there was no place else for us to go. Anyway, we all liked it fine right there at the edge of the park where we could walk into the heart of the old city in ten minutes.

Hence we were receptive to Jorge's proposal that we mount a demonstration at the port authority headquarters nearby. He and Maria arrived at the Sunday potluck with cloth banners and paints and brushes that we painted with symbols and slogans while Jorge cooked a special paella in a huge wok, copiously garnished with chicken, mussels, and shrimp tucked into the steaming saffron rice bubbling over the open fire. We feasted, drank wine, and made our plans for the morning.

Bright and early we gathered. Almost everyone on the dock was there due to peer pressure—we were all in this together, and it was manifestly unfair to let a few do the work that would benefit all. Even Jerry was there, much as he loathed the idea of a demonstration. A staunch member of the John Birch Society, he had threatened to throw his children out of the house if they ever joined a civil rights or anti-war demonstration. Now he was afraid a picture of him marching for his rights would make it back to his hometown.

Marching a few blocks to the three-story Port Authority headquarters to greet the executives as they arrived at their assigned parking spaces, we set up the banners—"Queremos agua y luz!"—to either side of the entrance. We had props to symbolize our plight—light bulbs, water buckets, and our star performer, Blanca, a fiery young Peruvian mother who was a veteran of street protests in Lima and Santiago. She had her infant strapped to her front, a baby bottle in one hand, and an empty water bucket in the other. As the first suit arrived, he had to ease his car slowly over a dip into the driveway. We raised a loud chant—"We want power and light!"—and Blanca rushed over to his car window brandishing her baby and wailing, "My baby! My baby needs water!" Then she grabbed the metal bucket and beat it forcefully with a steel ladle, setting up one hellacious din, as unsettling as a baby's cry or a fingernail down a chalkboard. I recoiled in middle-class propriety, but there was no stopping Blanca. The bureaucrat parked and hurried into the refuge of his building, not glancing to one side or the other.

The other execs did the same, and soon we could see them huddled together in their offices and looking out their windows. We kept up our shouts, Blanca making a godawful racket at erratic intervals. A crowd gathered on the street. Within fifteen minutes we were asked to send in negotiators. Carlos, Blanca's husband, and I got chosen and were ushered up to an office on the second floor, where we met with the boss, a middle-aged man, out of shape, with worry lines on a basically decent face. We put it to him that while we took no position on the rights or wrongs of the case, nevertheless it *was* wrong to penalize *us*, innocent victims who came for winter shelter in all good faith.

As we made our case I noticed that every time Blanca suddenly bastinadoed her bucket he cringed, squeezing his eyes almost shut. He was scarcely listening to us, so agitated was he by the outrageously disordered noise outside his office. Within ten minutes he agreed to provide better water and power if we would just *stop that woman!* And he proved good to his word. The next morning workmen arrived to put in a bank of proper spigots and outlets.

While we were demonstrating, the only person left at the dock was Roger. He had staggered back late the night before, and about now he woke up with the usual splitting headache and disabling nausea—to a peal of Santos's barking. It was loud and frantic even by skipp standards, and it didn't subside—it increased.

"Sara, for the love of God throw a fucking *knife* at that bloody yapping freak!"

No answer.

He burrowed his head under his pillow. Each yip bullwhipped his cerebellum. No one was making even the slightest effort to hush the dog. Then he remembered. Everyone was at the demonstration. The dock was deserted. Santos went on, gale-force paroxysms of barks accelerating to a storm.

Intoxicated with fury, Roger finally bolted out of bed, grabbed a machete, and stormed on deck almost naked, pallid as a grub, grimacing with pain and hatred, screaming and cursing and brandishing the weapon. Two youths who were crouched at the base of a tree next to the dock looked up in consternation, dropped something, vaulted the old iron fence, and disappeared into the bridge traffic.

Roger stopped dead in his tracks. Pierre's expensive bicycle was chained to the base of that tree. A hacksaw blade, one end wrapped with tape, lay in the grass. The chain was cut halfway through. Adrenaline steam-cleaned Roger's brain when he realized that he'd singlehandedly run off two thieves.

He next realized that Santos had gone quiet. The little dog was poised at the stern of the boat, looking eagerly toward Roger, his stub of a tail jerking back and forth, only an occasional yelp shuddering out to vent his feelings.

This incident changed Roger's feelings about the dog—and life. When we got back everyone wanted to hear the story, and Roger and Santos were the center of attention. Roger gave the dog full credit, deprecating his own part. Pierre responded handsomely, thanking Roger profusely and giving him an excellent bottle of wine. Roger, naturally, enjoyed the attention—and started to mellow out about the dog.

"For once that perpetual noise machine had good reason to bark . . . once, after six months of din!" But he said it with a noticeable lack of rancor.

At the next potluck he continued to harrumph about "that noise machine" but added, in a conciliatory tone, "A nuisance but apparently a necessary one," and "certainly the lesser of two evils, by Jove." Sara felt emboldened to pat Santos surreptitiously, and by the end of the evening he lay on his back in her lap while she scratched his belly. The next week I noticed Santos wolfing down beans and ham hock from a plate next to Roger's feet, while Roger talked to a neighbor.

"Santos! What do you think you're doing? Come here! Roger, I'm so sorry—he doesn't usually do that!"

Roger looked a bit sheepish.

"It's alright. I . . . uh . . . gave it to him... put the miserable beast to some use cleaning up. . . . Saves rinsing. . . ."

From that time on a cloud lifted from Roger's brow. The early morning vomiting stopped. He and Sara attended the potlucks more frequently and became integrated with their dockmates. And when we left for the Aegean, he seemed sorry to see the dog go.

Santos had made his mark in Seville.

TWENTY-THREE

MEDITERRANEAN DASH

Breath proceeded from Seville downriver to Cadiz, then hopped along the coast to Almeria, near the southeast corner of Spain. From there we sailed nonstop to Tunisia, our longest passage through the Mediterranean. We readied the boat for anything, mindful of the old sea's reputation for changeability and violent extremes, but all began gently in a glassy early-morning calm as we pulled out of the stone-bordered harborworks. The walls and turrets of the Moorish fortress, old dark stonework contrasting with the pastel town below, grew smaller as a southwest breeze ruffled the mirror surface, filled our sails, and sent us slipping over smooth seas toward Cabo Gato, where the southeast tip of Spain falls in rocky coils into the sea.

By late afternoon we were far enough offshore to see behind us the high, white cliffs and broad sweeping bays of the Costa del Sol. Little white-washed villages, tiny in the distance, were tucked onto green swards atop the high bold promontories. Atop the most prominent capes the slim white tower of a coastal lighthouse pierced upward. The visibility went on and on down the coast as though we were seeing a part of the world's arc from space. The air was balmy with late spring and fresh with salt tang and clear as the sea beneath our keel, where shafts of sunlight wavered down to converge at some point far below.

The sun set, the stars began to glow, and the lights of the little seaside towns and hilltop villages came on, giving definition to the night geography. The clusters and strings of lights showed where people lived, how many, whether by the sea in fishing towns or high up in shepherds' aeries.

Land lights give a night comfort, reassuring sailors that humanity is still there, carrying on its accustomed routines, cooking supper, chinking crockery and silver, snoozing beside a fire, turning back the covers. All of it is there, awaiting the sailor's return.

The night grew a little chilly as it wore on, and when Dorothy arose for her predawn watch she dressed in thick trousers, wool jacket, and the Russian-style head muff she'd sewed together from old hot pads and some quilt material. She looked like a cheerful refugee when I saw her sitting intensely still and quiet as I came up for my watch, late because she hadn't called me. She didn't answer my greeting either, and then I saw why.

A little bird sat on her lap, in the lee of her jacket, sheltering from the wind, needing a rest on its Africa-to-Europe migration. It wobbled a little on its high black stilt legs, balancing its rotund yellow breast and looking around inquisitively. Dorothy had a pleased, tender look on her face as she watched the little animal hop around exploring. It had the whole boat to rest on, and it had chosen Dorothy as the best spot. No wonder my wife had sat still there in the chill dawn for an hour past her watch. Nothing seemed wrong with the bird. When Dorothy was finally ready to get up, she gently transferred it to the next person on watch, me. It stood on my knee, looked in my face, askance, pooped quickly on my pants, and flew off.

The wind continued fair and steady out of the southwest for another full day, and toward nightfall of our third day out we were approaching the African coast in the vicinity of Bone, Algeria. Twenty miles offshore we saw a lot of traffic. We were in the thick of the shipping lane that follows the North African coast about 12 to 25 miles offshore between the Suez Canal and the Straits of Gibraltar. Ships were in sight at all times, and the procession of tankers, container ships, bulk freighters, and the rest of them, flying all sorts of flags and manned by polyglot crews, kept our attention keenly attuned.

This shipping lane is an ancient route, older than anyone knows. In the millennia before modern navigation, all vessels followed the coast as a matter of course to keep from getting lost. How many years of this traffic had furrowed these waters? The Carthaginians knew these coasts like the backs of their hands. Before them the Phoenicians and before them the Minoans sailed these waters, preceded perhaps by the Egyptians. Who before them and in what boats we don't know.

The wind freshened and came around slowly to the northeast, and we closed with the coast, riding a lift that sent us working at a tangent to the shoreline, heading almost due east. Having left the shipping lane farther offshore, we turned our attention to the dry, bony coast and gazed with fascination at old hills and headlands that had been coasted by so many sailors time out of mind. A light started to blink at dusk—its characteristics were wrong for where I supposed we were, but my charts were old, since we had no intention of visiting fundamentalist Algeria with its reportedly militant Muslim take on visiting yachts.

So we tacked, not wanting to get too close and run afoul of local authorities. This time the easy breeze decided to give us a taste of Mediterranean medicine. Within minutes it stepped up from 15 knots to 30, then slowly increased to 35. I took a reef in the main and kept on going, charging to windward, throwing up sheets of spray into the dark night. The sea lagged behind the wind, making for exhilarating sailing with the boat heeled over and tearing to windward without much head sea to stop her. But soon solid water came washing down the decks and burst against the cabin. Dorothy appeared in the companionway.

"Is everything alright? It's blowing pretty hard, isn't it?" she said with concern, steeling herself to leave her warm bunk and enter the stormy night on the improbable stage of a wet, canted deck. I sent her back to bed and went forward to reef the main again. Our speed was awesome, the boat going full tilt.

We had run into one of the Mediterranean's quick-building storms. The sky darkened overhead as low, thick clouds slid over the stars and moon, cutting off the light like a heavy steel bank vault sliding shut. I wondered how long the blow would last. When it showed no signs of easing I let go the staysail halyard, pulled the sail down, and lashed it to the boom. Next I began to wonder about dropping the working jib and putting up the storm jib in its stead. The sea was building, and soon we'd be unable to go to windward at all.

Just as I was debating, we reentered the thick of the shipping lane and bearing down on us were the bright lights of a freighter. Its range lights—the lower one at the bow and the higher one farther aft at the bridge—were lined up one directly above the other, and the red and green side lights both showed, indicating a potential head-on collision. The ship closed with us steadily. Did he see us? The clouds were low overhead, the night dark. I slipped a loop of rope over one of the spokes of the wheel to hold its course and went below to flick on the masthead strobe light. It flashed brilliantly at the top of the mainmast, illuminating everything on the boat for a fraction of a second at two-second intervals. That had to be visible. I called over channel 16 to the approaching ship, asking if he saw the flashing strobe at our masthead. Immediately came back a reply in a strong Danish accent that, yes, he saw us clearly and made us out well on radar. That was a relief.

Through the next hour, as we plunged along heavily, sending up huge washes of spray, ship after ship approached, and each time I turned on the strobe and called the master and eased our apprehensions.

Then, as quickly as it blew up, the gale of wind settled down, and within an hour we were wallowing in sloppy seas without enough wind to steady the sails. We flopped about intolerably until I turned on the engine to restore forward momentum. Typical of the Mediterranean summer, the blow was followed by prolonged calms and light airs. We motored until the swell died away and then raised our biggest, lightest sails for the remainder of the passage, which was so relaxed that we actually managed to paint the deck and the dinghy before arriving at Tunis.

TWENTY-FOUR

SANTOS AT CORFU

Perhaps Corfu was an obvious place for ghosts to come swirling out of the past. Enough unsettled business has happened there in the last 5,000 years to saturate the ether with apparitions, and a slight jog, any disturbance, may precipitate out of solution some pathetic shade to hover dolefully, beating its wings and fanning forth the grievance of its times. Santos called forth such a spirit while we were there, innocently wandering the crowded warren of a bazaar. For once he didn't do anything to provoke it—he was just there, and, as it happened, that was enough.

We left Brindisi in the afternoon bound for Corfu, picked up a freshening breeze, and ran down the heel of Italy, past an empty coastline of layered cliffs with occasional towns situated high atop, overlooking the sea. The absence of seaside villages underscored a brutal history of piracy that plagued this coast for millennia. Towns built on the water got sacked. Towns built on the heights could see ships approaching in time to flee or prepare their defenses.

Piracy was a respectable occupation in the days of Odysseus, who pillaged innocent seaside settlements when opportunity offered. Later, when the Roman Empire declined, a long era of pillaging began anew, reaching its apex when much of the Greek, Italian, and Spanish coasts were depopulated by slave raiders from North Africa.

To sail down these shores and see the whitewashed towns still perched on their cliffs gave flesh to that history.

All night the breeze held up, and in the morning it freshened, driving us along the building seas toward the snowcapped peaks of Albania, brilliant in the clear, sunlit air. Close to our south the solid green mass of Corfu rose out of Homer's wine-dark Ionian Sea. By the time we reached the Albanian line and jibed, the wind had increased to near-gale force and we thundered down the long scenic channel between Corfu and the mainland. Wildflowers decked the summer hillsides. Long gusts fell off the slopes and laid *Breath* rail down, driving her hard through the flat water of the channel.

Next day we explored the town, Santos prancing and pulling at his leash, afire with eagerness to be ashore on an island so ancient with odors. After taking in the impressive town square with its stately stone buildings and broad promenades and wide avenues, we wandered away into a less pretentious and much older part of town.

We ended up in the bazaar, a maze of narrow alleyways still paved by cobblestones and lined cheek to jowl by tiny hole-in-the-wall shops whose tattered awnings stretched out over the street and blocked out the sky, a warren isolated in time and place, selling a curious variety of goods—linens, shoes, postcards, tools, jewelry, sandals, pots and pans, umbrellas, carvings , paintings, tin, and brassware. From the look and sound of artisans' work, many of the items for sale were being made on the premises. Dorothy and I went with the flow of people, enjoying the crowd, looking into the small shops while Santos walked close beside us. He was never enthused about walking in a crowd where he couldn't see and was liable to be stepped on.

A throng of people like a torpid river at full slack tide eddied into every nook and cranny. There were Greeks, Italians, and legions of tourists, especially British and German but most especially German. If the phrase "ugly American" was coined for and ever deserved by the Yankee tourist for being fat, affluent, heedless of local sensibilities, armed with expensive camera, and above all loud, in the Mediterranean that mantle had passed on to the German. The deutschmark reigned supreme, breeding an irksome self-satisfaction. Loud teutonic voices were an inescapable backdrop to the hubbub of artisanry.

As we slowly jostled our way down the narrow winding streets we came to the stall of a tinsmith. An old white-haired man sat at a worn workshop table shaping a funnel with a small ball peen hammer. He was bent over his work, oblivious of the crowd, and his wares hung in clusters about the front of his shop—teapots, funnels of all sizes, cups, bowls, plates, flower vases. Tap-tap-tap went the hammer as he turned the sheet of tin against a mold. This was hand craftsmanship little changed in centuries. I wondered who this tinker was, whether he'd learned the trade from his father, whether his family occupation reached far back to tinkers' guilds, medieval fairs, and farmyards.

He reached his arm out for a different hammer and my idyll on the harmony of history shriveled. His forearm bore a grisly tattoo, the infamous thunderbolt and prisoner ID number. I'd seen it before on ravaged old men riding the New York subway, clinging to an overhead strap, and it always sent a chill of horror through me, like a recurring nightmare when the face of a stranger sitting next to me at a bar turns and smiles and morphs into the face of the devil, full of unimaginable evil—smiling at me.

This old tinsmith had survived Hitler's death camps. Loutish teutonic voices haggling in the street suddenly seemed insupportable.

I decided to buy a funnel—a boat always needs another funnel.

When I spoke to him in English, he looked up eagerly, as I thought for a sale. But no, his first words were a question.

"English? You English people?"

"No," I said. "We're American."

"American!" he exclaimed with outright joy. "Oh Americans . . . the best people! American soldiers save me. I love American!" He jumped up and almost embraced me, and urged me out of the street into his shop. Just then Dorothy appeared at the shop front with Santos on the leash, still hidden behind the counter.

"My wife," I said.

He gave her a look that resonated with feeling so intense it startled her. But he mastered himself and urged her kindly, "Come in, please, come. . . ."

"Thank you, but I have a dog . . . this little dog . . . is it alright?" she asked cautiously. Santos appeared in the doorway, a ray of light from a gap in the awning illuminating him. The old man gasped.

"Pauli!" he exclaimed. "Pauli. . . ." followed by endearments in what sounded like Italian. He dropped to his knees and held out his arms. Santos, usually aloof with strangers, was happy to escape the trodding crowd of feet outside, and he trotted amiably over and nuzzled his arm as the old guy ran his fingers through his ruff and scratched behind his ears as if he'd done it a thousand times. When at last he got up his eyes were glistening, and he told us, almost dreamily, "Before the war I have dog, like this . . . just like this."

We asked about his war experience and it came pouring out. He had been an Italian Jew caught up in the clutches of the "final solution." He spent nearly three years in Auschwitz, and in the last month it was touch and go whether all the prisoners would be exterminated before the Allies arrived.

"Look. What the American planes send to us." He disappeared

in back and reappeared immediately with a square of folded paper, incredibly worn and handled, almost ready to come apart where it had been folded. He showed it to us with a portentous look—the line drawing of an ugly, gross pig. Then, winking and giggling at us, he unfolded the paper and the drawing became the visage of Adolph Hitler. The old man laughed a shrill, eerie laugh.

"See? Hitler . . . the pig! Dirty swine! See?" He kept folding it back and forth to show how the picture of Hitler folded into the pig and vice versa. We laughed and admired it, wartime propaganda dropped by Allied bombers as they passed deep into Germany. The man had found it and kept it as a sacred icon. His passion was so strong he still trembled when he held it. One would have thought he'd have lost it many years before.

We talked a little more and bought a funnel and a teapot. Then Dorothy asked if he was married . . . and the light went dead in the old Jew's eyes. A look of uttermost anguish contorted his face.

"I was married. Before the war. You wait, I show you." He disappeared once again into the back and returned with an old, handcrafted hardwood box that had tatters of velvet on the top and mother of pearl inlay along the sides. The top still fitted tightly, and he carefully prised it open. Inside were folded documents and a very old photograph that just fit the box.

It was a sepia-toned family portrait of a man and wife and their four daughters. They were all dressed in their best. He must have been in his early thirties, slim, intense, a little self-conscious, and manifestly proud of his family. His wife rested her glossy dark hair against his chest and looked out with a serene gaze. They were seated, and kneeling in front of them were their bright-eyed, eager girls, the oldest holding the youngest, and the other two stroking a little black dog.

"My family . . . wife . . . daughters," he pointed at them with a shaking finger. "All died in the camp. The Nazis . . . gassed.. my girls! . . . all! . . . all!" His voice was a wail. His chest heaved and he gave an involuntary sob, his mouth working up and down soundlessly.

Dorothy and I were transfixed.

"And see—Pauli!" Sure enough, the dog looked a lot like Santos and could have been part schipperke or spitz. Tears had welled up in his eyes and one dropped on the photograph. Alarmed, he fumbled for a cloth under the counter and hastened to wipe it, ever so carefully, then dabbed sternly at his eyes. Tears were in my eyes too as we stood there in the fading afternoon light, tears of sympathy, pathos, and rage at the unspeakable horror perpetrated on that poor old guy; and how a twist of fate, the German economic miracle, rubbed that sad catastrophe in his face every afternoon. Even now, a German group, tipsy and loud from a late liquid luncheon, came barging down the street in high spirits, roaring out a drinking song.

We were silent in communion until the noise moved away, and then the heartbroken old tinker looked at Dorth and asked softly, "Why the bambinas? Why?"

TWENTY-FIVE

WALKING THE DOG

Walking the dog, morning and evening, was sometimes a chore, but it did reliably get us off the boat and expose us to experiences and places we might otherwise have missed.

Our worst morning walk was in Tarifa, a lovely Spanish town, where neat white houses climb a hill behind the port and look across the Straits of Gibraltar to the coastal mountains of Africa. Our berth at the dock opened onto a cobblestoned street, which on this particular morning had just been cleaned by the resident housewives, each sweeping the sidewalk and street outside her family's dwelling and then actually washing it with soapy water and long-handled brushes. A residual dampness clung like dew to the stones, and everything glistened, fresh and clean. The ladies stopped chatting for the moment as we passed and smiled in welcome. I for my part tried to convey heartfelt admiration for their town, their street, their culture that evoked such sensibilities.

As we smiled and exchanged pleasantries, I felt Santos's leash tighten—the dreaded dead weight. Without looking back I knew my dog had chosen this mortifyingly public, assiduously cleaned street to dig all four paws in and hunker down with that chagrined grimace on his face—a chagrin that nonetheless never gave him the slightest pause. No, no matter how I yanked the leash or implored or sternly commanded him to cease and desist just for a moment, he had chosen this place to embarrass the hell out of me.

The best dog walk, hands down, was off the southernmost bulge of Turkey.

We lay to our anchor in a pleasant cove not far from the town of Kas (pronounced cash), known in ancient times as Antiphellos. It was a beautiful and well-protected anchorage looking across blue sunlit water to another whitewashed town at the foot of the towering Anatolian massif. Directly behind our stern, a steep hill, almost a cliff, rose up a couple of hundred feet and then leveled off in an extensive ledge, shady with trees, a vantage point that would command the coast for many miles. There looked to be a goat path up the hill that we could ascend.

So, early one morning with no one else up except Santos, who was gazing silently out to sea, I got out my shoes and dropped them softly on the deck. He sprang to attention, recognizing the sound of leather, two impacts. Shoes on deck always meant walk.

We pulled the skiff up on the gravel beach and started climbing along the trail, Santos with his nose glued to the ground as he traveled. Telltale droppings and the tinkling of earthenware bells above us spoke of goats, but the trail seemed somehow more substantial than a goat path. There were several spots where steps and handholds had been carved into the rock, and where I had to give Santos a boost, but I gave it no thought until we reached the ledge, a shelf of about a quarter acre overgrown with trees and shrubs. The view was spectacular, clearly the best along this stretch of coast, following the regular trend of the shore where the monolithic mountain sloped bluntly down to meet the sparkling sea.

Santos disappeared behind a bush, and I could hear him scratching at something. I peered around the trees and saw his nose pressed under a huge boulder where no doubt a lizard had scurried for safety. The rock was overgrown with foliage but had an unusually regular shape—then I noticed its feet, carved out of the rock, feet like a lion. Pulling away the tangle of dead vines revealed a lid of heavy stone, ponderous and ajar; it was a stone coffin—a sarcophagus.

I had read about them in books and seen pictures, but that hadn't readied me for the impact of this massive casket carved out of a single block of stone, as elaborately chased with grooves, facets, and panels as though it had been routed out of soft pine. There were symbols at either end, some resembling the sun, and lines of writing all along the bottom edge; and the whole of it was shaped handsomely, with a balance and grace that belied its weight. The lid had been lifted and cracked, by grave robbers probably. As I marveled over it I caught sight of another one, also obscured by foliage. Eventually Santos and I found half a dozen of these sarcophagi, each one weighing tons, all with their lids cracked or broken, some plainer than others but every one of them an amazing piece of work.

The lonely ledge was an ancient necropolis. The same promise of beauty that had drawn us up here had drawn these people to their final resting places, where they might gaze forever down that clear coast. What a wonderful mentality and concept. The massive stone tombs and the view spoke of eternity and peace in a language we could no longer hear, but could still understand two millennia and more later.

Most of the Turkish coast was ideal for exploring with a dog. Uninhabited coves wild with rock, slope, and forest might yet have ruins, with steps worn into the stone testifying to thousands of years of prior footsteps. One never knew what relic might crop up in a field or under a ledge below the sea's surface. Seeing so many ruins along the coast dramatically illustrated the wealth and extent of that ancient civilization. Fine touches of sculpture were so profuse that 2,000 years later they're still turning up in farmers' fields. In the U.S., an artifact that old would be locked in a glass case and attended by a full-time guard, its environs declared a national historic site employing curators and parking attendants—but in Turkey the ancient past kicks around underfoot, with only Zeus knows what else lying beneath that likely-looking mound of dirt, waiting to be discovered.

A couple of weeks farther down the southern coast of Turkey, *Breath* was moored stern-to a small island a stone's throw from the mainland in water that stayed deep right to the shore. As dawn spread across the sky, once again the only two awake were Santos and myself, both of us watching the sun rise. Early-morning light touched the silvery-gray boulders and dark green pines, then the water began to glow as the sun climbed. Overhead the sky was cloudless, another hot, dry day in the offing. The foliage looked tinder dry, the pines concentrated with pitch. On the opposite shore the foothills of Asia Minor climbed steep and high to mountain masses out of sight.

While making a cup of coffee below, I heard Santos start to growl, again and again, in an odd sequence. Back on deck we had been discovered by a swarm of big yellow and black wasps, desperate for moisture due to the summer drought, who clustered thick over his water bowl and buzzed my full coffee cup, making me spill it as I flinched away. Although they didn't sting us, they were distinctly unsettling to have around.

Santos must have had previous painful run-ins with wasps, because he became extremely agitated, snapping frantically, whimpering as they buzzed his ears and eyes. He ran down the deck growling and snapping and finally bolted to the caprail and dropped into the water.

When he surfaced he headed straight for a rocky beach at the island, leaving a widening V behind him in the glossy water. I didn't want to call him back loudly because of the sleepers down in the cabin, and he either didn't hear or felt free to ignore my sotto voce commands.

Leaving my coffee on board and grumbling about the hassle of pets that were as time-consuming as children, I jumped in the dinghy and rowed to shore to fetch him, but by that time even more wasps surrounded him, attracted to the beads of water on his coat, which they kept checking, hoping it was fresh. He was more agitated than I'd ever seen him. Now, as more of them gathered around, he ran off into the pines that grew in back of the beach. What was there to do but follow?—so follow I did, calling his name and whistling to no avail. The bees stayed on the beach, and I enjoyed a pleasant jaunt over a low rise, the sunlight filtering through the trees. There was little undergrowth and the path seemed well worn, yet there was no sign of anybody else using it—no footprints, no trace of trash— except, as I began to notice, shards of pottery everywhere around, not only on the path but in the grass—in fact everywhere I looked, almost a carpet of them.

The path descended into a copse of ancient gnarled olive trees through which came the glint of marble. I pushed forward and forgot all about Santos, dumbstruck by the sudden profusion of ruins that lay about among the trees. There were a few standing walls, low and broken, waist height at most, but on the ground were layers over layers of carved stone, interspersed with fragments of sculpture and bits of mosaic. As I examined it all, I noticed that some of the blocks lying near the top were incised with the distinctive crosses of the Byzantine era. Beneath that layer were Roman mosaics intact enough to show a face or a robed figure. And beneath that stratum, carefully overturning the blocks of marble, I came upon examples of what looked like typically Lycian script from the centuries before Christ. The inescapable conclusion was that this must have been one of the sacred groves where temples had been built, one supplanting another, for a thousand years or more, spanning three great civilizations.

I stood there, my head spinning, mesmerized by the history that lay in heaps about me, when I caught sight of one mosaic, more intact than the rest, that lay under a broken section of wall. As I got on my knees to peer under the collapsed structure to see the rest of the mosaic, there was Santos, lying on the cool tile in the dim shade, looking up at me, defensive but defiant. He'd finally escaped the wasps and was damned if he'd come out.

I explored the enchanted grove for another hour, by which time the sun was high and the bees gone to shade. Santos and I returned to the dinghy and rowed to the boat. Everyone was up, and it was hot, so we decided to take a swim right off the boat before we moved on.

When we donned masks, we saw more shards scattered everywhere over the rocky bottom. I dove down and explored under a series of rock ledges about twenty feet deep—and there was the top half of an amphora, complete with both handles. I carefully extricated it and brought it to the surface, where it met the air for the first time in perhaps two millennia. We all took a good long, loving look at the beautiful artifact—and then, mindful of the Turkish penal system as dramatized, unforgettably, by the movie *Midnight Express*, I dove back down and gently worked the amphora underneath the ledge, there perhaps to lie for another millennium.

TWENTY-SIX

SANTOS AND THE RAT OF CESME

For years we had heard that schipperkes were gifted ratters, doubly necessary where barges carried grain as cargo. We'd read of schipperkes in rural areas bringing back rats, their necks neatly broken, as trophies or presents for the master. Pierre, our Dutch neighbor in Seville, swore by this and put all his faith in Santos, giving him full credit for keeping rats off the dock.

The dog certainly put on a convincing display of how to break a rat's neck as he growled and shook some toy from side to side in a blur of speed. We always wondered what would happen if a rat was ever bold or unfortunate enough to board the boat. What battle royale would ensue, what sound and fury would herald Santos at long last getting his teeth on man and dog's most hated enemy?

We never guessed the half of it until one day a torrential downpour sluiced through the gutters in the ancient Turkish city of Cesme.

Raffy was gone after a three-week visit and Diego was on his own, wandering about the teeming and ancient city of Cesme, while *Breath* lay in the excellent natural harbor below. Turkish cities offered great free entertainment for a boy and a dog. For one thing, an honest-to-god storybook castle dominated the heights above the town. A walled and turreted fortress built by Crusaders back in the 13th century, it was still mostly intact and wholly accessible. There was no admission fee, no guards, nothing off limits, no warning signs or guardrails—why it was almost as good as a shopping mall for hanging out, exploring, and daydreaming, though the local Turkish kids probably would have disagreed. Anyway, Diego and Santos were sitting on a turreted wall when they saw heavy clouds moving in. Since I was gone too, he was the man of the boat and started making his way back to *Breath* to help his mother in case of sudden bad weather.

Down the steep cobbled streets went boy and dog, headed for the waterfront where tourists congregated and vendors sold everything from little bronze pepper grinders to glass candle lanterns to the Turkish carpets that are everywhere along the coast. They stopped to watch a portrait artist rapidly sketching the likeness of a woman sitting self-consciously in a chair while everyone else peered over the artist's shoulder at the conjuring feat that is art.

A dancing bear shuffled down the crowded street, not actually dancing but nonetheless a real live bear restrained only by a leash and its master's will. Diego kept a wary eye out for this Turkish phenomenon and took considerable pains to keep a wide distance between his own little black bear and the big shambling beasts he so resembled.

Then there were the ice cream sellers, who dispensed not only ice cream but also merriment and sleight of hand. Turkish ice cream is not great by Italian or American standards—too sticky and congealed —but it lends itself to an amusing act. The ice cream seller digs out a wedge of his product with a two-foot-long wooden spatula, presses it into the cone, and then extends it to the child, the ice cream cone sticking to one end of the spatula while he holds the other. When the child tries to grasp the cone, the seller with a deft twist of his wrist turns the cone up. The child's hand grasps at empty air and everybody laughs—even the child. Again and again the cone is proffered, the child reaches for it, and some other sleight or antic whisks it away just as the fingers close. It is a deft and amusing performance, and the Turks never tire of it.

Santos and Diego's favorite Turkish food was the diner—lamb sliced into wafer-thin pieces and stacked hundreds on a skewer from which the vendor could slice shreds off the outsides to make a very tasty sandwich. This was the Turkish answer to a hamburger. Since Diego was a generous soul, he always favored his dog with a few shreds of lamb, with which Santos was always well content.

That, by the way, is one of the admirable spiritual qualities of a dog. A dog is happy to be remembered with a share, even so much as a crumb. It's the act of the gift that brings the shine to a dog's eyes; one never hears a dog whining that it didn't get its fair share. A pauper who shares a morsel of his dry crust receives the same grateful devotion as a pasha who clogs his lapdog's arteries with marinated sweetmeats off a golden platter.

Diego and the dog made it back to the boat just before the storm broke overhead. Thunder and lightning were accompanied by a downpour of such intensity that the streets flooded and gutters and storm drains overflowed and poured like rivers into the harbor. Diego checked on the anchors and their chafing gear in the wild deluge, getting soaking wet before going below to his mother's praises and a steaming cup of cocoa. With hatches pulled shut and portholes dogged down, the three of them ignored the pounding rain outside, had supper, and eventually went early to bed.

The next morning all went normally. Santos appeared at the aft cabin porthole, jumped down onto the bed, and said hello. Breakfast happened and the day's work began, which involved painting a badly worn section of the foredeck. Diego went up into the cockpit to get the paint and brushes out of the cockpit locker, and when he lifted the lid found himself staring at a rat. It cowered behind a paint can, petrified.

"Santos! A rat!" Diego called out. Santos sprang up to the box, looked inside, and sprang back barking—but did nothing. Both Dorothy and Diego were amazed, having assumed Santos would be on the vermin in a flash. They encouraged him to attack, but Santos kept his distance. When Diego poked the thing with the nearest implement, a tube of caulking, it jumped out of the paint locker and ran down the deck, Santos howling in pursuit. But when it took shelter underneath a coil of rope, the dog screeched on the brakes and refused to get any closer than a couple of feet.

Impasse. Santos wouldn't kill it, the rat wasn't going to fling itself overboard, and the real possibility existed that it would suddenly break and bolt through a hatch and once down below get irretrievably lost—a nightmare prospect. Reluctantly Diego fetched his BB gun and hit the rather small, young, and pathetic rat with three pellets, killing it. After watching it awhile to make sure it was dead, they flipped it into the harbor with the blade of an oar.

What to make of Santos's behavior? The phrase that came to mind was "All sound and fury, signifying nothing." This blowhard of a dog. We couldn't believe it. Then we began thinking—we'd never seen him hurt anything at all. If he were really so vicious as he pretended to be, he would have killed something by now. Santos could have hurt chickens, baby goats, lizards, little kittens—all of which he adored to chase but had never made the slightest effort to harm. All he ever did was to nose them, encouraging them to run, with a bemused quality on his face, almost a tenderness.

Our dog, in his heart of hearts, didn't have it in him to kill another animal. The great warrior, vanquisher of elephants, counter of coup on hogs and donkeys, the bane of all ratdom, was a pacifist. Now it all fit together. He chased things strictly for sport and ego validation. He couldn't stand the sight of blood.

We wondered how the rat had gotten out to our boat and concluded that it must have been washed out of its nest in a sewer by a flash flood and carried into the harbor. Blinded by rain, swimming by instinct, deafened by the scream of the wind and the loud splatter of thousands of raindrops on the surface, it had paddled in circles, getting weaker, until it bumped into our anchor chain. It must have climbed the chain, got on deck via the knightheads, and found the best shelter it could in the cockpit box.

Maybe Santos could tell this was no brazen in-your-face rat but a pathetic displaced animal, young and afraid and eager to get off the boat—if only there weren't all that water. Maybe he felt sorry for it.

I don't know. I'd had a theory about Santos for some while, and this seemed to back it up. Let me preface it by saying I do not believe in reincarnation, since as far as can be ascertained no one actually *knows* what's going on in this world. But the idea of reincarnation has been around for millennia, and it's entertaining, explains a lot, and is at least as feasible as the belief that wine and bread turn into actual blood and flesh in a communicant's throat or that heaven is a place where one can get gloriously laid (Muslim) or never laid (Christian) or spend the rest of eternity with harp in hand intoning "alleluja!" and "selah" to a deity who enjoys the adulation.

For a long while I presumed Santos was so developed as a dog that in his next life he would come back as a human. Now I began to reconsider. Perhaps he had been a human in his last life, maybe Alexander the Great, a brilliant and charismatic individual who'd fallen way back on the evolutionary scale by using his gifts for violent purposes. So, in this, his present incarnation, the old charm and martial spirit remained, but with it was mixed a horror of violence.

The little dog's persona took on a new depth. He seemed suddenly more vulnerable, more admirable, his pursuit of ferocity a lifelong bluff that masked a gentle nature in a small body. In retrospect we were sort of glad he hadn't ripped the terrified little mammal to pieces and stained his muzzle with its blood.

Now we loved him—and respected him—more than ever.

TWENTY-SEVEN

GREECE TO GAMBIA

When we finally left the Aegean, October was well advanced and autumn gales became a threat. Consequently we sailed when we could and holed up when the weather got bad. Beautiful weather ushered us away from Kos and kept us moving across the Aegean, leaving Kithera to the south and Cape Malea to the north. Skirting the Pelopponesian capes, we arrived at Methoni. This key location in the Venetian spice trade was fortified so mightily that from a distance the walls and towers of the citadel, lifting above the horizon, seemed to have been built on the open sea.

We were still getting the dinghy into the water when Alon swam out to us. The 18-year-old son of friends, he was taking a year off before starting college. His presence on board changed the dynamic of the voyage—now Diego had someone to relate to who was not three times his age. Alon knew how to play Go! and was good enough to often beat Diego. He was also an excellent high school gymnast, strong and lithe, though short. This inspired Diego, who was enjoying a growth spurt, getting big and strong enough to be of considerable use. Suddenly he took pleasure in working the boat, being an authority, showing Alon how to raise the sails and haul on the anchor.

From Methoni we sailed across the Ionian to Sicily and coasted around its south shore, continuing on past Malta because the island had a fanatical "no pets ashore" policy. Attractive as its anchorage and famous fortifications were, we took no chances, staying well out to sea and making our next landfall at Bizerte, in Tunisia.

Bizerte had been a major port when the Barbary pirates were depopulating the coastal regions of the northern Mediterranean with their slave raids. Long before, in Roman times, it had been the second city of the Carthaginian heartland. Its excellent harbor offered equally good protection from weather and enemy raiders, and its location at a Mediterranean chokepoint positioned it to intercept shipping between western Europe and the Levant. Between the inner and outer harbors, an impressive fortress wall encircled a small city. We spent some interesting hours wandering through this medieval stronghold.

But there was something odd about Bizerte.

While we waited for favorable weather we finally figured it out. There were no other dogs, and there weren't many dog enthusiasts. Unlike in Greece or Spain, no one asked about Santos, what breed he was or whether he would grow bigger . . . the usual questions. The place was eerily quiet. Instead of dogs, there were cats—cats sitting on the ledges of apartment windows, picking their way along glass-topped walls, and peering out of gloomy doorways. All those cats put Santos off. He was more subdued than we'd ever seen him as we passed through the gloomy, high overhung narrow streets. He didn't fling himself against his leash, he kept his head down to avoid making eye contact, and the smells in the cobblestones streets held no delights for him. He gave no chase to cats—he knew he was in enemy territory

To tell the truth, we too were a little uneasy walking the town. The buildings were run-down and seemed too quiet. People stared with open hostility. Old ladies talking to friends would see us coming and quickly draw their veils over their faces, holding them in place with their teeth so that all we saw of them was their burning black eyes, fixed suspiciously on us. Tunis was the capital of the Palestine Liberation Organization, which had distributed an anti-U.S. propaganda poster that was displayed in many shop windows. It showed Uncle Sam devouring babies, with blood dripping from his mouth—a startling image for us gringos. Our desire to be gone increased daily.

Twice we left but had to put back because of bad weather and unfavorable winds, but on the third try we got up and around Africa's northernmost point and made good progress to the west. Late in the afternoon, however, we saw a long wall of black cloud moving toward us.

As the roll cloud approached we took positions at the shrouds with halyards in hand, ready to douse jib and main. We just got them down before the first blast of cold air hammered us. Under staysail and mizzen we reeled to the punch but rode the rest of the wind easily enough, motorsailing through the leftover slop. We arrived off Sardinia's south coast two days later, having motored most of the way, and put into San Pietro on its west side for only a few hours. Alon and Diego took the dinghy ashore to give Santos a walk and buy some supplies, and then we set sail again. A northeast mistral was predicted to sweep down the channel between Sardinia and Menorca, and we wanted to catch it. The passage would be rough and stormy, but the wind would drive us west for free—and diesel prices had climbed to as much as $4 a gallon as we traveled westward.

We reefed down and changed to the small jib at dusk to prepare ourselves for the predicted gale, but the wind never really materialized. Instead we got lightning.

It flickered ominously in the distance all night, and during Diego's watch it passed overhead. As he sat there nervous in the dark, guiding the boat, a brilliant flash of light would illuminate the sails and a bolt of unimaginable power would rivet the sea. The image lasted only an instant but was so bright and intense that it quivered in the mind's eye until replaced by a new stroke, and all the while the tumbling, tearing crack of thunder sounded like the very fabric of the firmament being ripped asunder.

"Dad! There's lightning!" he called out, as the rain poured down, seeping its way through the seams and openings in his raingear.

"I know son. You OK?"

"I guess so. It's kinda scary."

"You got that right. But I think it's passed over now." Within a minute another heart-riveting crack of doom drilled into the sea directly ahead of the bow.

"Wow, that was a close one, Dad! What'll we do?"

"Nothing. There's nothing we can do. We're in God's hands now. If he wants us we'll go peaceably."

"My boots are filled up with rain. . . ."

"Make sure your trouser cuffs are outside your boots so that rain can't run into them."

"OK. . . ." He sounded so forlorn and bedraggled that I braced myself to leave the relative comfort of the cabin and join him.

"Want me to come keep you company?" No answer.

"Here, just let me find my foul-weather gear," I said. "Aaahh, damn! It's wet. . . . Just a second, I'll get a dry one. . . ." But before I got to it, he called again.

"Dad?"

"Yeah."

"You don't have to come up. I can handle it...." He trailed off, dubious, then came back stronger. "I've already got company. Santos is under my rain jacket. Every time it thunders he. . . ."

A searing flash of white illuminated Diego's awestruck face for a stark, stroboscopic instant, followed by a dreadful crack like the sound of an ancient oak exploding at its core, struck by inconceivable voltage that vaporized the sap of every cell in a heartbeat. Cascades of thunder quaked and ricocheted through the far reaches of the heavens, shook the sea, rumbled in our blood.

"Good dog . . . good dog! That's a boy!" Diego was clutching the dog with both hands, his eyes wide, a quaver in his voice. "Are you scared of the thunder? Huh? Don't worry, our watch is almost done." He kept up a brave patter meant to reassure the animal—and himself. Thankfully the next stroke sounded farther away, and the next. After awhile I went back to my bunk, leaving my brave son and his loyal companion to steer us through the night.

* * *

When Raff got word that we'd be going to Africa he promptly took a term off from Dartmouth and traveled to Isla Formentera in the Balearics, a Spanish archipelago off the eastern shore of the Iberian peninsula. He arrived waving enthusiastically from the top deck of the ferry from Ibiza. As soon as he debarked onto the dock he stripped down to his underwear, and with a great shout dove in to swim out to the boat—his preferred way to rejoin us after any long absence. He patted Santos affectionately.

"Remember me, boy? Eh? Eh? That's a boy!" as the dog leaped about on his hind legs and chewed at Raff's hands with an exuberant growl.

The brothers were delighted to be together again, and Santos, as always, was the littlest brother, the pride of the family. We sailed for Alicante, fast-growing port and tourist destination on the Spanish mainland. After one look at the city's broad waterfront paseo, with its patterned cobblestones and exotic palms and bustling sidewalk cafés, Raf returned to *Breath* declaring, "OK Santos, time to saddle up the doggus!" Out came the flashy red harness and leash while Santos pranced on his hind legs, groaning with anticipation. The three boys paraded Santos around for hours every day and never lacked for senoritas to talk to. Raff, having learned Russian, was now working on Spanish. Always eager to meet new people, he hadn't forgotten Santos's effectiveness as an icebreaker.

Our last stop in Spain was at Tarifa, a beautiful whitewashed town on a hill not far past Gibraltar. There, tied up to the old stone quay, we prepared for our thousand-mile sail to the Canaries.

Santos recognized only too well the preparations for a long voyage—the buzz of activity as shopping bags with extra provisions were brought aboard and stowed in lockers below, our hose extended to the shore to fill the tanks with water, extra fuel jugs filled and lashed to the cabin sides, the dinghy hoisted on deck and tied down, anchors and lines lashed, loose gear taken below. A sea voyage was definitely in the offing. That in itself was bad enough, but what was worse, his mistress had taken out her old leather suitcase and was filling it with clothes—never a good sign. He hung around her needfully the whole day before we left, insinuating himself onto her lap, getting underfoot, whimpering. When I called to him he pointedly ignored me—the author of his troubles—and gazed steadily up at Dorothy with pleading eyes.

When Dorothy stepped off the boat with her suitcase and sat on the seawall, and then the engine went on and the boys started casting off dock lines—and then the boat started moving while his mistress was still on land! waving goodbye! the distance between her and the boat widening alarmingly!—Santos gave a mournful cry and dashed to the stern, teetering on the rudderhead, balancing on three legs while beckoning helplessly with the remaining forepaw. Diego reached him just in time and bundled him into his arms, reassuring him. Even so the little dog stood for a long time on the after deck, gazing at the diminishing town.

He got over it, and the boys spent a lot of time with him on the ten-day voyage. And some time later, after we had reached the Canaries, Dorothy returned—she had flown to the States to be with her aged parents for Thanksgiving. Santos was suffused with joy for days after her return.

* * *

We spent two weeks in Tenerife, tied stern-to the quay in the fishing harbor behind the long, massive breakwater—a great spot. It was free, for one thing, and very sociable, with cruising yachts tied up to both sides and big ships coming and going, their polyglot crews walking by at all times of the day or night. Here Raffy's best friend from childhood, Amos, tracked us down after quitting his job and catching a flight.

Fired up by the prospect of adventure, the four boys clicked into a great crew. They cooked breakfast every morning—invariably French toast—worked on the boat until mid-afternoon, and then knocked off to swim off the breakwater in the clear sea, work out, play tennis at the fishermen's club, and play uproarious hands of whist until late in the night. Young Diego, a necessary fourth at cards, basked in his camaraderie with the older guys.

Santos loved Tenerife. He was constantly at the center of attention, patrolling our deck as he did and giving a short flurry of barks at anyone who came by—sailors, lovers strolling the waterfront, locals bringing their families to see the boats.

Every morning he and Diego made the pre-breakfast bakery run for hot loaves of long Spanish bread. They left at dawn, before anyone else was stirring, the boy riding a borrowed bike down the empty seaside boulevard, the dog running alongside on a leash, the early-morning breeze fresh in their faces, the island of Grand Canaria sitting blue on the horizon across the calm sea. On a side street lined by orange trees they bought the day's supply of warm bread for several boats. On the way back they would stop at an overlook and watch the sun come up, eating warm, fresh bread with butter, then hurry back to the port and an enthusiastic reception .

Lastly my buddy David, a lanky affable south Georgian, managed to squeeze five weeks off from his Atlanta business. Not long after he arrived in the Canaries, we completed our inoculations, stocked up on water, diesel, olives, wine, chocolate, and ham, and set sail for Africa.

TWENTY-EIGHT

DENTON BRIDGE

We made the 900-mile run to Gambia in six days with the Portuguese trades boisterous at our backs. Every night stars gleamed and the black sea leaped with phosphorescence, but on the last night, closing with the coast, we felt a change. When the compass light grew dim, I tapped the glass and light shone through bright where my fingertips had been. I traced a line in the dust.

Harmattan.

The word carried freight— danger, desert, masked bedouins— associations with the Sahara, from which this hot, dry wind blew, dessicating the already marginal fields of the Sahel, carrying a thick pall of fine red silt far out to sea, even as far as the West Indies.

Daylight revealed a deplorable amount of Mauretania's precious topsoil on *Breath*. Mud grimed the deck where spray had landed. Grit filled our nasal passages and irritated our eyes.

Worse, we couldn't see more than a mile through the clouds of swirling dirt. The Admiralty coast pilot warned that this was a dangerous coast to approach in harmattan weather because it was low and featureless, a mangrove swamp fronted by the aptly named "Stop In Time Bank." A vessel might be sailing in three to four fathoms and abruptly go aground without seeing land and with no warning from the depth finder.

Furthermore, we were unable to see either the horizon or the sun. Without either one, my old faithful sextant was useless, and I had yet to buy a GPS. Fortunately the continental shelf in this area declines so regularly—with the notable exception of the bank—that by taking soundings we could gauge our distance from shore, giving ourselves a rough longitude. Armed with that I managed to take a noon sight for latitude and got a position fix that guided us close enough to spot—and follow—a cargo ship heading in to port.

We used the engine at speed to keep the freighter in sight.

Attracted by *Breath*'s bow wave, a pod of a dozen dolphins showed up to ride it. They came jumping and breaching, full of the joy of life. All took an obvious interest in Santos, cruising by and rolling up to watch him with one eye out of the water, while he knew nothing to do but bark incessantly. A big bull, the obvious leader, was distinctly larger than the rest, and we could discern a clear pattern of white scars on his flank, perhaps the result of fights with sharks. He hung amidships on the starboard side, his speed exactly matching that of the sailboat. Santos stayed by the boat's waist, up on the deckbox, a position of power, his slowing bark strong and staccato. Dog and bull dolphin were three or four feet apart. For several long minutes the bull stayed near, eyeing us occasionally. He seemed to be enjoying the dog's frenetic racket.

"Look at him checking Santos out," I said to Dorothy. "He must have seen other mammals on a boat before, and perhaps he is trying to categorize him, an ocean Linnaeus."

Dorth laughed at me. "Yeah. . . . And don't you think his winking at us was a sign to show he was our equal as we watched the silly barker together?"

I went below to consult the charts, and while I was gone Dorothy heard a distinct clicking that she thought was communication addressed to the dog. She had worked with dolphins for a short while and was also closest to the dog, so the rest of us skeptics had to concur.

Raffy went down to consult the encyclopedia and found out that these were Atlantic humpback dolphins. They travel in small groups, frequenting the shallow waters of the continental shelves, and the humps on the backs of this pod made us fairly confident we were identifying them correctly.

These dolphins have a traditional tolerance of man, and for centuries a symbiotic relationship linked dolphins with shore-based fishermen. Carthaginian fleets of the sixth century B.C., exploring for gold down the Atlantic coast of North Africa, reported that fishermen would spread their long seine nets as far into the ocean as possible—one end on the beach, the other seaward—and would signal dolphins by beating the water with flat sticks. This set up a vibration that dolphins could sense and summoned them to herd schools of fish into a more compact ball that the seine nets could get around. Then the people on shore would start pulling in the seaward end, corralling more fish for humans and dolphins.

Dolphins have been reported many times to help people swim back to land. There is a story from Greek antiquity of the famous singer Arion, from Corinth, who was going to be killed by pirates. He sang a song and jumped into the sea, and dolphins came to rescue him. Since then, stories of dolphins have been told in many parts of the world, and there are plenty of examples in modern times of dolphin rescues. Dolphins relate to man like no other animal that is living wild and free. Later we would have reason to wonder if they also relate to dogs.

* * *

We had heard about The Gambia from the Italian sailor and doctor who had wintered with us at the dock in Seville. He had rhapsodized about the great river, unusually navigable for hundreds of miles. It's a watery artery to the African heartland, home of hippos and crocodiles, marvelous birds, towering riverine jungle, and villages that had never seen a tourist. Our goal was to get as far upriver as our draft would allow, but first we had to clear customs, find a chart and tide tables for the river, take on fresh water that was safe to drink, replenish our vegetables, and get a feel for what we would need. Accordingly we anchored off Banjul, Gambia's capital.

The port wasn't impressive at first sight. Offering the only landlocked harbor with a deepwater entrance in a thousand miles of coast, its quiet backwaters enticed old tramp steamers and barges to their final resting places. They lay where they had foundered, in the mud on the shallow bottom, their superstructures filigreed with rust.

Environs ashore struck the same note. Dust billowed up from Banjul's streets, exhalations rose from its open gutters, and plaster peeled from its buildings. Goats and sheep lived in the town, cheek to jowl with their owners in tightly packed dwellings. Once we looked past appearances, however, the place began to grow on us. Little children bolted out of their dwellings to grab us merrily by the hand, and old men nodded courteously from where they squatted around open fires brewing strong tea. The drab streets emphasized the brilliant dress of the women: long skirts with batik patterns in red, green, and blue with matching blouse. Often we'd see a contrasting wrap around the middle, with two baby feet sticking out on each side of the mother's waist. One young mother wore a robe of midnight velvet splashed with gold. She looked like a princess put to drudgery, walking past an open ditch with a baby strapped to her back and a bundle of firewood balanced on her head.

A throng flowed through the narrow aisles of the public market, where women sat behind jute sacks stuffed with rice or peanuts and giant calabashes holding exotic produce whose uses were a mystery to us—clods of earth, peeled twigs, clumps of bark, brightly colored powders. Fabric vendors unrolled their wares with a blaze of color, while ragged "small boys" hawked kola nuts, an ancient stimulant, to a crowd diverse with Bambara tribesmen from Mali, traders from Senegal, soldiers, beggars, housewives, Arabs from Mauritania, refugees from Liberia, and, most notably, "marabouts"—bearded holy men in pristine white robes with piercing eyes and hypnotic amulets of polished brass, antelope horn, and finely worked leather that swung from their necks as they jostled past housewives haggling over fish for supper.

* * *

Santos kept up his guard the whole time he was in Africa—it was not his favorite place. For one thing, in Africa animals occupy quite a different niche in the social order than in the U.S. or Europe. People take an intense interest in them, but instead of being adored pets and soulmates, animals are valued for their utility as food or labor—or feared. Wild animals are still a part of life in Africa, or at least a vivid part of the cultural memory. People told us of hyena attacks, women being "sexed" by baboons, hippos upsetting dugouts, crocodiles dragging a child from the riverbank.

There were no other dogs that even remotely resembled Santos. Time and again we would leave him outside a store in a village and come out to find fifteen or twenty people standing around the dog, speculating loudly. They might have been wondering what kind of animal he was, or, for all we knew, whether he'd make a decent meal. We were eventually relieved on that score when an informant told us that no one would consider eating him because he looked too much like a wild pig, and most Gambians are Muslims, restricted by religion from eating pig flesh.

When we first landed at Oyster Creek a crowd gathered around him and a lively debate raged in Wolof, until one of the policemen from the bridge checkpoint asked in careful English, "Excuse, sah. What kind of animal it is this one?"

"A dog. A boat dog."

"Aha! They think he is baby 'buki' . . . hyena, sah." And once they mentioned it, the resemblance was unmistakable—the erect pointy ears, no tail, high shoulders, and scaled-back hindquarters.

Santos's all-time personal low took place in Africa. The animals he had dominated so easily back on St. John were quite another story here. He was walking on the leash at Dorothy's side, minding his own business. No sidewalk graced the roadway; the normal throng of people was hemmed in by slow-moving traffic to one side and the festering ditch on the other. People brushed past each other, almost the way ants in passing briefly touch each other's antennae.

Embedded in the oncoming stream of people came an unusual sheep, traveling on its own recognizance, on a mission. It was dirty and ragged—forget about wool—and it looked intelligent . . . and belligerent. A most unusual sheep. When it saw Santos it took immediate umbrage, and far from shying away, lowered its head for battle and went for him. Santos had not put anything to flight since he'd arrived in Africa—he sensed the pastoral vibes—and he had made no provocative move toward this animal whatsoever. He tried to ignore it and retain his dignity, but if he hadn't sought ignominious shelter behind Dorothy's legs he would have been bowled over by this . . . this street sheep! Aggressive, touchy, this was a sheep with attitude, like none he had ever seen at East End.

And if that wasn't bad enough, he had a run-in with an attack chicken in a village upriver—a hen with chicks that made a beeline for him, enraged to see him on her turf. What was he supposed to do? He wasn't going to kill it, so he had to retreat . . . from a lousy chicken.

Africa was a topsy-turvy place for a First World dog, but all that was nothing compared with what was about to happen.

* * *

After clearing in with the officials and getting a feel for Banjul, we moved the boat to Oyster Creek, a serpentine but navigable waterway that branches off from the Gambia estuary and empties into the Atlantic several miles from the city. The coastal highway crosses it at Denton Bridge, a low fixed span set on large concrete pillars. Just before it gets to the bridge, the creek widens enough— about 200 yards or so across—to form safe anchorage for small craft. The police checkpoint at the bridge, where all buses and taxis had to stop, made it convenient for catching a ride to the tourist hotels or back to Banjul. Here we spent the last week of 1990, our young crew enjoying the nightlife and New Year's Eve in the hotels.

Nick, an English sailor we'd become friendly with, who had lived for years in The Gambia, offered to let us tie alongside his boat to fill our water tanks from his hose ashore, which ran to a house hidden at a distance by trees. This was a kind offer. Safe drinking water was nothing to take for granted in Gambia, and since the alternative would be to fill our five-gallon jugs from a spigot at the police checkpoint and lug them out to *Breath*, we accepted the offer with alacrity. We had nearly 400 gallons to load. In the morning, with the tanks full, we would begin our voyage to Basse Santa Su, over 200 miles upriver.

We tied up outboard of Nick's boat at slack tide, deploying a stern anchor just in case something went wrong. As we started to fill, the water pressure dropped off to a trickle, and Nick invited us to spend the night tied alongside. The pressure would pick up after midnight, he assured us, and by dawn we'd be full. We could then get away on the flood tide.

All this attention to the state of the tide was important because Nick's berth was quite close to the first of two high-voltage powerlines that hung in parabolas over the river from pylons on the bank. These cables, about 100 feet apart, carried the power supply to Serrekunda, the Gambia River's biggest town.

"How high are those powerlines, Nick?" asked David during the supper we shared together.

"Don't rightly know, mate. Lower in the middle of course. I've been through close to shore where they rise higher, but my mast is a good deal shorter than yours."

"What would happen if we hit it?" asked Alon.

"Don't even think about it," said Dave. "Four people in a 22-foot daysailer in that lake near Atlanta . . . ya'll hear 'bout them? When their mast touched electric wires?"

"No," I replied. "What happened?"

"Fried. Toast. Had to scrape 'em off the damn deck with a spatula. And that was just ordinary wires. This here's high-tension wire." He pronounced it "wahr."

After supper we talked about the river, learning from Nick where the best anchorages were and which villages had the best markets. Before turning in, Dorothy and I sat on deck and watched the full moon rising in the clear sky. Its light had turned the muddy waters of Oyster Creek to quicksilver; not so much as a zephyr stirred the surface. Just a week ago we had sailed in off a thousand miles of ocean. Snugly anchored behind mud banks and mangroves, we could still hear surf thundering on the bar just beyond the highway bridge.

Santos lay contentedly in Dorothy's lap, into which he'd climbed as soon as she sat down. For a brief while he let his attention flag as his mistress scratched behind his ears. When we retired to our bunk in the aft cabin, Dorothy bent low to nuzzle him goodnight. He touched his nose to her face, his ardent eyes flared , then he returned to his chosen station on the cabintop, from which he could see the whole boat, and which he vacated only in the worst weather.

* * *

We were sound asleep just past midnight when our dock lines began to creak. At first I thought a passing boat may have sent a wake, but Santos would have barked at any boat that came by. The creaking got louder, and by the time I got on deck to investigate, the ropes had gone from creaking to groaning with stress. Santos was gingerly sniffing at the loudest cleat, bristling his ruff, expressing his misgivings with a low, sporadic growl.

On such a still night there could only be one cause—current— and a glance over the side at the small branches speeding past the hull alarmed me. The ebb tide had tripled its usual maximum rate. *Breath* was caught in a freak tidal phenomenon with her long, deep keel tied up stern-to the stream, the wrong way, like a 20-ton weathervane with its feathers to the wind.

The current took an ever more powerful hold on her keel, determined to wrench it the right way around. Within fifteen minutes the groaning of the lines was turning into shrieks, and the cleats on Nick's boat looked ready to snap. Nick appeared on deck distraught. He had never seen such a sudden acceleration of the river before and feared for his boat. His lines were already stretched bar taut to stakes in the bank. If anything gave, both boats would spin off grappled together, helpless to avoid destruction. It was incumbent on me to cast off from Nick, turn *Breath* around, and anchor bow-to the stream—right away, before things got any worse.

That was easier said than done, however. We were in a difficult spot. Just a few boat lengths downstream, the first of the two high-tension powerlines hung across the creek, and the other was only a hundred feet or so beyond. Close beyond them loomed Denton Bridge, its low fixed span resting on massive concrete pillars. If our maneuver went wrong, if we couldn't complete the turn in time, our mainmast might trigger the live wires. And if the boat somehow made it under the wires and hit the bridge beyond, both masts would be pinned by the roadway while its hull was sucked under and sunk.

And just beyond the bridge lay the bar, pounded by the heavy surf of the open Atlantic.

I called everyone up on deck to move the boat. As they hurried topsides, Santos sensed something wrong. Why was his mistress up and about after midnight? Why was she starting the engine at this hour? Why was the normally bantering crew so quiet? He stood by, poised to react.

We cast off the lines and hung briefly to the stern anchor we had set that afternoon as a safety. Tethered from her stern, *Breath* yawed violently out into the stream, then veered back again, almost hitting boats to either end of her giddy arc.

The anchor was dragging, but very slowly. We had time to try motoring hard astern while my strong crew hauled on the line. Hopefully we could work the boat backward to gain more room from boats moored nearby to make our turn. We needed it; *Breath*'s long straight keel and heavy displacement were more suited to making long steady runs on the high seas than sharp turns in constricted waterways.

We succeeded, taking in rope, but most of it smoked through my crew's hands when they went to cleat it. The hydraulic forces were enormous, stretching the nylon line like a rubber band. Each time they managed to cleat it, it writhed against the teak bitts and screeched like an animal in agony. Santos hovered around the boys' heels until he got tripped on and added his sharp yelp to the rope's shriek.

"Come here Santos!" called Dorothy, a center of calm sitting in the cockpit as shouts flew overhead and bodies lurched back and forth. She held him in her lap and tried to soothe him. He was quivering with excitement.

Again three of the boys won and lost rope in the struggle to cleat it without crushing a finger. Then, as the boat sheered out from shore, the rope ran amok. In rapid succession it pinned Dave against the mizzen shrouds, almost nipped Alon's thumb off against the cleat, and jumped to the rudderhead, threatening to break it off until Raff, making a dangerous leap, wrested it free.

My friend Marco sprang to mind—one-legged Marco, whose thigh had been caught in a coil and instantly severed while docking a ferry in strong winds. Our own line was out of control. If it snapped, its backlash might take an eye, or even a life. We needed to be free of it. I shouted, "Cast off the anchor line!" and out it snaked, irretrievable.

I gunned the engine into a turn and almost turned the boat around, but the current ran even swifter near the middle of the stream and suddenly threatened to skewer us on the sharp steel bow of a derelict racing yacht riding to its mooring there. I steered to go around behind it, but halfway into the turn realized we were going to hit the wire. In desperation I steered back toward the bank where the drooping wire rose higher to the pylon. Dorothy clutched the dog and we all held our breaths.

We just tipped it. There was a flare of blue flame, a meteor shower of sparks, and we were through, unharmed—but the second wire was coming up fast, and directly behind it loomed the stone bridge. I flung the helm over hard and jack-hammered the diesel, but we struck anyway, a long, scraping skid, the top six inches of our mainmast pinned hard against the powerline.

Forty thousand volts exploded down the shrouds, a hideous incandescence lit up the sky, and a powerful roaring and hissing filled the air. Time stopped. Transfixed, we watched welding fires flare every four feet down the mainstay. We heard a racket down below: the switchboard spewed molten aluminum, fuses shot from their sockets, popping like automatic gunfire, and smoke began to billow out the hatches.

Cars on the highway screeched to a stop, and police came sprinting from the checkpoint across the bridge. Nick stood rooted in horror to his deck, while Louis, his wizened old watchman, sobbed, "Boss! They're dying! They're dying!" All watched as blue fire glowed about the rig like a deadly spirit. No sound came from the boat save the crackle of electrocution.

Suddenly the fireworks stopped. The current had pulled the boat's hull downstream until the cable had rolled over the mast top, and now we were headed through the perilously narrow corridor between the second wire and the bridge, toward the far bank, which was looming up inexorably. The good news was that the wire had pivoted the boat on its mast, and we had turned enough to face the current and for the first time gain control of the boat. But the bad news was that we had no way out.

For a long moment we were frozen, between worlds, unable to speak; even irrepressible Santos was stunned into silence. People watching from the shore, seeing no movement and hearing no sound, assumed that we had been killed. Then, from the foredeck, Dave gave a shout.

"Watch out for the wire—it's close!" That broke the spell and we surged back into action.

Santos immediately wriggled free of Dorothy's arms and dashed up to the foredeck.

Dorothy addressed the boys, almost casually. "Fire. Fire below. Get the extinguishers." They flung themselves down the hatches to blast everything that moved with dry chemical.

I couldn't see the wires because the awning was still up. Guided by shouts, I brought her carefully around in that narrow aisle, afraid to hit the wire but absolutely terrified of hitting the pilings with our rudder. We proceeded back toward the other bank, minds racing, wondering what to do. We were trapped. There was nowhere to go but back out, under the wires. We'd survived it once, we'd have to brave it again. *Breath*'s Airex foam core between layers of fiberglass would provide the same dampening protection on the way out that had apparently saved us on the way in.

Wheel hard over, throttle full blast, we braced for impact. The masthead hit the cable, erupting like a volcano and sending a torrent of fat red sparks to the deck. They floated down like fallout from a giant sparkler. Dave ducked back under the shelter of the awning, but Santos, eyes fixed ahead, stayed to defend the foredeck. He was still growling for all he was worth when the fiery rain of electrified harmattan dust landed in his fur. Uttering a short shriek, Santos sprinted down the side deck with cinders glowing in his coat, panic in his eyes, and plunged into the water. When he surfaced he was already swimming with all his might for the boat, his paws pumping the water at a desperate rate, his eyes fastened on Dorothy—but the current swept him away.

There wasn't a thing we could do.

An instant later, a blast like a small thunderbolt arc-welded the mainstay just four feet above where Amos had instinctively grabbed it for balance. His body contorted, arched backward, and disappeared over the side into the river. Raffy, at the forward shrouds, flipped backward and fell overboard off the foredeck. Dave fell to the deck, and I was flung back hard against the mizzenmast. We felt the cold quiver of AC voltage tingling in our cells. Directly behind us loomed the stone pillars of the bridge, mere feet away from the vulnerable rudder. The night was on fire, the *boat* was on fire!

A horrible moment followed as I wondered whether Raff would be swept against the hull by the current and be chopped by the big prop that was churning through the muddy water. I couldn't stop or the rudder would be smashed against the concrete pillars, the boat would be sucked under, and people would be killed. The big Ford diesel was redlined, roaring full blast, the night exploding with flashes, when I hit the pitch control of the Hunderstadt propeller for maximum torque.

In the water, Raff felt the prop coming nearer as he bumped along the hull. He managed to position his feet firmly on the hull and gave a mighty shove. Had he neglected to tuck up his legs he would have lost a foot. He surfaced in the roiling water of our prop wash shouting, "Are you all right? Are you all right?" as he saw flames leap and smoke pour out of the main hatch.

Dorothy sat in her frozen calm and said "Fire! Fire!" and Alon leaped to the big main hatch and literally dove through it head first. How he kept from breaking his neck I'll never know, but he landed on his feet and seized a fire extinguisher. Diego had already started spraying an extinguisher when the mosquito net had burst into flames, and now the two of them blasted away, back to back, and quickly quelled the flames as I steered toward safety.

Then we were through . . . off the wire . . . engine hammering steadily in the quiet night air.

Raff, a college swimmer, struck out for the bank, swimming for his life, and barely made it, his hands touching then clutching and clawing at mud and shells even as the current struggled to pull him away. Meanwhile, Amos spread-eagled himself against a bridge piling. He was in just his jockey shorts, and the piling was covered with sharp oysters. He called out at intervals for help, saying, "I'm all right, but it's getting harder to hold on!" We tied up alongside a trawler whose crew handed us lines, looking at us as if they were seeing ghosts. One of them went in a sturdy skiff to rescue Amos.

Against all odds we were safe and sound—all the humans, at least. But there was no sign of Santos.

* * *

Dave and Raffy went that night to call for the dog along both shores. Dorothy and Diego were out the next morning searching the riverbank to the sea and roaming well down the coast before the African sun blazing down on the empty beach drove them back.

A loud knocking on the hull had waked us early in the morning. A policeman was standing on the barge, looking official and expectant. I worried that we had broken some rule, harmed the city's power, or committed some other infraction of which we were unaware.

"Good morning," he said, gravely. "I've come to see if we can help you in any way. Is everyone safe here?"

"Oh yes. We're all here and OK. But we did lose our little dog. He went down the river." "Oh . . . well," said the policeman, "the dog. . . ."

Still, there was hope. An old fisherman mending his nets told Alon that the current had probably set south at well over a knot. The ebb tide had started around midnight and went six hours before reversing. We measured it off on the chart. If he was right, Santos could have been carried six miles down the coast by dawn—to Cape St. Mary, a long bulge of coastline marked by white sand beaches and a number of tourist hotels.

Dorothy put on her walking shoes and said, "I hate to leave you with this shambles, but I won't rest easy until I've searched around Cape St. Mary. Maybe at one of the hotels. Somebody must have seen him!" She gave me a crooked smile and set out with Alon.

They took a transport to Cape St. Mary and walked for miles down the beach, making inquiries at every hotel. She went from the Sunwing to the Senegambia, talking to beach attendants, tourists, and vendors, but nobody had seen or heard of a little black dog. Personnel at the reservations desk bridled at the suggestion that a dog might be in their hotel. Finally, tired and dejected, the seekers sat on a high dune overlooking the sea and faced the likelihood that he hadn't survived—or that if he had, we would never find him. Somehow that seemed worse. Dorothy started to cry, and soon Alon too was blinking back tears.

Yet she came back persistent—offering a reward over the radio, notifying the Denton Bridge police, nailing up hand-printed signs on trees and telephone poles. She asked Samba Sey, a young Gambian who made a living as a yacht agent, to put the word out along the coast and to keep his eyes open.

It was touching, but futile. In plain view beyond the bridge was the Oyster Creek bar, broad flats of hard sand on which pounded row after row of breakers that mounted up like penitentiary walls, massive, forbidding, collapsing with such force that they sent tremors through the earth. The mental image of Santos funneled helplessly into that cauldron made me wince. True, we'd lost him before and he'd always turned up, but this time everybody except Dorothy assumed a shark must have found his battered corpse.

* * *

When we had repaired the damage, it was time to leave Oyster Creek if we wanted to cruise upriver before meeting a deadline in the Virgin Islands. Santos still hadn't turned up. Though he'd never been gone more than a day or two before, Dorothy clung to the hope that her dog would appear unexpectedly.

"Honey," I pleaded, "we've got to get on with our lives . . . do the river, cross the Atlantic, get back to work."

"But what if he survived?" she said. "He was such a strong swimmer. What if he somehow finds his way back here—and we're gone!"

"I find it hard to believe he survived that surf and then swam until dawn," I said flatly. I didn't mention sharks to her.

"Mom," said Raff gently, "I hate to say it but I think Dad's right. Amos and I went out at slack tide that day to see if we could surf those breakers. No way! It would have broken our necks." Amos nodded somberly.

"Sure we would be the first to hear if he had made it," Dave added. "He was the most distinctive damn dog I've ever seen, and y'all put out the word for him up and down the coast. And the reward—a month's pay for a workin' man here—you think they ain't been scouring the bushes for him?"

That stopped her. There was a painful silence as she searched our faces, looking for a reprieve from reality. Then her eyes flooded, her shoulders shook, and her voice broke.

"I just didn't want to abandon hi-hi-him!" Tears rolled down her cheeks. Her agitated sons hugged her, Alon and Amos turned away embarrassed, and Dave gripped my shoulder, concern creasing his homely, honest face. Next morning, with heavy hearts, we hauled the anchor for our long-awaited trip upriver.

Our loss really hit home at a side creek 50 miles upriver where we were anchored awaiting a favorable tide. Suddenly we saw a strange face peering in at the porthole, inquiring politely if we wanted to buy a fish. The fisherman had paddled up silently alongside in a dugout. When Santos was alive that could never have happened. Now we missed the zealous barking we'd so often tried to hush.

And the next day, when Dorothy and I returned from buying bread in the village, the skiff was tied behind the boat and the guys were all down below playing whist and listening to rock and roll. We stood in the dust and the sun, calling in vain for a ride, until one of the boys happened to come on deck and hear us. Santos would have shrilled the alarm for his mistress even before she got to the riverbank.

I remembered then very suddenly what Jean had said when she gave us Santos back on the Indian River in Florida. "Your ship needs a schipperke!" The word "needs" had seemed a little pretentious at the time, but Santos had proven her right a hundred times over. We needed him in myriad ways, from watchdog and ratter to companion and friend, to protector, and even . . . does this sound fatuous? . . . even as mentor, as exemplar.

It came into sharper focus a couple of nights later, when I woke to an empty bed, got up, and found Dorothy sitting in the moonlight. From the way her eyes glistened, I could tell she'd been thinking of Santos.

I sat down and put an arm around her. After a while she spoke.

"You know what I miss most? His shaggy mane filling the porthole. He liked to watch me cook. Now every time a shadow falls over that port it reminds me of the love in those bright black eyes. . . . I miss his little spirit."

"He was as noble in spirit as any person," I said. "Maybe that's what makes me wonder. . . ."

"Wonder what?"

"Well . . . do you realize how incredibly lucky we were? Both our boys could have been killed. Can you imagine calling Alon or Amos's folks to tell them their only son just died? God help me—the captain! So many things could have taken our lives, but we all survived unscathed. It's too . . . too . . . this is weird, but. . . ."

"But what?"

"Somebody had to die."

"Huh?"

"Blame it on my religious upbringing, but I keep seeing Santos as a kind of sacrificial lamb. A bold, warlike sacrificial lamb. You know how I've said that we've always been so lucky—none of our family has even ever broken a bone? And Santos all these years has been heedless of danger, braving it, defying it, almost inviting it. He's been a lightning rod for trouble, who focused it on himself, absorbed it . . . like a mother bird faking a broken wing to draw off the wolf. I mean, the commotion, the excitement has always revolved around him—he's the one who gets lost or kidnapped, not our kids. He's the one who falls overboard—not our child."

We sat quietly for a moment, contemplating the horror. We knew two cruising families that had lost a young child to drowning.

"He's the one who gets hit by cars," I continued. "We've had accidents but not a scratch on our persons. We've had this incredible little creature who's always getting into trouble, while the rest of us live charmed lives. And now, at Denton Bridge, when there must have been thirty different ways we could have died—if the engine had failed, if it had been raining, if the cable had broken—there's Santos again, at the bow, point man, pressing into danger, barking out his challenge: 'You wanna mess with somebody, you got the cojones, try me!' And he took the full weight of it and went into the black void, to be beaten by the breakers, giving up his body to be devoured by sharks—leaving us once again without a scratch. That preposterous little hero!"

My voice broke. Tears flowed down Dorothy's cheeks.

"It's almost like he was sent to us . . . to be a guardian angel . . . in deep disguise. He gave us the last of his luck, then took our place in the jaws of death. He rendered his greatest service at the very end of his life—what a way to check out!"

We watched the moon slip below the treetops.

"Farfetched," said my wife sleepily, "but it's a comforting thought."

"Speaking of farfetched. . . . I haven't told anybody this. When we got off the wires and were steaming up to that trawler, finally safe, I was steering, and I felt a warm light glowing just behind my right shoulder . . . strong. I felt a definite presence in that light. I didn't want to turn around, because I was afraid it would disappear. I don't know what to make of it . . . probably a stressed-out thyroid gland. But at such a moment, hanging between life and death, if one ever gets a glimpse beyond . . . if there is a beyond. . . ."

* * *

Two weeks passed as we made our way 150 miles up the Gambia to Georgetown. On another calm, bone-dry, hazy savanna day, *Breath* was anchored near a large tree overhanging the river. Dorothy and I were reinforcing the awning and watching monkeys cavort while the boys played a boisterous game of whist at the table in the main saloon.

Suddenly I heard an engine. I looked up and saw a yacht motoring upriver, the first we'd seen since Banjul. It was a catamaran flying Italian colors. When they saw our flag, they veered across the river to come near, inspecting us with binoculars before hailing us in a stentorian voice.

"Hello . . . are you the Americans that lost the little black dog?"

"Yes . . . ?" I answered, cautiously.

The whist game below went dead silent.

"I don't say if it is yours, but Samba say that tell you—the police at Denton Bridge have a small black dog was found on the beach."

For a couple of seconds we were struck speechless—then a wave of incredulous joy broke over the boat, and the entire crew tumbled up on deck shouting, "Oh my God! Yes . . .YES . . .YES!"

Could it possibly be? Dorothy and I immediately resolved to return to the coast, but before we left I cautioned the crew.

"Remember, someone might easily have found a stray mutt that was black and brought it in, hoping for the reward. Don't get your hopes too high."

We set off well before dawn the next morning, crossing the river by silent dugout, listening as the birds awoke and began to call. An ancient school bus, rusted to the bone, took us past a couple miles of desolate bush to the central road, where an erratic series of transports took us the rest of the way.

At long last we rolled into Banjul. With hope and trepidation we caught a taxi to the bridge to see if Santos had truly survived. The police officer on duty greeted us warmly.

"You have come for your dog!" he announced, then turned and called peremptorily, "Small boy! Go to fisherman Ceesay's compound and tell him . . . bring the dog!" A ten-year-old barefoot lad who'd been hanging around the door dashed off with the summons. We spoke with the officer, who had been on duty that fateful night, and waited on tenterhooks to see the dog.

Then, there he was, unquestionably Santos, coming down the path from the highway, led on a ratty, frayed piece of polypropylene string. He seemed listless, and he walked with a limp, his head held down. But when Dorothy dropped to her knees and called "Santos!" a charge went through him as if someone had flicked the power back on. His head shot up, his ears snapped forward, his eyes caught fire, and his whole body trembled as that beloved voice registered. Then, like a jet catapulted off a carrier's deck, he leaped into her arms and covered her hands and face with quick, deft licks, squirming with delight. Dorothy buried her face in his thick ruff and hugged him a long time.

This time, when she looked up, the tears in her eyes were a balm to my heart.

The fisherman seemed a good sort. I wasn't sure he was telling the truth when he said that the dog wouldn't eat African food and he'd been obliged to buy a tin of corned beef every day to feed him. If so the mutt had never had it so good, except for his trip with the Thompsons. I protested weakly, the fisherman insisted it was true, and I paid up, ten days times a dollar fifty. Why quibble—one of the family was back from the dead!

The police officer told us that early in the morning after we had hit the wires, a Swedish tourist staying at the Sunwing Hotel, five miles down the coast from Denton Bridge, was walking the beach looking for birds and found Santos. He was battered and exhausted, and the Swede deduced the obvious—that the little animal must have fallen off some vessel and then had some kind of ordeal. He smuggled Santos back into his hotel room and fed him. Thus Santos was at the Sunwing that afternoon when Dorothy arrived to inquire if anyone had seen a small black dog. Nobody had—the Swede had been careful when he violated the hotel rules. When he had to fly home, he gave Santos to the police, who kept him in the station for a couple of days and then gave him to a fisherman to keep until we might return. They had also notified Samba, the self-appointed yacht agent, who passed the word to the Italian catamaran.

We offered the police a cash reward as well, but the officer said, with pride, "No sir, thank you, we are just doing our job."

We spent that night in a Banjul hotel. Dorothy got the key, opened the room, and then came down the back steps to the fence, where Santos was passed over to her. A few minutes later I joined them and saw Santos sleeping blissfully in Dorothy's arms.

"Peter, look at the hoarfrost around his muzzle He looks much older," she said. "And when I was holding him in my lap and patted him along his back, he yelped."

"Something may be wrong with his spine. Not surprising when you remember what that surf was like. Those waves were immense. A maelstrom. Poor guy . . . tough guy . . . lucky guy!"

"I wonder what actually happened to him," she said.

"Well, given the strength of that current, we know he went through the breakers—Raffy barely made it ashore himself, and he's a powerful swimmer. No way Santos could have stemmed that current. And we know that the current was setting strong toward Cape St. Mary, where the Swede found him at dawn. He went overboard about 1 A.M., and the speed, set, and duration of the current dovetail perfectly with the idea that he rode the current until dawn, found himself close to shore at slack tide, and swam in to the beach. He probably dogpaddled toward the lights of shore the whole time the current was whisking him down the coast."

"So all the times he jumped off the boat and swam to some event ashore stood him in good stead," Dorothy exclaimed. "Even the boys throwing him into the breakers at Cinnamon Bay when the north swells were crashing in—and I reprimanded them for having fun at his expense!"

We kept trying to piece together what could have happened after our little dog went overboard, surfaced, and despite his best efforts was carried rapidly away from *Breath* and Dorothy's gaze. Perhaps he saw the orange glow of flames at the portholes and the billow of smoke coming from the hatches, but quickly receding. Then the bridge loomed overhead, and maybe he heard the hubbub of onlookers' excited voices. Maybe he bumped and scraped against one of the 12-foot-diameter stone pilings, cutting himself on the sharp edges of the oysters that grew in profusion there. If so he would have scrabbled frantically for traction, but to no avail. Then the current sucked him through, able to see nothing in that black undercroft except perhaps the red eyes of pigeons, glowing eerily from their nests atop the pillars. Swept back into moonlight, he saw the lights and traffic on the bridge fading into distance, and heard the ominous roar of the surf growing louder, like thunder in an approaching hurricane.

Then the roar was upon him and he was entombed in the cataract, wrenched from air and night, his body slammed against the hard sand bottom. He felt a huge jolt of pain through his left front paw and shoulder. All sense of direction was gone. Lungs bursting, gagging, he popped into the night air at last, gasping and choking, bobbing between breakers, catching his breath, summoning his will once more. Then the next breaker reared up, and tons of furious white water pounded him down once again, scraping him against the sand, knocking the breath out of him, and holding him down as he struggled desperately to find the surface.

Somehow he survived that battering onslaught that would have broken any of our necks. Maybe his body shape, compact and muscular, helped him absorb the impact of being slammed against the sand. Maybe his buoyant ruff hair floated him back to the surface. One thing we knew—he was an incredibly tough, resilient little dog.

Swept out through the surf line at last, he would have been just a small piece of still-living flotsam amid the weed, spew, and trash of an urban delta. Exhausted and bleeding, he may have been scarcely conscious at first, his limbs barely moving while only his buoyant fur kept him afloat. Then, perhaps, he began to swim a measured dogpaddle under the calm, star-shot night, heading for the lights of shore to the south while the current carried him steadily westward toward Cape St. Mary. When dawn and slack water arrived, he must have been close enough to the beach to reach it before the east-going flood tide picked up.

"But what about the sharks?" Dorothy wondered, voicing that thought for the first time.

"Yeah, I know . . . That's what the rest of us were thinking all along . . . that even if he survived the breakers. . . ."

"Isn't this coast notorious for sharks . . . from the slave trade and all?"

"Well, maybe back then. I mean, none of these beach hotels would agree with you. It can't be that bad...." I fell silent. The police had told us that the Swede found the dog torn and bleeding. Santos must have trailed a blood line on his five-mile drift down the coast—a small one, to be sure, but that was all a shark needed.

"You know what?" Dorothy said. "Remember those dolphins we saw at the approach to the river? I'll bet they found him and protected him, kept the sharks away."

"And I thought I was the one with farfetched ideas."

"Well, dolphins have done it before—pushed humans to shore after they fell off a yacht."

"Yup—I wonder if they would relate to a dog though. It's possible...." And yielding to sleep in the warm night, Santos at our sides, we left it at that.

* * *

Next morning we caught a group taxi upcountry. Santos sat quietly on our laps. A fellow passenger, noticing Santos, warned us that if we arrived too late to the Georgetown turnoff there would be no transport, and we would have to walk the two miles of lonely bush to the river crossing in the dark. Hyenas roamed that area at night, and the scent of our dog would surely attract them.

I began monitoring our progress with a tinge of anxiety. A succession of police checkpoints delayed traffic; our driver got detained for having a forged chauffeur's license; and then the car ran out of gas. While we got gas I bought several packages of matches, what passed for a newspaper, and some kerosene, with the hyenas in mind. Sure enough, we arrived at the Georgetown turnoff just after the sun disappeared below the horizon.

Night fell fast. All around us stretched empty bush. We hurried along, three pairs of ears acutely tuned to the evening noises. In the distance something howled. It was answered by a bark—but not from a dog. I soaked the rolled-up newspaper at its end with kerosene and got the matches handy.

About a mile from the river, Santos stopped dead in his tracks and started to growl. The hackles bristled like porcupine quills on his neck—and on mine. Something was hiding in the tall grass just ahead. Santos started to bark, and we heard a whining growl from the bush.

With shaking hands, Dorothy struck a match and touched it to the paper. It blazed up instantly, and I feinted toward the bush waving the flames in front, while Santos barked and Dorothy shouted. The grass shook as something grunted and bolted away. Santos flung himself against the leash and barked frantically even as we dragged him off unceremoniously at a half jog. Then, to our relief, we saw headlights coming and hitched a ride the rest of the way.

* * *

When we got to where we could see the lights of the boat, we gave a shout for the boys and heard their answering blast on the queen helmet shell.

"Do you have him? Did you find Santos?" Raffy called. Dorothy urged the dog to bark. His unmistakable voice rang across the calm river, to be answered by a cheer of wild exuberance.

What a joyful evening it was. Dorothy had bought some treats in Banjul and we had a celebratory supper, toasting Santos with lemonade and Guiness. The little dog's big spirit had carried him through yet again, and his survival hammered home the lesson his whole life exemplified—that with a lot of pluck and a little luck, miracles can happen. The critical factor is not money, size, or anything you can conquer, inherit, or purchase. The critical thing is attitude. And this lesson was Santos's greatest gift to us.

Santos resumed his place in the crew, uncowed by his narrow

escape. A week after his return we were 200 miles upstream, exploring a jungle-choked creek. Rowing and drifting in the skiff, we surprised a troop of baboons sunning themselves on a dead branch overhanging the water. True to form, Santos leaped straight off the bow, a bloodcurdling growl in his throat, and surfaced swimming full tilt. The baboons grudgingly moved into the forest, flinging many a scornful backward glance at our fiery dog, as we headed him off from the riverbank with an oar.

That night, back on *Breath*, a solitary baboon gave a hoarse bark from the riverside forest. Santos bristled with affront and hurled back a piercing retort. In unison the whole baboon clan erupted with a howl of invective, which Santos returned lustily, bouncing stiff-legged off the deck with each passionate bark. For a moment uproar filled the fragrant air, then silence drifted back in.

We praised our doughty dog for upholding *Breath*'s honor and then retired to our beds, leaving Santos back on station, forepaws draped over the cabintop, keeping his watch over the night.

TWENTY-NINE

RUNNING DOWN HOME

It was not until we left Africa that we found out how much that night at Denton Bridge had really affected our dog.

We left the mouth of the Gambia at slack tide in light airs and drifted seaward on the ebb, past Stop In Time Bank into clear soundings and a pronounced swell from the northwest. Sometime after dark we gave up trying to sail and motored until midnight, when we started to catch some breeze. By dawn we were reefed, flying the small jib and making heavy going of it as the brunt of the Portuguese trades in full winter force whistled down from the north—Africa's bulk had kept them some twenty miles offshore. The boat heeled deeply and took steady spray. The motion was unaccustomedly violent after months on the river, and the crew was prone to bed. No one exhibited any interest in a meal, especially not in cooking one. Well into the morning this lethargy persisted, with only the helmsman alert for anchored dugouts that might contain sleeping fishermen— the continental shelf extends a long way to sea off West Africa.

Late in the day we started to get our sea legs.

"Hey Pete! What's the fishing like in these waters?" asked Amos.

"Supposed to be real good, according to what I've read and heard."

"Mind if I get a line in the water?"

"Be my guest. . . . You the man!"

Amos was the best fish cook and the most motivated fisherman, he being the closest thing to a genuine West Indian aboard. He went forward, steeling his stomach to rummage about in the fo'c's'le for fishing line and the yellow feather lure, and emerged looking pale and gulping fresh air. He strung the rig together and ran the monofilament well out, then stuck a matchstick into a retaining loop of the nylon so that it would break when a fish struck. Then he settled back against one of the cockpit uprights, fished out a box of Marlboros, and flicked up the top. He showed me the contents.

"Last one in the pack, eh?" I said.

"Last one in my life!!"

"Seriously?"

"Yep. It's now or never. I threw away the rest. This trip is my best chance. No cigarettes on board and no possibility of scoring any until we get to the Caribbean." He cupped a match and lit it up, smoked a few long drags, and flipped it in a high arc out over the sea.

Next morning, about 250 miles west southwest of Cape Verde, we hooked a big one. The matchstick snapped with a sharp report like a tiny pistol shot, galvanizing the nodding watch to bellow out, "FISH! FISH!" Everybody below stampeded up on deck, some up the companionway and others vaulting up through the main hatch. A great shout went up as the fish, a bull dorado, leaped flailing into the air, slinging off showers of droplets that caught the sun like diamonds, his body glistening gold, blue, and green.

"Slow the boat down! You'll pull the hook outta him! Come into the wind!"

"Don't give him any slack! He'll shake the hook out."

"Look at him jump! Outasight!"

"Amazing! Beautiful—watch the boom! Sheet it in! Sheet it quick!"

"Ohmigod, feel the pull!"

In it came steadily, its beauty and its struggle eliciting a stream of shouts. People ran about the deck, getting in position to heave it over the lifeline, a ticklish maneuver without a gaff. When that was done it commenced to thrash on the deck, making an incredible racket. A 40-pound game fish has a tail that can break a man's arm. When it beats on the deck, wet, trying with all its might to escape, it sets up a powerful, rapid-fire battering that transmits desperation—the noise is unbelievable, especially inside the cabin drum. With the shouts of the crew, it's the most pandemonium the boat ever, normally, sees.

We ran below for a bottle of cheap rum and poured it liberally into the gaping, gasping gills of the poor creature—taking care to avoid the snapping teeth and lashing tail—and immediately it ceased its flogging, fell back in a swoon onto the deck, and peacefully expired, dead drunk.

In the sudden silence we realized what was missing—the dog. Ordinarily he would be barking madly and making dashes at the fish, doing his part to the best of his ability, and we'd be having to fend him off lest he get accidentally bit—but this time he hadn't made a peep. In fact he was nowhere to be seen on deck. We called and whistled, but there was no response.

"Oh no!" Diego said. "We'd better go about and do a reverse course. . . ."

"Wait," said Dorothy. "I'll bet he's down below—let me check."

In a minute she called up through the main hatch, "He's here . . . but he won't come out."

I went below to see, and Dorothy pointed under the main saloon table. I bent down to peer into the gloom, and there he was, backed under the table as far into the corner as he could get, with fear in his eyes and trembling in every limb. Now we began to understand the psychic toll that Denton Bridge had taken. The pandemonium created by killing the fish on deck had triggered memories of that night, and he had taken immediate shelter in the most protected corner of the boat.

* * *

The wind took us close to the Cape Verde Islands, so we stopped at Praia. The port officials warned us to beware of thieves, so we took precautions, always leaving one or two crew aboard, who ferried us ashore and then returned to *Breath* with the dinghy instead of leaving it on the beach, where boys might play in it or steal the outboard. When the shore party returned to the beach, we'd call for Santos, who would be alert on deck and would start barking.

He was quite useful this way because the crew down below couldn't hear what was going on topside, especially when playing an uproarious game of whist and listening to some godawful noise on the tape deck. Santos, on the other hand, was usually alert on deck, especially when Dorothy was ashore. He often gleaned a good idea how long she would be gone by observing what she carried; her canvas grocery bags meant a routine shopping trip, not more than a couple of hours, but the well-worn brown leather suitcase was his cue to misery. Fortunately, that was rare.

Well before she got back he'd start pacing the deck, poking his head into the portholes to confirm that she hadn't somehow slipped aboard. When the breeze was from the shore, he could detect her with his nose even before she arrived, and we'd hear him giving the alarm while we were still walking. His high-pitched bark would cut through anything, even earphones blasting heavy-metal music.

The next day everyone wanted to go ashore to ride the bus the length of the island, so we took a calculated risk and left the dinghy in the care of the local guardia.

The bus drove the whole way on a highway made entirely of cobblestones. We saw peasants bent under loads of wood and farm produce, others leading donkeys, and very few cars—similar to the West Indies of seventy years ago. We saw no other tourists and only one small resort, a complex of cottages that badly needed paint, on a beach with a big swell.

The Cape Verde islands seemed a poor place but abundant in pork. As a former Portuguese possession and hence nominally Christian, the islanders were free to eat pigs, which can be fed on a household's organic garbage—the symmetry of swine. We saw pigs everywhere, running down the deserted streets in the heat of the noonday sun and congregating in mud and rotting fruit. The sight raised one's appreciation for the predominantly Muslim culture of West Africa, where the only pigs are wild ones in the bush.

When we got back to the boat in the late afternoon, Santos was wound up tight as a crossbow and hoarse as a crow. A man came over from a nearby steel ketch with a Belgian flag, the only other yacht in the harbor, to tell us that our dog had fended off a rowboat with two youths on board for at least half an hour, barking and snarling for all he was worth, until the Belgian realized what was happening and came by in his inflatable to confront the would-be thieves.

"Your dog is schipperke, no?" he said, pronouncing the breed name in an unusual way—the correct way I presumed, he being Belgian.

"Yes, it's a Belgian barge dog—your country's dog."

"Hmm. . . ." he frowned. "Is Dutch dog, I think . . . but thees one ver' good . . . strong dog."

I never could figure out why the Belgians we met always claimed the schipperke was a Dutch animal, while the Dutch proclaimed it to be Belgian. Neither country seemed eager to claim the honor.

* * *

The next morning we pulled up anchors and headed for the island of Fogo. Its contour lines drawn on a chart draw and catch the eye—about ten tightly drawn concentric circles, each representing a thousand feet of elevation. And the island lived up to our expectations. It was visible from afar by way of its astonishingly steep and perfect 10,000-foot cone, the most emphatically volcanic island any of us had ever seen. We looked for an anchorage, but the island is just about round, devoid of coves and headlands or any kind of harbor. There were only landing places on beaches with more or less surf, where we'd feel uneasy leaving the boat for even an hour, much less the entire day it would take to climb the mountain. I could imagine being on top of the mountain, almost two miles high in the rarefied exhilarating air, and looking down to see the boat dragging anchor toward a line of breakers.

So we reluctantly carried on to Ilheu Brava in a wind that had grown stronger by the day since we'd left the African coast and was now blowing a near gale. The only anchorage with a safe approach was a cove on the leeward side, into which we tucked with two anchors on a narrow shelf of sand. There we sat for over a week, rolling in the swell at the foot of precipitous green mountains, off a scattered little village that lined the beach. We waited for the weather to moderate, but each day the wind whistled, and gusts shrieked through our rigging. When we walked a short distance up the road we could see the rocky north tip of the island and watch the tumultuous seas sweep past the point, lavish white crests cascading down the faces of the tumbling waves. I didn't want to start our passage in seas as rough as that.

To while away the time, the four boys took Santos on a hike up into the hills. They planned to be back by lunch but didn't even make it for supper, and when darkness fell, Dorothy and I were glad they had taken the dog. Otherwise one of us would have had to wait on the beach for the boys' arrival. Not until late in the evening did we finally hear Santos's piercing yelp over the moan of the wind. I rowed in with the skiff, and the boys waded out to catch and hold the skiff bow to the surf while they all jumped on board.

The exhausted but exhilarated crew had climbed past ancient stone terraces and extensive rock walls to the very top of the island, some 5,000 feet up, where all was swathed in the swirling mist of the continuous cloud cap, then walked down the other side to a beautifully preserved old Portuguese town set in the hills, where they met interesting, friendly people with whom they drank a lot of beer and got a ride back to the boat. They brought back a discouraging report though. Everybody they'd asked had agreed that the weather would stay windy until April. The wind howls all winter there.

We finally had to leave. Raffy had a non-refundable flight back to Dartmouth from the Virgin Islands, timed to the start of the spring trimester, and we had to be back by mid-March.

The wind, if anything, had increased, so we prepared for rough seas, placing the weather boards in the companionway, dogging down all the hatches, and screwing shut all the portholes except the two above the galley, which we left open to let a little fresh air below. We set only the reefed mizzen, staysail, and storm jib and went out into the easterly gale. The boat handled well and went fast, riding the growing seas handily until we were about five miles west of the island.

There the seas, which had parted at the island, came back together in a pattern of enormous cross-swells that battered the boat from side to side. One big sea, about 15 feet high and steep as a wall, broke against the starboard hull and knocked the boat almost onto her beam ends. At that same instant a big, surly cross-sea boarded us from the port side, and suddenly half the deck was underwater, seawater well up over the portholes, even over the cabintop, and filling the lower half of the cockpit while those of us on deck clung to handrails, stanchions, and the wheel. Simultaneously came a startled scream from the cabin as Dorothy saw water shooting as if from two six-inch fire hoses through the open galley portholes and straight across the cabin to the door of the head.

"A hundred gallons in about two seconds!" she called, awed. Diego flew to the bilge pump while Alon slammed shut the offending ports and rinsed the stove burners with fresh water. On we sailed, gradually getting away from the treacherous cross-seas and into the more regular but still huge swells of the southeast North Atlantic. For several days we carried on without the main, but by the time we were halfway across to the Leewards, the weather mellowed into a steady force 4 or 5 breeze—11 to 21 knots—to which we raised all working sail.

* * *

Three days out from Brava, with the self-steering sail set, the boat surfing down the burgeoning swells, the crew mostly dozing or reading below, and Alon, whose watch it was, occasionally looking around but otherwise occupied with the dishes, there came a sudden howl of barking from Santos. Alon jumped up through the companionway and gave a shout of delight to see a young humpback whale about the size of the boat. By the time we all got on deck it was coming from directly behind us, heading with a burst of speed straight for the rudder. We gaped, but just short of the rudder, it dove close under our hull and then surfaced showily just in front of the bowsprit and sped away. Then it made a wide arc and came back again to launch another run. This time we knew it was playing and delighted in seeing such a magnificent animal so close up. It kept up the game for almost 40 minutes before coming close alongside, so close we could see down his blowhole. Santos had been barking all the while, and now the whale rolled partway onto its back and looked straight at him with a good-humored grin—how it conveyed that or we perceived it I can't say, but so it seemed to us. Santos, instead of being cool, kept barking a storm. We were a bit ashamed of his churlishness when the whale wandered off to another patch of ocean.

That was the highlight of the trip.

The low point was when we discovered that the propane tank shut-off valve had been turned the wrong way and had broken, so there was now no way to shut off the gas at the tank—a basic safety arrangement. Fresh from Denton Bridge we were gun-shy about catastrophe at sea, and since I had a shut-off valve that would fit the hose, we took council and agreed we should replace it. We prepared everything in advance, but inevitably a cloud of propane shot out of the severed hose before we quickly jammed the ends onto the valve barbs.

Four days out of St. Maarten we ran out of cooking gas. Within half a day everything tasty to eat that didn't need to be cooked had been eaten by the four hungry boys—cans of tuna fish, peanut butter, crackers, and cookies. A stringent budget had dictated what we stocked the boat with in Banjul, and we had relied heavily on rice, onions, potatoes, and pasta—all of which needed cooking.

Amos tried using a kerosene lamp to heat up soup but mostly managed to soot up the galley until it looked like a shepherd's cave blackened by centuries of cook fires. The boys used all our aluminum foil to construct a solar oven, which succeeded in shriveling thin slices of potatoes that nonetheless stuck in our throats. Half of us decided to fast the rest of the way, and the others kept experimenting.

The only one who kept on eating a regular diet was Santos, for whom we'd bought a huge bag of dried dogfood in the Canaries, afraid we wouldn't see any in The Gambia. It had lost its crunch, smelled stale, and by now was a candidate for weevils, but he ate it happily twice a day while the rest of us watched him with, if not envy, a sudden surge of hunger. As far as I know, none of the crew made any midnight raids on Santos's stash.

We reached land early in the evening on the fourth day of our fast, but by the time we had carefully rounded St. Maarten's outlying dangers and dropped anchor in Philipsburg's Great Bay, it was 10 P.M. We had already launched the dinghy as we motored into the bay, so we leaped in, all six of us and the dog, and motored full speed for the town dock.

To our dismay, all the restaurants were closing and no grocery stores were open. However, the Häagen-Dazs outlet stayed open until midnight, and in we stormed, counting out the last of our money. We ate ice cream greedily, and then discovered a Burger King, which had cold cheeseburgers and greasy fries, the night's leavings. Dorothy declined any such fare, but the rest of us wolfed it all down, chased it with cold beers, and counted ourselves lucky.

Such are the exigencies of seafaring.

* * *

Arriving back in St. John in late February, we started calling U.S. Customs well before dawn, and they were waiting for us when *Breath* pulled into the dock. Having come from "very foreign," we were met by several agents and a drug-sniffing dog, more heat than I'd ever seen at Cruz Bay Customs. Everyone but the captain was required to leave the boat. Santos, leashed to the rigging, went ballistic when the Doberman boarded his boat. The big dog backed off, looking young, not fully trained, and much confused by the small guard dog's vehemence. He skittered from sailbag to sailbag and ended up peeing on a tooled leather satchel that belonged to one of his handlers.

Two of our closest friends—Andy (Amos's father) and John— happened to be going through town when they saw *Breath* pull up to the customs dock in Cruz Bay. They jammed on their brakes, and as soon as the boat was cleared, took us to Andy's home for a celebration.

Wine flowed as freely as the conversation. We all told the story of Denton Bridge, blow by blow, each of us chiming in with details. Toast after toast was proposed and drunk to deeply. Andy toasted us all, the boat, the voyage. John toasted me, the captain. I toasted my crew and especially my wife. We all toasted each other, especially Amos's mother and sisters.

Diego, who, ever since our stay in Spain had sometimes had a little wine with meals, had a full share that day as the bottles kept uncorking and the glasses were indiscriminately filled. This celebration of the voyage, burnished by its brush with death, made him for the first time a little tipsy.

"I wanna make a toast!" he said, raising his glass and standing up with a scrape of the chair. He was met by a chorus of "Hear, Hear!" "Let the man make his toast!" "Speak Diego, speak!"

"I wanna toast the smallest member of the crew!" Immediate laughter and cheering rose up. "Yeah, Diego!" "You da man, Diego!" "More wine for Little Big Man!"

"No, not me! Do you think I would toast myself? I wouldn't toast myself!" The alcohol was showing a little. "Santos! I'm toasting Santos—the seagoing schipperke!" Cheers interrupted him. "For showing . . ." Diego got just a touch maudlin at that point, and everyone quieted down."...For showing you don't have to be big . . . to be brave!" That brought the house down with clapping, table pounding, stamping of feet. Diego, the youngest and smallest, had shown himself true blue in the crisis, convinced we were going to die but giving his all. Alon jumped up with Santos in one arm, and with his other clasped Diego around the neck, shouting, "Little guys unite!"

On the voyage back I had lost no opportunity to point out that Alexander the Great had been small in stature too, and that a big dog might well have perished in the surf at Denton Bridge, whereas Santos had survived. Speed and agility can be more useful than sheer mass—and spirit more important than any physical attribute.

Santos was hard proof. The admiration he inspired was precisely because he was so brave and adventurous *despite* his tiny size. He was a prime example of a central concept in every religion, every culture—that spirit is what really matters—not money, size, birth, or even intelligence. With spirit you have everything—without it, nothing.

THIRTY

CORAL BAY

When we returned home to St. John, the house at East End had
been rented by someone who showed no intention of moving away.
And, lovely though it was and remained, East End too was chang-
ing. A big chunk of it had been bought by stateside developers to
build large houses—"villas," they were called, with the intimations
of luxury and hedonism called up by that term. Concrete trucks were
rumbling down the heretofore secluded road, droning like enemy
bombers come to wipe out an old culture. East End was losing its
traditional West Indian character.

Coral Bay looked good though. Many of our friends were settled
in the hills and valleys surrounding the tiny village, and we decided
to put down our mooring there until Diego graduated from high
school.

Diego was recruited to captain a team of young St. John sailors
in the Governor's Cup Regatta in St. Thomas. All the Virgin Islands,
including the British Virgins, had youth sailing programs, and every
year they raced each other in St. Thomas. Diego had been a member
of the Coral Bay KATS (Kids and the Sea) before he'd left and was
still young enough at 15 to compete. The Coral Bay KATS had a
promising crew but lacked a good skipper, and when Diego returned
to the scene with thousands of blue-water miles under his belt, he was
the logical choice.

The Coral Bay team competed in the big Youth Regatta, and they
swept the events, due largely to Diego's abilities not just as a sailor
but as a leader. And for his efforts, he won a thousand-dollar U.S.
saving bond. Not bad for the little boy who got so seasick, and whose
mantra had been, "I hate this boat!"

Santos returned to his Coral Bay community. A short walk from
the dock was his all-time #1 most favorite place to hang out, Skinny
Legs, a popular—actually a beloved—bar, grill, and community

center. Skinny's motto, "a pretty OK place," set its tone, as did its promise of "same day service." A bumper sticker on an adjoining wall made it clear: "We're all here because we're not all there." Notwithstanding, Doug and Moe, the owners and partners, ran a smooth operation with the best hamburger on the island, live music on weekends, and two huge TVs for watching sports, movies, and—during hurricane season—detailed storm reports.

Sometimes the bar and grill seemed a cover for Skinny's function as civic auditorium and social welfare center, so many meetings were held there, so many benefits to raise money for good causes and sad cases. Doug and Moe had hearts of gold and were a classic instance of doing well by doing good. Skinny's thrived; it was thronged by locals and tourists alike, and by Santos whenever he could get there.

Dogs were forbidden from the premises by the health department, of course, and Moe and Doug tried, at least perfunctorily, to kick them out when an inspector was in rumor, but that kind of heat came in waves, every other year for a week or two. The rest of the time the prohibition was tough to enforce in an open-air bar with no doors whose patrons owned the dogs.

We did what we could to keep him out, but it was hopeless seeing that Ron, the chief bartender, was one of Santos's particular friends. Ron always just happened to have some tasty leftover he'd saved. The draw was irresistible, especially at dusk, when we'd get out of our truck and be lugging supplies to the dinghy, enjoining Santos to come along. If we took our eyes off him for a second, he'd be gone.

We always knew where to find him—trying to be invisible under a table. The dead giveaway was seeing a table whose occupants were looking down at their feet.

Santos knew the rules: no dogfights, no barking, try to remain inconspicuous—and no obnoxious begging. As a result he was allowed to stay when other dogs got the boot. The way he begged—politely—and the extreme care with which he took food—never snatching it from the hand—endeared him to parents of little children, who are always fascinated by a dog built to their own scale.

When *SAIL* magazine published an article about his going overboard in Venezuela, he became locally famous. If Skinny's was anything it was a sailor's bar, and since *SAIL* was the preeminent sailing magazine, the story got read not only by local sailors but by the cruising people passing through.

Then *Reader's Digest* reprinted the *SAIL* piece, and his renown took a leap upward. With a circulation of 20 million, *Reader's Digest* introduced Santos to all kinds of people, not just sailors, and the story was translated into a dozen languages. He became a conversation piece for the bartenders and waitresses, who pointed him out to tourists as the dog that had been featured in *Readers Digest*. There'd be the occasional whoop of delight.

"I read about that dog!"

Everybody seemed to know him. Saturday mornings, when the youth sailing program was under way, he would be up on deck as one Laser after another sailed by, the children calling out his name while he barked them through his territory. Often we'd be walking Santos somewhere and people we'd never seen before would greet him, "Hey, Santos!" Cap'n Fatty Goodlander, the irrepressible marine journalist, talked about him on the radio.

Friday happy hour at Skinny's was the high point of the dog's week. People from all over the island crowded the bar. Santos had a legitimate function then that might even have won health department approval—he devoted himself to keeping the floor at the feet of the patrons free and clean of spilled chips and dip.

* * *

Santos had mostly stopped chasing cars by now, but every once in a while a motor would go by that touched two live neurons together in his brain and shorted out his common sense. That happened one afternoon when I was down by the dock, painting the bottom of our skiff. Chutney came running to me, calling, "Peter! Peter! Santos is hit!"

I looked around for the dog, but he was gone. I felt a familiar angst grip my stomach and give it a twist.

"What?"

"Come quick! Santos . . ." she gasped, her cute freckled face contorted with distress, her husky voice panting. "Santos—he's hurt bad—can't move!"

"Where?"

"Up by Skinny's—on the road!"

I ran back with her up to the road.

"What happened, Chutney?"

"He got hit . . . Prime truck. . . ." Later I learned that the Prime restaurant supply truck had made its weekly delivery and driven off. For whatever reason, Santos, who had seen the truck many times before, took off after it this time with a burst of speed and attacked the rear tire. He must have caught one of the heavy treads with his teeth, and it flung him hard against the back bumper. The truck driver never realized anything had happened.

A knot of people stood looking at the ground. In the center knelt Judy, our local nurse practitioner.

"How is he, Judy?"

"I'm not sure. He's alive but in shock. His right hind leg looks bad. You'd better get him to the vet, quick."

The same leg he'd broken before . . . poor Santos. He looked awful, almost in a coma, not recognizing me, his eyes glazed over, apparently paralyzed, his breath coming rapid and shallow.

Suddenly Dorothy was at my side, comforting her boy with the sound of her voice.

"Call Andy Williamson before he leaves his clinic for the day. Tell him we'll be on the next ferry. We've got to hurry," she told me. I went for the truck. Ron, the bartender, ducked into Skinny's storeroom and came back with the perfect-sized cardboard box for a cradle, then stripped off his shirt and lined the box with it, moisture in his eyes as he beheld the still form. "Forget it," he said to me when I tried to refuse the shirt. "I got another one in the office." As we drove off he was calling the vet.

On the ferry, Dorothy spoke to Santos in a low voice close to his ear, and before the boat docked at Red Hook he'd come around, lifting his muzzle up weakly toward her face, his eyes showing the glint of recognition through the pain.

Once again the vet came through, meeting us way after the end of a normal week's work. We left him to it, returned to St. John, and stopped at Skinny's to return Ron's shirt. Ron came right over, concerned, oblivious to the crush of clamoring customers at the bar.

"How is the little guy?" he asked.

"He's going to be alright. Andy's fixing him up—another broken leg—same one as before."

"Then it's celebration time!" His face broke into its characteristic wide grin, his bushy hair flaring out from an old beret, and he thrust both hands into the cooler and came up with three ice-cold Sam Adams.

"On me! Here's to Santos! May he never chase internal combustion engines again!"

It proved a prophetic toast. Santos had learned his lesson at last.

* * *

Down by the dock in Coral Bay was a congenial place for dogs. Large trees shaded much of the foreshore, and dinghies stored upside down in the grass made great spots to take a nap. Nearby, the garbage dumpster offered hope of scraps. Dogs could wander into the sea to cool themselves off or wander down the dock to greet the boat people as they came ashore.

Though he didn't get overly friendly with many of the Coral Bay dogs, in part because most of them were transients, Santos did have two canine friends he valued. One was Elwood.

Elwood was half pit bull and half Rottweiler, but despite its threatening bloodlines, it was the friendliest, most laid-back beast in Coral Bay. She (yes, she) belonged to Coral Bay Marine, the little marine store at the head of the dock that had at one time or another employed just about everybody living in the harbor. Allen, the co-proprietor, had named her in jest after an Oklahoma uncle who had never seen the ocean.

Though she was, of course, a powerful dog, with jaws that could take off an arm, shelacked the disposition of a guard dog—which is probably just as well in a potentially lethal animal. She had to be urged to go after the donkeys, which she did half-heartedly, ambling up toward them where they despoiled the garbage and giving one deep-throated WHOOF!, which would jerk their heads up and send them into the tall grass snorting and braying their protests. This kind of reaction would have had Santos exultantly springing after them in full throat, but Elwood had no chase instinct either.

She was a tiny puppy when she first met Santos, whom she worshipped from the start. He was so intelligent, so well traveled, and so completely in charge of the Coral Bay dock dog hierarchy that he seemed godlike to her. Every morning Elwood would wait on the dock for him to arrive by dinghy, sometimes peeing herself with delight when the big dog—he was larger at first—leaped onto the dock. She loved to play with him—jumping up on him, running into his side to rub flank to flank—real puppy stuff, which Santos would reciprocate for a couple of minutes before taking off on his rounds.

After sailing to Venezuela and being gone six months, we returned to Coral Bay, and when Santos came up to the dock there was Ellwood—huge now, but still grinning with delight, ears back, head bobbing with obsequious adoration. Santos was a bit taken aback. He could scarcely jump onto the dock—Ellwood was inadvertently blocking the way, licking him with sloppy tongue strokes that almost knocked him off the foredeck.

He ducked her greeting and made it onto the dock only to have Ellwood, who now towered over him, jump onto him the way she used to do, shoving him to his seat, whereupon she licked his face again with a tongue half the size of his head. He tried to get by her, but she rubbed against him flank to flank, her tail wagging her body from back to front in a sideways shimmy that nearly knocked him off the dock. He tried to slip around behind her in a deft end run but got stopped cold by her wagging tail, which caught him in the chops like a blackjack.

Santos endured it for a couple of days but was finally forced to lay down the law with a warning snarl and snap. Ellwood, as dim as she was lovable, eventually got the message but still met him every morning and followed him around respectfully, wagging her tail. For the rest of his life he had a devoted friend.

Perhaps because I was the one who frequently brought him ashore, Elwood made a point of welcoming me with the same enthusiasm. She had the knack of coming up when I was defenseless, unable to evade her attentions. One morning I had both hands locked to the dock, striving mightily to keep the dinghy steady as a slightly obese lady tried to board, when Elwood bounded up, full of joy after a long night's separation, and repeatedly slobbered a broad wet tongue across my mouth.

Santos's other close canine companion was the only dog older than he was. Old Luke was a black Lab who lived on the dock. Day in and day out he lay in the same spot, about halfway down the length of the dock. Through stinging winter squalls and blistering summer heat he was there, raising his head and giving a couple of thumps with his tail to greet the first skiff to come ashore at dawn and bid goodnight to the last one off in the wee hours.

Nobody knew how old he was. The visiting vet, who took the ferry over from St. Thomas once a week and treated him for free, guessed he must be 17, the equivalent of a hundred-plus in human years.

Old Luke looked every one of those years, gaunt, sway-backed, and arthritic, with loose folds of skin hanging about his neck and jowls and his mournful, clouded eyes peering out from deep in their sockets. When he had to move, he would heave a reluctant sigh, lift himself with visible effort onto shaky legs, and stand there for a moment, steadying himself, before moving off. Soon he'd be back to resume his vigil, sad eyes always looking wistfully out to sea.

He was waiting for Hardy, his master, to row up in his dinghy and tie it once again to the rusted black iron cleat he had always used in the past. The old dog waited patiently for years, becoming a fixture on the Coral Bay dock, but he waited in vain. Hardy was dead, or at least, that's what everybody thought. His body was never found, but one morning his sailboat was washed up in the surf at Drunk Bay, where its shattered hulk lies today, high and dry on the exposed rock beach where hurricane swells eventually lifted it.

Hardy had been a reclusive, gray-haired drifter with a face that had been battered by hard living. A skein of tiny red capillaries laced his nose, and his hands, normally clasped around a green Heineken bottle, shook slightly. He had sailed in with his dog one day on a battered old fiberglass sloop, and ended up staying for a year or so. Not many people got to know him, though. He mostly stayed on his boat and drank a bottle of rum a day, sometimes two bottles. To his credit, unlike some, he wasn't a loud roaring drunk, determined to give the sleeping harbor the benefit of his drunken epiphanies. He kept his boat apart, at the outer edge of the mooring area, and rowed to shore with Luke always sitting in the bow to buy groceries and more rum. So far as anyone could remember, he never left the anchorage until the day he died.

That day he left the harbor under full sail, too late in the afternoon, headed for St. Croix, forty miles south. The passage between the islands can be rough, and Hardy's boat was not particularly seaworthy, but on this day it didn't matter because he never even made it out to the open sea. It was Ram's Head that did for him.

Ram's Head is the southernmost tip of St. John, a great knob of rock, reminiscent of a medieval mace, at the end of a long, low peninsula that reaches far enough into the Caribbean to disturb the sweep of the oceanic swells that the trade winds have driven all the way from Africa.

Out on the deep ocean these waves are uniform and steady and roll harmlessly under a vessel's stern, but once they enter the shelf of shallow water that bears the Virgin Islands they grow unsettled and confused. They rub the rising bottom and meet the shock waves rebounding from the wall of rock that lies ahead, and their free-frolicking run across three thousand miles of open Atlantic turns ugly and violent. At last they explode against Ram's Head's implacable rock, and a hiker standing atop it can feel the vibrations of the impact.

Perhaps he missed his step in the steepened seas, the edge of his balance blunted by a long spell at anchor and too much rum. Perhaps he stepped over on purpose. But most likely he lost his grip on the rigging when he used both hands to unzip his fly. Falling overboard is the most common cause of accidental death at sea, and most drowned men who have fallen off yachts are recovered, if they ever are, with their flies unzipped.

At any rate, his boat washed ashore at Drunk Bay, where white-shouldered ranks of rollers shattered it against the rock beach. The beach is a long, gradual curve of smooth shiny rocks about the size of a fist that tumble over each other in the surf . . . nature's rock polisher.

The noise of that dense clattering, the rock rolling over and over, countless tons of granite in motion, may have been the last sound Jerry heard on this earth as he drowned—if that's what happened. His body was never found. Luke was found next to the wrecked hull, howling a woeful lament. Kind souls brought him back to Coral Bay, where he colonized that spot on the dock, the point at which Jerry had always tied up his dinghy, and waited patiently, determined to be there when his master arrived.

He was such a dear old soul, the epitome of a faithful dog, that the boating community took him under their care. Several ladies who lived on boats made a point of remembering him when they had bones to dispose of, and there always seemed to be leftovers in his bowl. Sandy, the proprietress of the marine store at the head of the dock, made sure he had water, and Chutney, her six-year-old daughter, would occasionally sit with him and brush his coat, then give him a hug, her little blonde head laid against his neck. Only then would Luke forget his vigil for a moment and turn his anxious gaze from the harbor to give Chutney a touching look of gratitude, his ears back and a grimace of a smile on his face as he panted a little louder, before returning to his watch.

Then one day the good old heart cracked, and at the cumbrous age of 18 he was gone. The next day someone had painted on the dock the outline of Luke's body in its usual position and written within it, "Luke, R.I.P." That image lasted a couple more years before the elements and people's feet wore it away.

By that time Jerry the drifter had been mourned and remembered more than many a wealthy, sober man.

After Luke was gone, Santos, at the age of ten, became the old-est dog in Coral Bay. Most uncared-for dogs succumb to some ail-ment sooner than later in the tropics—heartworm reliably kills a dog within five years unless someone gives it monthly pills, and tick fever takes others not lucky enough to have their ears and paws cleaned and inspected weekly. Every week Dorothy gave Santos a flea bath and went over his whole body, inspecting and brushing him. It was she who remembered to check his water dish and his food bowl, she who insisted on his regular walk even if it was rainy or inconvenient, she who remembered him with a pot to lick. She gave him a lot of love, the kind of love that takes on tasks and troubles itself with details—and Santos knew it. He was Dorothy's dog. He had a soul, and soul to soul he communicated with her on a level that ran deeper than words.

* * *

Breath kept making trips, and Santos found himself guarding the boat in Santiago de Cuba in the summer of 1991, in Cap Haitien in 1994, Lisbon in 1995, Guinea-Bissau in 1996, Puerto La Cruz in '97. The old seadog was a grizzled veteran by then, past his prime but still strong and alert. The only sign of a problem was a faint limp in his oft-damaged rear right leg. His limp got immediately worse when he was admonished for some misdemeanor, like making a mess in the cockpit with his supper or helping himself to a pack of cookies left overnight on deck. Then he'd drag his leg and shoot off mournful looks full of the weariness of existence. But when he spied any small boat nearing the danger zone, he leaped to his duty.

We crossed the Atlantic again in 1995, heading for the Azores and Spain en route to West Africa. The trip was a trading venture, in the wake of the 16th-century adventurers I'd first read about in the Hakluyt collection kept handy in the Tower Room of the Baker Library at Dartmouth. We were bound to Gambia and Guinea Bissau for a cargo of decorated calabashes and musical instruments—djembi drums, koras, balafons, African fiddles. Raff couldn't come with us. He was starting his second year at Harvard Law School—not a course of study from which he could blithely take a term off.

Diego helped us sail *Breath* across the Atlantic, but once we got to Europe he left the boat—and the nest. He was 18, had been accepted at an even colder college than Raff had attended, and left the first of September for orientation week at Colby College in Waterville,

Maine. Like his brother, he had won a scholarship for all four years. It's a great country, America.

That year, 1995, turned out to be the worst for hurricanes in over half a century. We weren't hit directly, but we got some days of nasty weather—and came as close to losing Santos as we ever had. We were running downwind at the time, occasionally rolling heavily and shipping green water over the foredeck. This created a problem for Santos, who needed to visit the anchor ropes, his privy of last resort, but was afraid to chance it. He would await his moment, get halfway down the deck, and come scurrying back as a sea threatened and the boat rolled.

Several times I walked him to the bow, where I sat in my foul-weather gear, holding on to the bronze staysail horse with one hand and his leash with the other while green water sloshed up my trousers. He could never perform on demand though, and having me sitting there, getting soaked, watching him and urging him to get on with it, constituted a pressure that puckered.

Finally, during Dorothy's watch, driven by desperation, he picked a relatively calm stretch and dashed forward, got into the prescribed position—inherently unstable—and a big wave toppled him over and swept him to the rail. His claws caught hold of a single coil of the rough, stiff anchor line, and that was the only thing that saved him. He clung to the rope for dear life, his eyes fixed on Dorothy's eyes while most of his body dangled over the side, the boat's bow wave foaming beneath him—then *Breath* righted herself and he regained the deck and dashed to the safety of the cockpit. And he still had to go!

For his sake we heaved-to, went below to stretch out for a couple of hours, and left Santos in peace. Then we carried on.

When we got to Iberia I bought a short length of fishing net and lashed it from the lifelines down to the rail to either side of the anchor lines, so that if the same thing should happen again he would fetch up in the net. That was the first adjustment to the boat we'd had to make for his safety. Always in the past he'd been too nimble and explosively energetic to need help.

A couple of other indications that Santos was not immortal came to us on that trip. At anchor in Portugal, as the fall chill became more pronounced, Santos still wanted to sleep all night on deck. He had the coat for it and enjoyed the brisk air—we'd see him at the porthole early in the new day with beads of dew bedecking his bristles—but he woke up one morning and couldn't uncurl his body. Dogs always turn in a circle a couple of times before they lie down, then go to sleep curled up, nose to feet. He didn't come to our porthole, not even when called. We found him at the head of the companionway, still curled up. When we tried to straighten him, gently, he yelped in pain and snapped. His eyes were morose.

With the warmth of the day, at most a half-hour after he woke, Santos would again be fine. But we knew something was wrong when the problem recurred more and more frequently. And when he grew more and more reluctant to make the springy jump in and out of the cockpit, we knew that the surf off the Denton Bridge inlet, the Lieutenant Governor's car, the Prime truck, and jumping out of moving vehicles had all taken a toll on his spine. I built him a step halfway up the cockpit coaming so that he wouldn't have to jump so hard, and that helped.

* * *

Portugal, Morocco, Canaries, Gambia—in November 1995 we were approaching the Gambia river entrance in mid-afternoon, sailing at hull speed, when dolphins appeared. At first Santos set up his pro forma hue and cry, but then he stopped short. Dorothy, who was on watch, hopped up the companionway to take a cautionary look around. She was delighted, as always, to see several of the ebullient mammals cavorting around *Breath*. Suddenly she called excitedly. "Oh Peter! It looks like the same dolphin." I hurried up on deck with the two friends who were sailing with us.

"Look," she said, "the big one. He's the same dolphin—he's got the same white scars on his flank."

"What do you mean?"

"Remember we saw that big dolphin with white scars on the way into The Gambia—the one Alon and I were watching? He rolled over and barked back at Santos, actually barked, and then gave me that look of shared amusement." Actually I did remember her saying something like that then. The scarred white lines had reminded me at the time of photographs of the Nazca highland lines in Peru, and now, almost six years later, the same sort of pattern was plain to see on this one swimming alongside.

Our dog, always the staunch defender of our boat, was lying quietly on the starboard seat amidships and watching the pod—unprecedented behavior for him. The big bull swam on his back or side, staying right alongside the boat's midships while the pod cavorted in the bow and stern waves. It is unusual for a dolphin to stay even with a boat for long—they usually move rapidly by and then come back for another pass—but this scarred fellow stayed alongside for a few minutes, looking at Santos while Santos looked back. The eye contact between dog and dolphin lasted a long time.

"Santos . . . do you recognize him?" Dorothy asked rhetorically. "That's the dolphin that saved you! Right?"

Could it have been? We'll never know, but the possibility went a long way toward explaining how a little dog survived the crumpling, bruising surf that night. The dolphins might have brought him through the waves or found him dogpaddling, close to death from injuries and pain. They might have saved him from sharks. Dolphins can kill sharks by hitting them at high velocity on their huge stomachs, which can be ruptured by a dolphin's hard beak. Seeing those scars on the big dolphin's flanks made me wonder. Stranger stories have turned out to be true. Since antiquity there have been consistent accounts of dolphins saving people—though perhaps Santos was the first dog to be carried to safety. As far as Dorothy was concerned, this proved her theory that dolphins had come to Santos's rescue on the night of his greatest peril.

One thing I'm convinced of: Santos knew that dolphin.

* * *

"Come on Santos, let's go look at some land," said Dorothy. It was a Sunday afternoon back in Coral Bay.

"Land?" I asked, looking up from the battery boxes where I was cleaning the terminals.

"Yes, land . . . flowers, fruit trees," she said as she hopped into the dinghy, lifting down her dog. I kept working. And thinking. Land—it was becoming an issue. Dorothy wanted it, but I wasn't so keen on leaving the boat. I'd gone with her a few times looking for a piece we could afford—which generally meant a piece with no view, a place in a hollow, or else an incredibly steep plot with loose, shaley soil. Each time I had been turned off.

When she came home, it was almost suppertime.

"Where did you go?" I asked.

"Someplace different this time. . . . See up there near that little peak?" She pointed to a spot high up the steep mountain that reared above Coral Bay. "It's beautiful. You should see it."

"Good for flowers?"

"Great. . . . It has rich, dark soil—I dug into it and even found an earthworm. Not many places on St. John have soil that good. And there were old terraces. It must have been a provisions ground way back when." A provisions ground meant a garden that had grown food. "I even found the head of a hoe—really rusted—where I was digging."

"What's the view like?"

"Well, the piece next to it is spectacular. The property I was looking at . . . if it had a house with a wide porch... would let you see some water. Mostly the view is mountains and the Coral Bay valley."

"Meaning houses, roads, and scrub bush?"

She pouted and said nothing, but rattled the dishes louder than usual.

"Well, what about the boat?"

"Well what about it?" she asked, a trifle coldly.

"You know—can you see the boat from that corner?" That was my only fixed requirement for a piece of land—that I should be able to keep an eye on my boat just in case someone tried to steal it, or the mooring failed, or a hose below the waterline let go. Boats tend to go downhill when nobody is living aboard, monitoring subtle changes.

"I don't know. . . . It's hard to see without climbing a tree. You ought to come see it. And you-know-who loved exploring all over the place."

"Santos, the old sea dog? Gettin' ready to swallow the anchor, are you boy?" He looked up quizzically at me, not sure what I wanted, then grabbed a sock from the floor and shook it briskly, growling, daring me to grab it. In the slanting afternoon light his muzzle was hoary with white hairs.

"It would be so nice to have a family base where the boys could come even if the boat were away . . . maybe build their own places in time." This was the best reason for a piece of land on St. John. The island was home to our sons.

"So . . . will you come?"

"Sure I will. Let's go up Tuesday afternoon."

A moment later I asked, "How much does he want for the piece? It's a half acre?"

"Yeah. . . . About $50,000, and maybe we could bargain him down to 45."

"Forty-five grand . . . whew. Where are we going to get that kind of money?"

"We could stop spending so much money on the boat, for starters."

"Heresy!" I exclaimed, partly in jest. "That's the trouble. We could swing it, but what would we have to give up? The boat will be neglected. We can kiss the book good-bye too—I'll have to spend all my time chartering and building the house."

"No you won't! We don't need a house right away. Just a piece of dry, stable land and dirt to get my fingers in. We'll pay for it over time." I realized with a start that she was close to tears.

Suddenly I felt like a selfish churl. She'd lived with me for well over twenty years on boats and in ramshackle houses. I couldn't count how many people had told me with a severe look that I was a *very lucky fellow* (read, "undeserving") to have a wife like her. And many a female charter guest had visibly blanched when it sank in that, no, these people didn't have a house on shore, this was it, afloat with the cumbersome ice chest, cold-water shower, tiny spaces, no dishwasher, and on and on, ad infinitum. To be sure, we were living consistent with our beliefs in a simpler life, consuming less, less pressure on the Earth to pump out everything from oil to crocodile skin belts to tropical hardwood dining tables for our needs.

But principles can be taken too far. I thought of Ghandi's wife, working her ass off to reinvent the wheel.

It wouldn't be a sellout for us to have a small piece of land and a little house.

"OK, let's go. Tomorrow. God knows I owe you. We can definitely swing it!"

The next day we went up an atrocious track that made the old East End road seem like a turnpike. This road was downright dangerous with collapsed portions where there was barely enough room to squeeze by, with boulders lodged precariously on the upper bank, ready to flatten an unlucky vehicle after the next hard rain, and with unguarded drop-offs that set butterflies to flight in your stomach if you so much as glanced down the abyss. The truck labored up a steep incline in four-wheel drive, higher and higher, until we swung around the spine of a ridge and caught a breathtaking glimpse of the harbor below and island after island stretching out to the east, with intricate, sparkling channels between them. The foliage closed in again, and then we came to a stop.

She led me down a slippery, overgrown path to a relatively level area that looked to have been terraced maybe a century ago. Big trees met overhead, blocking the sun except where shifting rays dappled the undergrowth. Glossy tyre palms nodded, and smooth, cool trunks of guavaberry were pillars in Pan's temple. It was excellent horticultural land . . . but the whine of mosquitoes gave me pause. This piece was in the lee of the ridge, and the east wind would be blocked.

Just then Lee showed up. He was a friend who lived in a shack nearby, an old hippy who'd recently quit the bottle.

"I know . . . you want to see your boat. How did I guess," he said, and led us to a large tree against which he had propped a ladder that reached a comfortable limb to sit on.

"Is this still the same piece of land?" I asked.

"Go on, take a look." Up I climbed.

"Whoa! That is gorgeous!"

"Nice, eh?"

"Fabulous. . . . Dorothy, come up and take a look." She climbed up and we gazed almost straight down together, at Coral Bay and at *Breath*, sitting pretty at her mooring. Beyond, the four landlocked pools of Hurricane Hole glowed with blue light, and beaches and coves lined the shore at East End. The Sir Francis Drake Channel spread a deep pile azure carpet all the way to Virgin Gorda. The view was so beautiful it was physical. It eased tension and produced a mild euphoria.

For years from East End, I'd looked across the interwoven shallows and deeps of Round Bay, gazing at these very mountains, admiring their bold rise. Sitting in the tree felt like flying a light plane above Coral Bay. A red-tailed hawk glided across the upwelling wind, his spotted barred feathers clearly visible before he banked and disappeared beyond the tree line.

I loved this place. Then reality set back in.

"So Lee—is this part of the other piece or no?"

"It borders on it—the very next one to the south."

"Same price?"

"A little more. . . . It's my sister's piece, and it's choice."

"So how much?"

"Eighty, but she'll probably accept a little less."

Seventy-five grand—we'd be paying for it forever. We returned to the boat, not saying much. I was surprised how much I liked the sister's piece. If only they sold quarter acres.

How to swing it? Try as I might, any way I cut it, the bottom line was that if we committed to that piece we'd be nailing our feet to the floor. I felt a rising desperation at the prospect.

But in springtime, when the wind often turned the boat sideways to the swell, we rocked back and forth, and Dorothy felt slightly nauseous for days on end. I felt *her* desperation rising, too. It was time to make a move. She wanted some piece, any piece—not one of the world's great views.

I finally gave up the struggle. We'd take the piece we could afford. When Raffy and his wife came for a visit, we took them up to see what we were going to buy. Dorothy and Thia dug in the rich, dark topsoil and speculated about where to put a garden, while Raf and I took machetes and cut some foliage away to look out over the green hills and beyond the ridge line to a bit of blue sea, where the beach of Sandy Cay was framed and glistening in the sun.

"Not bad," he said. "Damn nice in fact. So what's so special about the other piece?" I led him along the path to the big tree and sent him up the ladder. Long silence.

"It's nice isn't it?" I said. "Just a pity the zoning doesn't allow quarter acres. I could see my way clear to paying 40 grand, but not 80. That'd be enough for a good house and garden."

"So what is the zoning?" he asked.

"R-2," I replied.

"What's that . . . residential with allowance for two homes?"

"Yeah, I think so. That's what Lee told me. How did you know?"

"I took real estate law last semester."

"There's the advantage of a Harvard Law degree."

"Knock it off, it doesn't take an overpriced law degree to figure that out."

We sat in the tree and took in the archipelago that stretched to the horizon like a necklace of emeralds set in gold, spangled across a field of blue velvet.

"Dad. . . ."

"Yeah?"

"I have an idea."

"Uh-oh."

"You said you wished there were quarter-acre lots . . . ?"

"Right."

"Well . . . what if I share the cost of the sister's lot and Thia and I will build a house here someday?"

"Great idea—except you don't have any money yet, Raff. You're already deep in debt for law school, and you've got another year to go."

"My credit is good," he said, laughing sardonically. "You should see the offers I get every day in the mail now that I'm going to Harvard Law. It's ridiculous . . . diamonds on credit, time-share condos, luxury cars. So what do you say—can you stand me for a neighbor?"

"Raffy, are you serious?"

"Absolutely. Look at it this way. This will be a good investment. Once that road is paved, this place will go way up in value."

"My boy . . . the astute capitalist."

"Somebody in this family has got to cultivate some business sense."

"I'll say!" said Dorothy. She and Thia had walked up quietly.

"Well . . . you'd better discuss this with Thia. After all, she's . . ."

"Actually, we discussed it last night. It might even have been her idea."

Dorothy was beaming. I was speechless. Thia said, "You'd better think twice. If we're nearby and have little children, we may abuse you as babysitters."

"That would be the day!" I exclaimed. "Do you think you could stand it Dorth?" She smiled beatifically.

"I take that as an acceptance of my offer. I'll be sending my legal team over in the morning." Raff clapped me over the shoulder, and we hugged, all of us, then went down to *Breath* to call Diego and open a celebratory bottle of Spanish Rioja.

THIRTY-ONE

THE DEATH OF SANTOS

Santos had led a charmed life for twelve years, but since our last trip to Africa he'd been aging steadily. By hurricane season in 1997 he was 13 years old, with hoar frost on his muzzle and cataracts clouding his eyes, and rheumatism in the two old breaks of his right hind leg caused him pain. Even with the steps I'd made him, he gradually became incapable of jumping from the cockpit to the cabintop. It was a slow progression; at first he would make several weak attempts, obviously in pain, then grit his teeth and finally make it. In time, he more and more waited for someone to give him a lift—although, if another dog came by in a dinghy, he could still get there barking.

I knew he was in bad shape the day I put the T-bone from a steak on the cabintop, told him to jump up and get it, and walked away. It was a test; I meant to turn my back for just a minute, but as it happened a friend came by to ask for a hand lifting a battery out of his boat. A half-hour elapsed before I got back, and there was the T-bone, untouched, and Santos in the cockpit, whimpering with eagerness, frustration, or sorrow. I lifted him up and he took it to the foredeck, where he worked on it happily for hours—his teeth were still excellent—while I remembered how, as a young dog, he leaped out of the cockpit without the slightest sign of effort as though he could switch gravity off and on at will. I wondered what indignity would come next.

Several years previously a charterer had given us the address of a woman in Texas who made sun visors for dogs. Dorothy sent for one right away. I scoffed—"Why not buy him a tuxedo and teach him how to smoke a cigar while you're at it?" A visor wouldn't last ten seconds, I thought, but was I wrong. He wore it all the time, even when it got knocked askew and ended up around his neck. That didn't halt the progress of cataracts in his left eye, though, which left him almost blind on that side—and the right eye, too, was showing the telltale spread of the bluish, milky film. We'd heard of someone who did cataract surgery on dogs up in New York City, but it was extremely expensive, and none of the vets we asked thought much of the idea.

When another hurricane season arrived, *Breath* was tied up in Hurricane Hole, in the smallest and most protected of the four creeks. About twenty vessels were spending the months of threat there; most weren't inhabited until a storm became imminent. Then the quiet little cove became a hive of activity, with boats streaming in to look for a spot and dinghies buzzing back and forth, setting out skeins of anchor rodes, taking lines to mangroves, diving on anchors to set them and route the lines to avoid chafe. Santos enjoyed the activity, the camaraderie of people coming by to borrow or lend tools and gear or just to chat about the latest advisory and the likelihood of a direct hit.

We had sustained one direct hit already. Hurricane Bertha had struck in early July, a category 1 storm, its 90-knot sustained winds strong enough to be hurricane-force but not devastating—not strong enough, for example, to transmute Newtonian Law by driving a straw through a telephone pole. It was a workaday storm, lasting from 9 to 5 with the eye passing directly overhead. Santos had stayed on deck with Diego and me for most of it, watching 90-knot gusts roar over the crests of the surrounding hills, flattening foliage, then race out over the cove, picking up water off its surface to send towering clouds of spume whirling like giant dervishes straight at us, laying *Breath* onto her side, stretching the anchor rodes until they groaned in their chocks, and tormenting the rigging until the shrouds shrieked.

Hermitage Creek was very still by mid October. It had been a quiet season, no storms were on the horizon, and the anchorage was deserted. No tourists roamed the island, and lots of locals had left for annual visits to parents or children on the mainland. It was the slowest, quietest time of the year on St. John, and the road to East End was the slowest and quietest place of all. Scarcely a car went by in an hour.

The day dawned blue and clear. Santos awoke to the sounds of a heron's croak and the soft splashes and sharp cracks of a school of mangrove snappers feeding. Diaphanous clouds of fry were gathered among the mangrove roots, and the bigger fish hit the mangroves hard as they struck at their sustenance. The water appeared to boil briefly as the fish broke the surface, then they moved on and left the creek lapping placidly at the sandspit where the heron was wading.

The old dog rose, gradually stretched his creaky limbs, and stuck his head down the companionway to see if anything was stirring below. All was silent, so he lay back down on the after deck with his face resting in the porthole so that he could see the sleeping form of his mistress, and snoozed in the cool morning air until he heard her stir. When Dorothy opened her eyes, the first thing she saw was the snowy whiskers on the muzzle of her devoted animal pushing through the porthole, a wistful look in his face. She patted the mattress beside her and he jumped in, onto the bed, as he had done innumerable times before, and promptly scratched at a flea until he woke me up. We both petted him and had a pleasant good morning, then got up and prepared our coffee and tea. The day was laid back—the only activity was hauling me up the mast to check all the strops and blocks—that and the cooking and cleaning in the galley.

After an early supper, Dorothy sent me into Coral Bay to Skinny's to pick up some ice, and I took Santos along. By 8 P.M. there was virtually no one left in the bar, and I read the paper and conversed with the bartender.

"Come here Santos," said Ron with his wide grin, his hair wild and grizzled. "Let me indulge you." Santos scrambled up from the wooden floor and presented himself eagerly. Ron held out most of a hamburger that a young girl with eyes bigger than her stomach had scarcely touched.

"Your lucky day, old boy," Ron said affectionately. Santos hesitated, as he always did, looking up at Ron to be absolutely sure this was for him, then eased it out of his hand and took it under a table and had at it, enjoying every morsel.

"And people wonder why I can't keep him out of this place," I remarked.

"Ah, what the hell. Santos is special. Anyway, tourists are all gone—we can do as we please. I love hurricane season!" And so saying, Ron slid a video of Jimi Hendrix in concert into the VCR, cranked up the volume, and cracked two Sams open, one for him and one for me—"at Doug and Moe's charge," he informed me with a cheery grin. "Great guys, your bosses," I replied, beer held high, and we poured long amber dollops down our throats.

We had the place to ourselves. Skinny Legs had been like a home to Santos all these years. There was no way to know that this time when we left, Santos would never be back. He'd had his last meal, and it was his favorite, served from the hands of an old friend.

We drove in the truck to Hermitage, and I parked to the side and started grasping ice and a bag of tools. I opened the door for Santos and said, "Come on boy, jump." He hesitated, made as if to jump, then pulled back. He did this several times, and I finally had to push him out of the truck cab, both of my hands encumbered with heavy bags. I shut the door and walked across the dark road. The moon wasn't up yet.

"Come on, let's get in the dinghy." I waited, but no dog appeared out of the darkness. Well, that was alright, he'd taken off down the road a piece and would be back when his curiosity was satisfied. I waited a moment and then called again. The sandflies were biting, the ice was melting, and I was tired. I walked back up onto the road, calling insistently, when out of nowhere, from around the curve behind the hill, a car appeared, moving rapidly. It had a very quiet engine—I hadn't heard it coming. It flashed by, not noticing my tentative wave for it to slow down. I stopped calling and waited in apprehension. If Santos had finally decided to heed me and come trotting out on the road, he might not see the headlights through his milky, blind right eye.

When the car was gone, I started calling again, but there was no response. I waited for awhile, increasingly apprehensive. He should have come by now. He was usually eager to go wandering but just as eager to get back to the boat. If you just waited a bit and didn't try to command him, he'd appear soon enough.

He'd frightened us before. The feeling in my throat and in the pit of my stomach was familiar. I remembered how we'd felt when we'd lost him at sea for a day—under a spotlight of fear and apprehension. I recalled in an instant all the close calls, the times he been hit by cars, the times he'd failed to come home and none of us knew if we'd ever see him again.

They'd all been false alarms, I told myself, and this would be another. The thought also came that someday the alarm wouldn't be false, and that this time the feeling was eery. But I reminded myself that in Gambia we were sure he was dead. This was nothing by comparison—a passing car, and he was used to those. I walked along the road, black asphalt, dark night—and there on the side of the road in the grass was a familiar-shaped shadow—quite still.

So this was it, I thought, with a sudden collapse of hope. I picked him up gently, to take him to Dorothy. He was still warm and limber in my arms—was there still a chance? I wondered how long it took rigor mortis to set in. I carried him gently through the darkness of the path through the mangroves and laid him down on a towel on the front seat of the skiff. He never moved.

"Dorothy . . . I have something bad to tell you," I said loudly as I approached *Breath* in the skiff. She could tell from my voice that it was urgent, and then she saw what was in my arms.

"Is he hurt bad?"

"Honey . . . I think he's dead." My voice broke. "A car. . . ."

She took his inert little form with infinite tenderness, her eyes glistening, carried him down below, and sat on the starboard settee cradling him, looking into his face. He showed almost no sign of trauma on his body, but his muzzle on one side was distorted, his teeth jutting upward at an odd angle and his tongue too far out of his mouth. "I'm not sure he's dead yet. He's in a coma. . . . He's still warm." She rocked him back and forth, softly calling his name, gently stroking his head. She was silent for awhile, holding him close, and then suddenly she spoke—

"Oh Santos!" I looked over in time to see the old dog with his eyes half open, gazing at his mistress's face. She bent her head close to his and whispered, "Goodbye, sweet spirit. . . ."

His eyes shut, this time forever, and in a few minutes his soul went out of him.

EPILOGUE

Yes, Santos had a soul, if you or I have one; and soul to soul he communicated on a level that ran far deeper than words, the better way even for humans. Dorothy and I miss him still.

We buried him on our land, high up the slope of Bordeaux Mountain, and made a terrace of his grave, and planted a lignum vitae tree upon it. Like the kings of ancient Lycia, he can gaze out in death over the land and sea that he loved in life. I shaped a slab of lignum vitae into a tombstone and inscribed his name on it with three lines from a poem Raffy wrote when he heard Santos had died:

SANTOS
May your spirit roam free
On the endless beaches
Of the Hereafter.

As we placed the tombstone at the head of his grave, I remembered that when we were first given Santos, I had thought to myself that I would probably see his whole life span pass—youth, prime, old age—an example, in foreshortened time, of how the years would deal with me; and that when he died I would be that much closer to my own death, both in time and understanding.

And so I am. And so are we all.

Our choice—to let him run free—had finally had its irrevocable consequence. But Buddy, at his graveside, put it best.

"It had been a real waste to keep that *game* dog tie up mos' a' his life for fear of risk. That were he purpose in dis life—he *came* here to take risks, to be the smallest and the baddest—fearless, yo hear? How tie he up? Not that dog! Braver heart in dog I never seen yet."

* * *

Diego brought two college buddies, Jason and Kyle, down to the islands in his senior year at Colby. They had the month of January off to pursue an independent study, and theirs was to come to St. John, put in six hours of work each morning, go free diving in the afternoon, and drink beer at night. By the time they went back to Colby, Diego and his two friends had framed a small house on the land. They turned a dream into a reality.

I did the rest with Dorothy's help and that of many friends. When we moved off the boat into the house, I took her down to look at one of the footings.

"Here, use this scrub brush—here's some water—and clean the dirt off the top."

She did it, then said, "There are letters carved here. What does it say?"

"Read for yourself—it's in English."

"I hope it's not obscene."

She scrubbed the letters clean and read "DOROTHY'S HAVEN."

* * *

Diego came down for a visit.

"How can we thank you enough, son?" I asked him. "What you did gives new meaning to the phrase, 'labor of love.'"

"Actually, Dad, there is something. Something you've never done for anyone else. Let me take *Breath* out for a cruise around the islands with my friends."

Fittingly, it was Father's Day when *Breath* sailed out of Coral Bay's harbor without me aboard. The wind was out of the northeast and Round Bay was fluky, but once Diego and his friends got clear of East End they picked up the unabated whitecap wind. Topsail pulling, the boat heeled to the wind, put her shoulder into the sea, and left a lace wake billowing behind her.

THE END

Peter Muilenburg was born in 1945, grew up in China and the Philippines, went to Dartmouth College in New Hampshire, went to jail in Mississippi, went to ground in the Virgin Islands, and went to sea whenever he could. He is grateful to his wife, proud of his two sons, and happy in his friends.

Peter is also the author of *Adrift on a Sea of Blue Light* (Afro-Indies Press, 2005; ISBN 0-9761397-0-7).

CPSIA information can be obtained at www.ICGtesting.com
Printed in the USA
BVOW020013110712

294767BV00001B/9/P